Locked In, Locked Out

THE CITY IN THE TWENTY-FIRST CENTURY

Eugenie L. Birch and Susan M. Wachter, Series Editors

A complete list of books in the series is available from the publisher.

LOCKED IN, LOCKED OUT

Gated Communities in a Puerto Rican City

Zaire Zenit Dinzey-Flores

PENN

UNIVERSITY OF PENNSYLVANIA PRESS

PHILADELPHIA

Published by_____
University of Pennsylvania Press
Philadelphia, Pennsylvania 19104-4112
www.upenn.edu/pennpress

Printed in the United States of America on acid-free paper
10 9 8 7 6 5 4 3 2 1

Library of Congress Cataloging-in-Publication Data
Dinzey-Flores, Zaire Zenit.
  Locked in, locked out : gated communities in a Puerto Rican city / Zaire Zenit Dinzey-Flores. — 1st ed.
    p. cm. — (The city in the twenty-first century)
  ISBN 978-0-8122-4513-4 (hardcover : alk. paper)
  1. Gated communities—Social aspects—Puerto Rico—Ponce—History—20th century. 2. Sociology, Urban—Puerto Rico—Ponce—History—20th century. 3. Ponce (P.R.)—Social conditions—20th century. I. Title. II. Series: City in the twenty-first century.
HT169.59.P9D56 2013
307.77—dc23
                                                                    2012041495

Para Lelolai Palmares y Caribe Macandel
Todo . . .

"¡Upa, mi negro, que el sol abrasa!"
—Nicolás Guillén

Contents

> I do not come with timeless truths. My consciousness is not
> illuminated with ultimate radiances. Nevertheless, in complete
> composure, I think it would be good if certain things were said.
> —Frantz Fanon, *Black Skin, White Masks*

When I set out to do research in the gated communities of the poor and rich in Ponce, fear was paramount. I grew up in Puerto Rico in the 1970s and 1980s, when carjackings were frequent and yearly murder counts headlined the news. Spaces of the poor, and *caseríos* (public housing) especially, were envisioned as places to be avoided. What was being ingrained in me during those years was to not venture into the unknown, to stay within the boundaries of my own social and physical circles. And, yet, I embarked on this project, and I set out to visit communities made infamous, communities that I knew only as symbols of everything undesirable.

Soon after I sat for the first time inside the community center of Dr. Pila, a public housing project, in 2003, having been informed that there was an active war between drug *puntos* (camps), a car alarm began to blare in the background. A rock had been hurled through a car window. Even before this very first day in "the field," fear—elusive yet obdurate—was a companion. Months into the research, as I approached Dr. Pila's gates to interview Gisela, a management company staffer and resident of public housing, and walk around the development, she asked me to leave. My field notes that day read: "Hoy no se podía . . . habían matado a un muchacho de Dr. Pila anoche en Portugués y ya habían herido un muchacho de Portugués. No se sabe quién fué, pero dijeron que tuviera cuidado hoy todo el día. Me dijo que era mejor que me fuera" (It can't be done today . . . a guy from Dr. Pila was killed in Portugués last night, and another guy from Portugués had already been wounded. It was unknown who it was, but we were told to be on the lookout all day. She told me that it was better if I left). So I left that day. But still I returned to interview Gisela and others. And it was Gisela who did me the favor of taking pictures of Dr. Pila when no other resident would volunteer to do so. The "war" had forced a self-imposed curfew. I was warned to leave the community before nightfall and I acceded. But, still, I returned.

An equally persistent, different fear was present in the private gated communities. Fear of not being recognized and preoccupations of being suspected and rejected because of my demeanor and the color of my skin occupied my mind and informed my comportment. I wrote the following field note, after an interview in a private gated community:

> The man had told me to make sure I was punctual. When I rang his house he explained everything I was to do. . . . When I arrived, I shook his hand and proceeded into his house. . . . The tall, White, light-eyed gentleman wanted to know . . . what was I doing and where was I in school, where had I gone to do my bachelor's and my master's degrees, why I went to Michigan after Stanford and Harvard and why I didn't stay in both to continue my studies. He talked about people he knew who went to Michigan and Stanford. He wanted to know my last name—"*es inglés*" (it is English)—and where my family was from. During the interview, at times I thought that I had to write something about "interviewing while black in Puerto Rico." Interesting feelings came up for me, as the man talked about most people in his neighborhood being "Caucásicos." I don't know what that's about! And I don't know if it is a reaction to me, if the issue would come up with a non-black interviewer. I think that's why so many questions were asked about me, my legitimacy, my roots, where I came from, how I had done what I had done, and if it was true, valid, and even possible. After the interview, he had more questions—what was I going to do with my degree. . . . I think that he was both interested and also interested in showing his intellect and knowledge. I could tell when he was uncomfortable because his tone changed. When he talked about the neighborhood he sounded like a politician. When we talked about people and the *residenciales* (public housing) he talked more from emotions, uncomfortable and with feelings of general disdain. A few times he caught himself and said that he didn't intend to be so negative . . . BUT . . . (you know what's next) it is negative. The interview

ended on a very friendly note and he wished me luck in my marriage, parenthood, and studies. GOODBYE!

In "the field," facing so much discomfort, I continually asked myself why I returned to these places. Throughout I wasn't quite sure of the extent of the insecurity, how true or real it was, whether I was in danger, and, if so, what type of danger it would be. Fear informs the method and the subject of this work. While "fear"—of crime, violence—has been used to explicate the global rise of gated communities, fear can be about many different things: of the unknown, of the Other, of contact, of crossing a boundary. These fears, I find, shape life in the twenty-first-century city in ways that curtail the city's potential. This book is not about fear per se but about how social beliefs and imaginings become real, frozen in space, and, in turn, reinforcements for social boundaries and social inequalities.

In the twentieth century, Puerto Rico experienced what has come to be a typical story of boom and bust and rise and fall in postindustrial cities. Between the 1930s and 1950s, the heyday was accompanied by an army of industrialists, researchers, urban planners, and technocrats who sought to build and showcase the island as a prototype of development and progress. But in the latter part of the twentieth century, *la isla del encanto* (enchantment island) gave way to what my brother Juancho calls *la isla del desencanto* (the island of disenchantment), with high indexes of poverty, unemployment, and crime. This duality of enchantment/disenchantment inhabits this book, as I convey the failed social promises of industrialism, urban life, the city, and new and modern public and single-family housing. The shiny buildings, smooth and wide highways, and concrete homes were meant to beckon a future of progress and success but instead became the hallmarks of fear, insecurity, segregation, and inequality. As a result, the purpose of a city has been lost; there are few encounters between classes, and neighbors seldom encounter the street or each other—there is nonurban isolation amid ultra-urban complexity. The house, not the city, not the nation, has become the locus of social life and the family, the central unit. Gated housing for the poor and the affluent has fostered the formal division of communities and has broken contact across class and race.

This book, thus, is about the way the built environment—housing, gates, neighborhoods—reflects and refracts social ideals, beliefs, and separations by race and class, and how it does this both physically and symbolically. Two private and two public housing enclaves in Ponce, Puerto Rico—one of each gated formally, one with invisible gates, and one with gates enclosing individual mansions—illustrate how gates look in and look out and affect both those inside and outside. Gates transform daily routines, reshape community experience, and reroute movement across the city, defining the boundary lines of class and race. Through housing and the gates, race and class cement themselves while remaining masked, a codified cartography of privilege and disadvantage.

You will find that this book is as much about me as it is about my scholarship. I didn't willingly embrace this realization because scholars are trained to be "objective," "scientific," "unbiased." In this work, I am none; I could not be any of these. I did not arrive at the research new, fresh-eyed, and unencumbered; instead, I was informed by a history and a web of relationships to the communities I studied. After seeing community gates continually spring up on the island's landscape, I myself found it hard to navigate the city. Controlled access points were established in previously open neighborhoods like the private *urbanización* (subdivision) where I grew up, or the public ones I was often discouraged from visiting, and I worried about the "real" and "imagined" motivations, in addition to the implications of such constructions.

In this volume my perceptions and views, like my fears, are echoed and reinforced, co-constituted with those of my informants. (In the interest of maintaining confidentiality, all informants' names are pseudonyms. All translations from Spanish are mine. Racial identifications, however, are the informants' own.) The book reflects my fears and hopes as well as my own intellectual, academic, and personal positioning as a black woman of Dominican descent, doing research in the city where I was born and where I grew up. Ponce is a place I continue to visit and continue to think of longingly, sometimes optimistically and other times morosely, as home.

The Native Outsider

It is as if, then, the beauty—the beauty of the sea, the land, the air,
the trees, the market, the people, the sounds they make—were a
prison, and as if everything and everybody inside it were locked out.
—Jamaica Kincaid, *A Small Place*

Roy Lichtenstein's painting *Interior with African Mask* (1991) caught my attention from the first time I saw it, as a college freshman at Harvard's Fogg Art Museum. It depicted a modern living room in the front plane, a dining room in the background, with firm geometric lines, symmetric patterns and prints, and bright colors. But the furnishings seemed incongruous with "Africa." And then I saw it—on a shelf was a West African mask. In an art class later, I learned about Picasso's adoption of African masks, the beginning of modernist art, and Orientalism and the Western artists' use of the "Other" to define their own art. The mask in the painting seemed to be the only live object in Lichtenstein's living room: It stared back at the viewer. I saw myself in it. Born and raised in Ponce, Puerto Rico, the daughter of Dominican immigrants, and proudly identified as *negrita* (black), I grew up in between boundaries, along social fault lines that drew me inside but that seemed to leave me, always, outside, staring back, like the mask.[1] I was incongruous, uncomfortable, a counter piece to be admired, or not. I was and am a native outsider.

My father, a civil engineer who built big concrete buildings in Puerto Rico, has experienced many worlds. He grew up in an English-speaking sugar-mill town on the outskirts of San Pedro de Macorís in the Dominican Republic (famous for world-class baseball players), and he mopped floors briefly in

New York City at the Empire State Building's Fanny Farmer candy store and at the Port Authority Bus Terminal before constructing buildings and housing projects in New York and Puerto Rico. Because he was an offspring of migrations from St. Kitts, Nevis, St. Thomas, he also lived between boundaries. My mother, a tried-and-true *capitaleña* (a citizen of Santo Domingo, the capital city of the Dominican Republic) and daughter of a self-made rich builder, made the best of her marriage-work exile in Ponce and dedicated her life to building a family and making sense of her position in the unmalleable Ponce society through crafts: sewing, baking, and interior decorating.

With three children (I am the middle child) and with occasional visits by an older sibling on my father's side, my parents bought a home in a solidly middle-class subdivision in the northern part of Ponce and sent their children to a local private college-preparatory school. The Caribbean School was established in 1954 by Americans of Ponce's petrochemical plant. It was the first layer of my native outsider status. Through my elementary school years in the 1970s, the school seemed to be a multicultural haven—Americans, Puerto Ricans, a smattering of global children from, among other places, Japan, Israel, Germany, and the Dominican Republic. It was a model of the growing industrial and racially and class-integrated society Puerto Rico could become—the very society that architects of the New Deal and Operation Bootstrap had envisioned and planned, four decades before I was born. Language and ethnicity were, to me, the first evident lines of my demarcation. At the Caribbean School, we moved, sometimes abruptly, sometimes smoothly, from an English classroom with American teachers to a Spanish playground with Puerto Rican students, to a Spanish home; mothers were "Mom," "Ima," "Mama," or "Mami." As I got older, everything grew or seemed more delimited. A new school policy (soon abandoned) prohibited the use of Spanish outside of the classroom; Spanish retreated to subversive spots in secretive whispers. Important and discrete class, race, and gender markings revealed themselves in many clues: I was told that I looked like a boy because of my short cropped afro; I was asked by classmates how it felt to be "negra"; I was assigned to play the only credible role for a negra in the elementary school Christmas play (a Raggedy Ann). Race had been drawn for me at six, in school, as a dividing line. Class now emerged as an identifying mark, and, much later for me, sexuality, too, became perceptible, fixed, with gender, increasingly obvious, unavoidable, durable, obdurate as a characteristic that separated one from another.

My parents compelled us to move in between all the lines of division, to circumvent them, to challenge them. Yet, ironically, their strategy, to me, led to boundaries that were impossible to ignore. My mother's decision to send my sister and me to an *etiqueta y protocolo* (etiquette and manners) class was certainly not explicitly a political but, rather, a cultural legacy from the Dominican Republic of what was expected of "well-educated girls." Every Saturday morning for three months, we left our middle-class suburban *urbanización* (subdivision) to go to *el pueblo* (the city center) of Ponce to learn proper comportment: how to place a fork and knife at a table setting, what color underwear to wear with a sheer white dress, how to walk gracefully down a runway, how to keep our legs together when we sat down. I remember both hating and loving the class. The teacher refused to pronounce my name correctly: "I like Zairé more than Zaire, so I will call you Zairé," she said in Spanish, and I cringed as the Spanish pronunciation of my African name became unrecognizable by emphasis on the last, not the first, syllable. Yet, very tall for my age, I dreamed that this class might lead to my being discovered as a model. It would be another boundary that could lead to excelling—beauty and blackness. Achievement, in school, in sports, and in fashion, could transcend boundaries.

My "need" to excel came from a precocious understanding of inequality, of hierarchy, of social boundaries. Within those status standards, I was not the same as I saw myself. I was deemed less than I was to myself and an outsider. So, in fashion class as in school, I paid close attention—fork to the right of the plate, knife with the cutting edge in to the left, *color carne* (skin-tone) underwear (hard to find for my skin color in the early 1980s) under white clothing, and a plié at the end of the runway. That promised a recognition of beauty, which, to me, meant being inside. At the end of the fashion course, in a big finale at a recently gender-integrated Catholic school, a fashion show would award prizes and, thus, break down another boundary. In our *bordado* (crocheted) dresses, which my mother had sent for from her native Santo Domingo, my sister and I strutted down the runway, sure of our reward. The judges awarded the prettiest dress, the best walk, and the best-looking model prizes to fair-skinned girls with long dark hair. These were the same girls chosen for lead roles in every school play and as María in the Christmas nativity scene. Two black girls of Dominican descent, of admirable height and comportment, would win no prize. We were outside the parameters of beauty.

The good old dogma of equal opportunity and hard work promised recognition within academic settings. I fiercely went after the top grades, determined to be smart, be "the best." In sports, too, I ran track as fast as I could, jumped as high as I could, played basketball and tennis, excelled at volleyball. Little did I know that I was confirming a racial stereotype that blacks (of course) are better at sports than those who are more white. But, even in that seemingly more democratic world, I felt like an outsider. In volleyball practices, I would move away from the chatter of jokes about Dominicans and from teammates who called a black girl on another team "Shaka Zulu." In the out-of-school basketball league my father founded and ran, which often played on basketball courts in public housing, people referred to my parents as "Dominicainos" (instead of "Dominicanos"), thus making fun, inaccurately, of a regional Dominican accent in which the "i" sound replaces "r" and "l" phonetic sounds. The fact that he drove a new silver Volvo (in his most profitable period) made no difference. Because he, the most honest person I have ever known, was a black Dominicano who also provided funds for the league, he was nicknamed "Mafia." In tennis, I felt like Zina Garrison or Lori McNeal, who were both black tennis stars. But I played at tournaments in suffocating elite country clubs against blonde-haired, pigtailed Puerto Rican opponents, petite girls adorned with pastel-colored ribbons who talked to me in English, assuming, because I was at an upper-class contest but was black that I must be from the English-speaking Caribbean, or an American—an outsider, for sure. Therefore, I got to the courts just before match time, with not a minute to spare, and, at final score, I got out of there as fast as possible. How far outside I was. One night, when I was about eleven, my sister and I and other children were picked up in a car by a classmate's mother, for whom race did not seem to matter much (for friendship, that is), for a "disco party" at a private country club called El Club Deportivo. Some of us were members, some were not. Every child was admitted hospitably, except for my sister and me. The guard at the gate told us we could not enter. Our classmate's mother drove us home. Days later, after another white parent complained, the club sent a note of apology and promised free admission to the next disco party. We did not try again. Though, in fact, we were insiders, we had been seen and identified as outsiders.

Our home was a cocoon, a buffer against the worlds outside—inside-out. At home, race, class, and gender dissolved; girls could be both gentle and strong, *negritos* were always beautiful, and class and national borders (Dominican and Puerto Rican, in particular) were inconsequential. Unknowingly, serendipitously, my native outsiderness and my parents' attempts to move us between or across and over boundaries had established an important identity and relationship to boundaries that turned out to be tremendously useful for research, at Harvard and at the University of Michigan—I could inhabit, to some degree, quite different communities, and I could cross boundaries as a native outsider. My identity as a chameleon allowed for movement, inside and outside, in between. I was inside but never ceased to feel, in some dimension, outside.

Scholars have debated how insider and outsider statuses shape the research enterprise; outsiders are understood to have a detached, and thus, objective view that makes them privy to underlying theories and relationships; the insiders are understood to be unable to get over conscious and unconscious attachments.[2] Those who value the insider view suggest that it brings insights routinely overlooked by the outsider; those who value the outsider view assert an "objective," clear-headed, unbiased view of the phenomena examined. But an "egocentric predicament," Robert K. Merton suggested, makes all knowledge—from insider or outsider—subjective, inherently biased. Alford Young, Jr., suggests that insider and outsider identities are not fixed; at times, researchers are inside and, at times, outside, and each identity allows special insights or creates blind spots.[3] We are all permanently interlocked in "overlapping" identities that position us differently in relation to situational realities; identities are in motion, in flux, and in transit.[4] Yet identities become somewhat obdurate—and, especially, in research in places of an ongoing relationship; there, our identities and relationships can coagulate, become settled, in our minds and in the minds of others, shifting but in place. This is what I think Patricia Hill Collins means by the "outsider-within" label for the perspective black women scholars bring to the academy—outsiders who are inside.[5] Am I a native outsider or an outsider within? The ordering of the noun and adjective is important. In many ways I do not enter these communities from outside to be admitted inside. I'm from here, I have a preexisting relationship. But the view, to me, and from me, identifies me. In some ways, I am—like the African mask—an outsider-from-there.

The native outsider status reveals a degree of fooling, of deep-set emotions, of codification, of hiding, of shame, of not being able to reveal. This is why I write about gates. Gates "freeze" shameful ideas of separation, of race, class, gender inequality; they keep out things that are embarrassing, not readily accepted. The freezing is not necessarily conspiratorial but rather an accepted myth of inclusion and exclusion. To some, this serves as a "color-blind" perspective (where institutional racism and discrimination are considered made obsolete by equal opportunity).[6] Therefore, it becomes an individual's problem, not the society's. But color blindness masks inequalities and maintains white privilege by pretense. It gives the privileged "psychological comfort" and hinders redress, removing public debate on programs intended to address racial inequality.[7] What David Roediger calls the "wages of whiteness" and racial privilege are, in Puerto Rico today, compounded in such a color-blind ideology, denying intent, yet hurt is manifest. Isabelo Zenón Cruz captures this duality in his 1973 work on racism in Puerto Rico:[8]

> Un discrimen que no aflora a la conciencia debe hallarse demasiado arraigado en nuestro ser; es tan nuestro que ni siquiera advertimos su presencia. Sin conciencia no hay maldad en un acto dado. Sin embargo, puede producir mucho mal sobre aquellos seres contra los que va dirigidos. Un rayo no tiene la culpa de matarme pero causa mi muerte, me produce ese mal, me priva del bien radical de la vida.

> (A prejudice that does not reach the conscience is probably located too deep in our being that we do not even notice its presence. Without conscience there is no wrong intended in an act. However, it can produce significant damage over those who it is directed to. It is not lightning's fault that it kills me, but it causes my death, it produces that damage, it takes away my radical right to life.)[9]

When children from public housing, who attended the public school next door to the Caribbean School, walked by the gate of my private school it was better to pretend not to see or hear them, not to invite them in or acknowledge them. Not heeding the protocol, I created occasions for us to meet—as president of the Student Council, I made sure representatives of the top public high schools were invited to our ceremony; I sought integration wherever I could find it. I hung out with friends who lived in public housing communities, and my first romantic interest was a boy who lived in a *caserío* (public housing project) in Ponce. I entered and exited those spaces, ignoring warnings to stay away. I found comfort there; sometimes, there, I was beautiful, and sometimes I was seen as belonging. Sometimes I felt I was finally inside.

Home is where the heart is, where "everybody knows your name." This correlation between self and housing, the longing for "home" and a sense of being outside, is probably why, in this book, I focus on homes, housing, and space. Homes and neighborhoods offer a sense of belonging, a basis for identity and community.[10] But even a home can exclude. Indeed in Puerto Rico, in the United States, in Latin America, and in much of the world, homes and residential neighborhoods have been a vehicle for race, ethnic, and class exclusion.[11] Dogmatic (racist, sexist, heteronormative) notions of the home, of the family—mother, father, and child—are contained in and imposed through housing policies, real estate market practices, and urban plans. From postwar redlining mortgage policies that excluded African Americans from participating in the wealth-building practices of homeownership in the United States, effectively segregating them in poverty, to the "fortified enclaves" of the rich in Brazil and the racially homogeneous gated enclaves of South Africa, homes help sort populations by race and class, distributing inequality.[12] This book shows how race and class are elaborated through space in modern-day Puerto Rico and, in turn, how space codifies and masks these inequalities.

Stuart Hall writes that Caribbeans are bound in their colonial and violent history; they cannot preexist oppression or "go back through the eye of the needle."[13] As Jamaica Kincaid navigated the world of colonial Antigua, she noted the power of being inside and outside of home, of country.[14] Kincaid is unable to read herself outside of the English language or to experience "home" without oppression: she is inside but always outside. This inevitable native outsider sense of structured identity was useful as I visited public and private housing communities in Ponce. José Luis González wrote, in his influential work *El país de cuatro pisos* (The four-storyed country) that in Puerto Rican society the foundation and true culture is the Afro-Puerto Rican society, despite its overlay and camouflage by three upper levels of local and foreign white elite interests and practices.[15] Growing up in Puerto Rico, I straddled these levels and worlds, moving between the elite and the working class. From the intentions of my parents, I obtained metaphorical visas to enter different communities. I could, in my research, now move between *urbanizaciones* and *caseríos* and converse with those in each. In private homes, I employed the lessons in comportment from my etiqueta y protocolo class and from accumulated upper-middle-class affiliates. In *caseríos*, I could cross gates to experience a popular and communal Puerto Rico. I could inhabit a world in between those who lived behind the gates and fences of poverty and control and those who hid in colonial mansions behind self-imposed electronic gates and walls. As a researcher, I could gain access to both, as an observer and as a participant, while I observed both myself and those I interviewed.

Chapter 1

Fortress Gates of the Rich and Poor: Past and Present

> With every foundation of the city one should expect definitions and boundaries.
>
> —Lewis Mumford, *The City in History*

On November 8, 1993, Dr. Manuel de la Pila, the largest public housing project in the city of Ponce in Puerto Rico (the second-largest public housing authority in the U.S. federal system), became a gated community. Up until then, gates had kept people out rather than keeping people in. Gates had become the exclusive privilege of the affluent communities; their residents, for at least a decade, from about 1987, had been quietly erecting gates and fences to surround their homes and communities. Gates of the rich protected elegant homes and gardens and shut out intruders. In 1993, the first new gates of the poor in Ponce went up noisily under the supervision of law enforcement helicopters engaged in drug raids on public housing and under the eyes of television cameras. To some government functionaries, the public housing gates gave the poor in Puerto Rico access to a privilege heretofore exclusive to private homeowners; the residents of public housing disagreed. While the gates of privilege locked out urban chaos, in the words of a Dr. Pila resident the public housing gates simply "lock up" and in.

The public and private housing gates of Puerto Rico are visual symbols of a historical trend that has lasted for centuries within unequal communities around the globe. Gates have been an integral part of city design from Rome to Britain to the colonies of the New World.[1] In San Juan, Havana, and Santo

Domingo, gated fortresses protected the new colonies from impending attacks from the sea. Gates controlled and banished the powerless from being able to access the cities. Modern gates in residential communities have a similar function in the United States, in Latin America and the Caribbean, and in Europe, Asia, and the Middle East. Most have been erected as private enclaves, in the name of protection from crime, locking out an increasingly complex city.[2] The gated communities in public housing extended the gating apparatus to non-privileged communities. Gates to control the poor have been erected in New York, San Francisco, St. Louis, and Washington, D.C.; in favelas in Brazil; in the fortresses that mark racial and ethnic cleavages in South Africa; and as strategic camouflaging within slum cities throughout the world.[3] In private communities, gating arranged by insiders keeps others out; in public housing, gates are controlled by outsiders to gain protection for themselves from those inside. In locking themselves in, the privileged lock undesirables out. Gates for the poor reverse this order; they shut undesirables in. In both, the gates are erected in the interest of an upper class and, in modern cities, of the primarily white.

The Enemy Outside and Inside

Historically, gates have assumed an enemy: an enemy inside, an enemy outside. In elite neighborhoods, retirement communities, resorts, and even on military bases and bulwarks, gates have been intended to create a safe and protected sanctuary. In prisons, as in poor neighborhoods, and even in schools, gates are mechanisms of control and discipline of those inside. Gates are symbols of power that defend and protect monarchs, governments, religious institutions, military posts, colonizing migrant bodies, and empires; they afford power by segregation, locking in access to resources and material wealth. Lewis Mumford wrote that fortresses originated as symbols of exclusivity, reserved for medieval aristocrats: "As late as 1750 BC in Palestine the tribal chieftains occupied fortresses, while most of their subjects lived in surrounding hamlets, and moved into the fortified enclosure only in times of peril."[4] But the gate quickly became "a practical necessity, not just a symbol" that "magnified the selfish absorptions and the anxious preoccupations of the city's king or governor."[5] By the fifteenth century, the old citizen-policed walls had become vulnerable to the new artilleries of European power mongering, "a complicated system, with enclosures within enclosures," with "outworks, salients, bastions, in spearhead forms."[6]

Elaborate gates—external and internal—were considered necessary when constructing the foundations of colonial America. In San Juan, as in Havana and Santo Domingo, centuries ago, fortresses and gated towns helped imprint the Spanish empire on American geography. "The new colonial towns . . . looked backward, not forward—for they followed the standard Bastide pattern"[7] of southwestern France's thirteenth- and fourteenth-century towns. Towering coastal fortresses proclaimed to invaders from the sea that a land had already been claimed. Protection and defensibility were crucial to urban planning throughout the colonizing enterprise; central to building "the New World" was a concern with defending it—outside and in. The Spanish Law of the Indies made clear that the towns of the New World were to be built behind four protective walls, each with a guarded entrance.[8] Puerto Rico, for example, "was considered a *presidio* . . . a place whose strategic location demanded skillful fortification, a strong garrison, and the needed artillery."[9] And, with more or less support, by the sixteenth century the island had become protected by garrisoned fortifications distributed throughout, including La Fortaleza, Santa Elena, and El Boquerón. Of El Morro (the most elaborate of all forts) the governor-captain of the island, General Menéndez de Valdés, wrote to the Council of the Indies, in a letter of November 20, 1590, that "when it [El Morro] is completed will be the strongest that his majestie hath in all the Indies. And now the people of the country sleepeth in security."[10] By the eighteenth century, San Juan's city wall had been completed, with walls "seven and a half meters high and about six meters wide," and seven bulwarks, the castles of El Morro and La Fortaleza, and three gates.[11]

Threats to colonies also came from within. Colonizers built fences, walls, and cages to defend themselves from people inside their walls who threatened the colonial pursuit and their mercantilist accumulation of wealth. The Law of the Indies instructed settlers to, "with greatest possible haste[,] . . . erect jointly some kind of palisade or dig a ditch around the main plaza so that the Indians cannot do them harm."[12] Homes, too, were to be fortified: "All town homes are to be so planned that they can serve as a defense or fortress against those who might attempt to create disturbances or occupy the town."[13] Gates, fences, and walls were sorting mechanisms: "The wall . . . served as both a military device and an agent of effective command over the urban population. . . . Socially it emphasized the difference between the insider and outsider."[14] They sorted physically and also symbolically: "Nor are the Indians to enter the circuit of the settlement until the latter is complete and in condition for defense and the houses built. . . . They will consequently fear the Spaniards so much that they will not dare to offend them and will respect them and desire their friendship."[15] In order to expand the outward defense machinery, those considered insiders were allowed to hold posts in the garrisons; natives—by the eighteenth century "a motley laboring class" of mixed European, Taino/Carib, Arab/Moor, Canarian, West and Central African, and Creole—had been prohibited from holding posts as guards.[16] Kelvin Santiago-Valles notes that one of the principal penal structures of eighteenth- and nineteenth-century Puerto Rico held prisoners sentenced to labor in construction projects; the function of the first *presidio* in Puerto Rico was to "shelter and control the felons working on . . . fortresses." [17] The very act of defense from an enemy outside required the identification and control of potential enemies inside.

In colonial San Juan during the eighteenth and nineteenth centuries, the wall distributed power and aided in segregation, distinction, and control of a growing urban population. Sorting out, by walls, was regulated by governmental institutions with a panoptic design, that is, "arrang[ing] spatial unities that mak[e] it possible to see constantly and to recognize immediately."[18] Developed by Jeremy Bentham, in England, panopticism became the guiding architectural and philosophical principle for carceral institutions of eighteenth-century Europe. Panoptic institutions, like prisons, were government-controlled environments, structures that limited and monitored movement and that had regulations to monitor behavior and daily routines. Panoptic architecture was the chosen design for social regulatory institutions, from state-run psychiatric asylums to penitentiaries and reformatories, schools, and, to some extent, hospitals, all intended to facilitate control.[19] In San Juan, panoptic structures established order.

One of Puerto Rico's first penal institutions, the presidio at La Puntilla, was built between 1809 and 1820 as "a house of correction . . . modeled to the institutions established in Spain under the *Reglamento de prisiones* of 1807."[20] The felons were "supervised and guarded by the soldiers stationed in nearby artillery post and barracks." In prisons, inmates were not kept in panoptic rooms but in *galeras* (open halls), segregated and regulated by gravity of the offense, by gender, and by class.[21] The military groups faced outward, too, to protect the city from attack. By the nineteenth century, the *Casa de Beneficencia* (the Beneficence House) was the panoptic structure, disciplining and controlling function of all government-run social institutions in Puerto Rico. Initially intended as a center for rehabilitating "vice-ridden" women, the Casa de Beneficencia eventually provided "shelter, care, occupation, instruction, and moralization" for a wider range of undesirable men and children—"'delinquents,' 'invalids, orphans, paupers, abandoned old people,' 'the demented,' 'deserters,' 'patricides and infanticides,' and 'unruly slaves [until 1873]' of both sexes who populated as well as wandered throughout urban centers of the island, particularly San Juan."[22] Punitive corporal punishments were imposed: "Manacles, iron fetters, and similar forms of chained restriction were commonplace . . . as were whips for flogging and booths provided with streams of high-pressure water at extreme temperatures. All of these punitive technologies were deployed to physically discipline and morally refashion the inmates, on whose colonized bodies the Truth of medical cures and Christian repentance were being inscribed in the vernacular of pain."[23] Built in a poor shantytown, the Casa de Beneficencia provided housing and discipline, serving the purpose of sorting the poor and identifying communities that required surveillance, regulation, and confinement.

Who was labeled as undesirable responded to social and economic demands. In San Juan, the wall sorted people by social class and race. As the nineteenth century progressed, a growing middle class and entrepreneurial elite dictated the use of space inside and outside the military wall:

> The well-to-do—the old "nobility by birth" (with distinguished family names), the new landed and commercial wealth, and the professional class that flowed from both—lived *intramuros* [inside the wall]. Relegated to the outskirts of San Juan after midcentury were the dwellings of working-class families (and some of their workplaces . . .). . . . Not only was this segment of the population more expendable in case of attack or accidental industrial disaster; it could also be forced to live further away from economic opportunity. The powerful, then, expediently controlled the space in which they and others lived—space which was not only safer but also advantageous by virtue of its location within the radius of profit circumscribed by the city wall.[24]

By using formal ordinances, mutual aid societies, charitable organizations, and other means, "social reformers and government officials directed the working class to their appropriate economic station."[25] Enforced by municipal guards, the ordinances of 1883 laid out an exhaustive and strict code of comportment in the city, regulating everything from dress to talking and singing to child-rearing practices. The historian Teresita Martínez-Vergne writes, "Whether these ordinances were intended as etiquette guidelines from a nascent bourgeoisie to their subordinates . . . or as a device of municipal officials to preempt potentially dangerous situations, they were unequivocally transmitted from the knowing to the ignorant, the powerful to the weak, the privileged to the unfortunate."[26]

Inside city walls, prolific government regulations and ordinances controlled the movement and decorum of San Juan's poor; however, race, inscribed through the institution of slavery, became a prime indicator of who was to be regulated in urban spaces. In Puerto Rico, "Whites, slaves, and their descendants" were clearly demarcated from each other and intensely surveilled. "Newly arrived Africans (*bozales*)" and free people of color were strictly and especially regulated by being restricted from some city spaces; they could not travel together and could hold dances only near city walls and at restricted times of day.[27] Even after the abolition of slavery in 1873, ordinances of 1883 imposed a special onus on "colored folk," who "were always to walk on the street to allow Whites the use of narrow sidewalks at midcentury."[28] The institution of slavery required marking and identifying, as well as disciplining, because slaves were considered a threat to the city's order, power, and capital. City spaces were prime sites for disciplining, controlling, and reaffirming the institution of slavery in San Juan, as in other urban centers across the Caribbean and in the United States.[29] In the city of Bridgetown, Barbados, centrally located urban cages confined slaves, disciplining blacks and reminding them and others of their inferior and subservient racial and class position.[30] The cages to hold slaves, like fences and walls, became a new version of the "spectacle of the scaffold"— to punish the guilty and remind "the potentially guilty" of the unequal social order.[31]

Crime and Enemies of the Twentieth Century

Marking power and establishing control through walls and gates continued on into the twentieth century, quarantining rich and poor. In 1983, the writer Edgardo Rodríguez Juliá, "a white guy with a chubby face, a handlebar mustache, and glasses," walked into the largest public housing project in San Juan, Luis Lloréns Torres, to attend the funeral of Luis Rafael Cortijo, a famous black Puerto Rican musician from "Lloréns" (as the project is popularly known). The projects were seen as danger zones, "legendary symbols of all the criminality."[32] Like Rodríguez Juliá (self-described as white), I myself, a proud *negra* was nervous when I entered the public housing projects of Gándara and Dr. Pila in Ponce in 2004 to interview residents, my first time there in more than a decade.

Fear reflects how public housing has been imagined, symbolized, and stigmatized. Public housing communities have been presented publicly, and through policy, as places to be dreaded and from which to escape. With the growing public and private preoccupation over crime, public housing communities have come to be perceived as accomplices to crime, their infamy cemented through policy approaches that segregate and label them as threats. Outsiders warned me about entering such spaces. I encountered similar concerns from public housing residents themselves, members of the Resident Council, and others in Dr. Pila who all urged me to leave Dr. Pila early after a night of shootouts, and I did not dare trespass internal gates to go beyond the areas that had been sanctioned by the Council for my research. I walked fearfully on silent streets to reach the one access gate in that forty-acre project. To avoid crime, one had to avoid public housing communities—the meaning was "both blurred and perfectly clear."[33] Cordoning crime required avoiding and segregating the poor, or those people who had committed no crime but who were presumed to have done so.

After a dramatic rise in violence during the 1960s and 1970s, a consequence of drug consumption, Puerto Rico seemed, by the late 1980s and early 1990s, to be drowning in a crime wave.[34] Its murder rate was three times that of the United States; in 1994 it was the U.S. murder capital and a runner-up for the world's highest per capita homicide rate.[35] The city of Ponce reflected the islandwide trends, with an unprecedentedly high crime rate in 1991 and 1993, followed by an erratic decline through the rest of the decade. The print and TV media rode the wave by describing the frenzy and sustaining the fear with daily reports of homicides, carjackings, house hijackings, and armed robberies. Jorge Rodríguez Beruff wrote:

> El crimen se convirtió en el modus vivendi de un tipo de periodismo sensacionalista. . . . De esta manera, para los ochenta y los noventa las noticias televisivas se convirtieron en un interminable desfile de cadáveres y violencia, mayormente de hombres jóvenes de residenciales y barriadas, así como el medio de poner en escena la acción policiaca a través de operativos, redadas, allanamientos, arrestos, ocupación de drogas.

(Crime had become the modus vivendi of a type of sensationalist journalism . . . by the eighties and nineties, television news broadcasting mounted an interminable parade of cadavers and violence primarily of young men from public housing and barrios, as well as the means for staging police actions conducted through operatives, raids, levelings, arrests, and drug confiscations.)[36]

Daily life was marked by crime or the fear of crime and what Theresa Caldeira has referred to as "the talk of crime."[37] In Ponce, in my high school years, we sprinted from our cars to our front doors, afraid of becoming victims of a carjacking. Residents in barricaded mansions in Alhambra told me of being held up at gunpoint on the streets outside their walls in the late 1980s and early 1990s, as they entered their sanctuary on foot or by car. During one of my interviews, two residents traded stories of guns someone had waved at them. Eda talked about an afternoon approach by car to her driveway: "Yo entré y el tipo me siguió con la pistola y abrí los brazos, esperando que me disparara el tiro" (I went in and the guy followed me with a gun. And I opened my arms, waiting for him to shoot). Antonia had taken a quick walk one morning to deliver mail to her neighbor: "De pronto viene un muchacho y me pasa por el lado. . . . 'Esto es un asalto.' . . . En ese momento yo me he vuelto una fiera. Me eché hacia atrás . . . y yo moviendo las piernas empecé a gritar como una gata loca" (Suddenly, a guy comes to my side. . . . "This is a holdup." . . . At that moment I turned into an animal. I moved back . . . and moving my legs started to shriek like a crazy lion). The situation, everyone assured me, was a disaster, an emergency.[38]

Crime came to have an ecology, a geography, a time and a place. Media tended to focus on barrios and on public housing sites as sources of crime. Perpetrators and victims were to be found in sites of poverty and at night. "*No pases por ahí*" (Don't go there) was the standard line, one I heard numerous times during my visits. At night, I was banned from the projects by the residents themselves who told me they locked themselves in their homes.

The media's view repeated and fed a perception, also held by people and affirmed to those to whom I spoke, that crime was sited in barrios, *barriadas* (barrios, shanty town, or public housing), and public housing. A noted political analyst, Juan García-Passalacqua, argued that "everybody knows" that public housing sites are "war zones . . . controlled by the drug lords,"[39] and everybody, including residents of public housing, talked of avoiding such "war zones." When, in 2004, I was shooed away from public housing sites, many residents themselves spoke of people staying away: "*No te metas ahí, te van a matar*" (Don't go in there, you will get killed). To be in the proximity of public housing sites was to invite crime. "Crews from the sewer department, the telephone company, the electric company and other utilities were too fearful to work in these projects," claimed the authors of a 1997 Kennedy School policy brief: "Residents were even afraid to sleep in their beds; instead they slept on the floor, to stay clear of bullets that sometimes came flying through doors and windows. Project playgrounds were empty of children, who, at a young age, automatically went to work for their local drug dealer." [40]

Private-Gate Permissions and Public-Gate Occupations

By the late 1980s, elite residents of Ponce, especially of many communities that found themselves adjacent to public housing because of New Deal policies of integration, petitioned for relief. On May 20, 1987, the government came to the rescue, permitting elite communities to "privatize" certain public streets with gates and thus control access for reasons of safety in order to "participate in their own protection." The Ley de Cierre (Closing Law) allowed municipalities to grant permits to residential communities to restrict public access and traffic to their neighborhoods, streets, houses, and pedestrian walkways via a controlled access infrastructure that would limit entry and exit.[41] The purpose of the law was explicit:

El propósito principal de la citada Ley es proveer a nuestra ciudadanía un instrumento adicional para combatir la criminalidad y así lograr una participación más activa de nuestras comunidades en la lucha contra el crimen. Se trata de un mecanismo que la Ley concede a la ciudadanía para que participe efectivamente en su propia protección, permitiendo que los recursos de la Policía de Puerto Rico se puedan utilizar adecuadamente en áreas de alta incidencia criminal.

(The principal motive of the cited Law is to provide to our citizenship an additional instrument to combat crime, and by those means to achieve a more active participation from our communities in the fight against crime. This is a mechanism that the Law concedes to the citizenry so that they can effectively participate in their own protection, allowing the resources of the Puerto Rican police to be utilized in areas of high criminal incidence.)[42]

No doubt, such strategies can be traced to the colonial trends that erected moats and fortification for protection. Although, at the end of the nineteenth century, gates and walls were commonly used by the wealthy in U.S. and European cities in order to seek refuge from the problems associated with rapid industrialization and urbanization, gates did not become more common for residential areas, retirement developments, resorts, and country clubs in the United States itself, primarily in Florida and California, until the 1960s, 1970s, and into the 1980s. [43] Edward J. Blakely and Mary Gayle Snyder suggest that an increasingly volatile and uncertain urban environment, plus a need to connect to the psychological core of individual life—the home—led to the gating of residential neighborhoods.[44] Other scholars maintain that the fear of crime is perpetuated by, and coincident with, segregation and discrimination.[45] The anthropologist Theresa Caldeira writes that the "talk of crime is contagious": "These narratives and practices impose partitions, build up walls, delineate and enclose spaces, establish distances, segregate, differentiate, impose prohibitions, multiply rules of avoidance and exclusion, and restrict movements."[46]

By the 1970s, criminologists, social thinkers, and policymakers were identifying gates as important tools for combating crime. Environmental crime prevention interventions—building gates to privatize space, building road bumps or other barriers to reduce pedestrian and vehicular traffic flows, removing plants and bushes, engaging residents in clean-up drives and neighborhood watches—became popular in the late 1960s and early 1970s as a means to reduce crime in neighborhoods considered to be havens. These environmental strategies have since become a staple in global efforts to police neighborhoods. Environmental criminology itself derives from an understanding that communities, particularly the spatial arrangement of housing and neighborhoods and their relationship to individuals and organizations, mediate crime and that community collaboration and community supervision are necessary to control and prevent it.[47]

Ecology of crime research, in the tradition of environmental criminology, has focused on social disorganization and on youth; "routine activities theory," an extension of this tradition, suggests that crime requires three conditions: (1) a motivated offender; (2) a suitable target; and (3) an absence of capable guardianship.[48] In the early 1970s, Oscar Newman discovered that temporary gates led to a greater sense of safety for residents in a New York public housing site, and he outlined steps to meet the three conditions. Newman argued that in certain residential structures and spatial arrangements residents could defend, and exert territoriality over, public spaces. He favored a growing privatizing of space with gates and other interventions to monitor space. Two "natural policing" strategies became popular: the first, following Newman, favored closed "impermeable" environments with strangers excluded; a second, posed by Jane Jacobs's work, favored open spaces where strangers with "eyes on the street" participate in policing.[49] This tradition resulted in practical ecological crime-intervention strategies referred to as Crime Prevention through Environmental Design, which include a range of architectural interventions aimed at increasing security and monitoring.[50] The impact of environmental interventions and of gating, in particular, on crime is dubious; some researchers have found no real decrease in crime as a result of gating.[51] Others have found that a sense of safety, rather than an actual decline in crime, has been discovered to be the greatest benefit of gating.[52] Nevertheless, perhaps because of their facility for implementation (Oscar Newman's discovery of the effects of gating on public housing was, after all, accidental), the strategies became commonplace worldwide, especially as walls served also to veil poverty.[53]

In Body and Mind: The Dimensions of Walls, Fences, and Gates

Walls are physical and symbolic; they concretize distinctions[54] and, in turn, reinforce and maintain them. They create barriers. A need to sort the world, to define and classify, drives their establishment; to use Michel de Certeau's concept, they politically "'freeze' continuous process into emblems" and social structures.[55] Fences make concrete "mental fences" of discrimination.[56] As J. B. Jackson notes, boundaries are "essential," "the most basic political element in any landscape," itself a "composition of spaces . . . also a composition or web of boundaries."[57] Gates help identify community outsiders and insiders, and they award power, just as fortresses, prisons and cages, moats and ditches, and walls of rich and poor gated communities over the centuries have created and reinforced the distinction of body and mind, visually, actually, and symbolically. Gates delineate social boundaries of inequality: race, class, gender, "good" from "bad," worthy from unworthy.

Imprisonment is, in Edward M. Peters's words, "the public imposition of involuntary physical confinement . . . physical punishments that restrict an individual's freedom of movement."[58] Foucault makes a turn from the physical to the mental aspect of confinement; punishment required not only a physical dimension, but also a mental one. It would become a sign, a regulation and law impressed throughout all social institutions: "This, then, is how one must imagine the punitive city. At the crossroads, in the gardens, at the side of roads being repaired or bridges built, in workshops open to all, in the depths of mines that may be visited, will be hundreds of tiny theatres of punishment."[59] A complex structure signifying physical restriction and psychological confinement requires a redesign and reinterpretation of the wall: "The high wall, no longer the wall that surrounds and protects, no longer the wall that stands for power and wealth, but the meticulously sealed wall, uncrossable in either direction, closed in upon the now mysterious work of punishment, will become, near at hand, sometimes even at the very centre of the cities of the nineteenth century, the monotonous figure, at once material and symbolic, of the power to punish."[60] Walls are symbolic, imbued with explicit function and implicit meaning.

"Cognitive maps" of surroundings are not a product of mere stimulus-response processes.[61] The urban planner Kevin Lynch has noted that "the environment suggests distinctions and relations, and the observer—with great adaptability and in the light of his own purposes—selects, organizes, and endows with meaning what he sees."[62] Lynch calls these images "public images," "common mental pictures carried by large numbers of a city's inhabitants: areas of agreement which might be expected to appear in the interaction of a single physical reality, a common culture, and a basic physiological nature;" "the form of the environment itself play[s] a tremendous role in the shaping of the image."[63]

Throughout Puerto Rico, fences and gates can be read in the city's landscapes, interchangeably and collectively, as edges, landmarks, and nodes. Edges because they are "boundaries between two phases, linear breaks in continuity . . . barriers, more or less penetrable, which close one region off from another," "strongest [when] visually prominent, also continuous in form and impenetrable to cross movement."[64] They are landmarks because they embody in place "frequently used clues of identity and even structure," strongest when located at a junction.[65] They are nodes because they are points of decision making for navigating, "the strategic spots in a city into which an observer can enter, and which are the intensive foci to and from which he is traveling."[66] "They may be primarily junctions, places of a break in transportation, a crossing or convergence of paths, moments of shift from one structure to another."[67] Edges, landmarks, and nodes reflect and direct decision making about breaks, discontinuities, and distinction. Ordering the world, they shape behavior and determine social ascriptions.

Fences and gates in Puerto Rico, through physical qualities and public images, shape the social lives of both the poor and the rich; they reinforce "virtual social identities."[68] Gates for the poor become "stigmata" that attribute disreputable or "spoiled" identities. Gates for the rich are "prestige symbols."[69] Both are reductive representations of communities, "perceptible" and "evident" and reproducible (the mass media is a central producer), with "public images" that take on a self-perpetuating life.[70] These social identities, the sociologist Gerald Suttles writes, "provide a final solution to decision making where there are often no other clear cutoff points for determining how far social contacts should go."[71]

As gates and walls establish and reinforce community boundaries and social permissions, they distribute power; they warn and discipline city navigators; and they shape and sustain race, class, and gender inequality and exclusion, determining and exemplifying a social hierarchy.[72] Herbert Blumer believed that race prejudice is rooted in a sense of group position, maintained by collectively rearticulating a sense of superiority that demeans a subordinate group, justifying social exclusion, solidifying claims to privileges, and sustaining fears and suspicion of that subordinate group.[73]

Walls protect distinctive lifestyles, constituting what Pierre Bourdieu has called a "habitus," a "system of differences, differential position, i.e., everything which distinguishes it from what it is defined and asserted through difference. . . . The most fundamental oppositions in the structure (high/low, rich/poor etc.) tend to establish themselves as the fundamental structuring principles of practices and the perception of practices."[74] "Principles of division, inextricably logical and sociological, function within and for the purposes of the struggle between social groups; in producing concepts, they produce groups, the very groups which produce the principles and the groups against which they are produced. What is at stake in the struggles about the meaning of the social world is power."[75]

The Power of Gates

Locking in and out, gates reflect and effect social relations; they shape race and class inequality. Like the housing they surround, gates are "social structures in the process of becoming," and they make "social rules legible."[76] In doing so, they convey, enforce, and codify social processes, and they reframe life in the twenty-first-century city. Jonathan Charley explains that "the spatial segregation of society along class, gender and ethnic lines . . . is similarly replicated wherever capitalist urbanization gathers pace."[77] Within a politico-economic order, Sharon Zukin agrees that "segregation and exclusion on every level are conceptualized in streets and neighborhoods . . . institutionalized in zoning laws, architecture and conventions of use."[78] Thus, urban policy, master city plans, and urban development programs seeking to control chaos, complement industrialization, and implement civic democracy reproduce the order of spatial inequality and exclusion.[79]

Scholarship on gated communities has recognized their effects, but it has mostly focused on how gates shape life *inside* the privileged communities that they envelop.[80] Behind some gates, community is insinuated and safety is assumed. But gates that service the rich also look out, physically and symbolically delimiting race and class for outsiders, as they do for insiders. Outside these gates of privilege, passersby are warned not to trespass, visitors are forced to make prior arrangements, and neighbors are prescribed to socialize in specific ways. Other types of gates, complementary in their function, enforce practices of social distinction: gates, fortresses, and walls restrain and hide poor communities in segregated residential enclaves, and prisons and cages throughout different historical settings banish undesirables—the poor, racially subordinated—from the city.[81]

A society that in the middle of the twentieth century appeared to be a model for social mobility, an example of what injections of colonial development policy could do (increased life expectancy, reduced fertility, low unemployment, higher per capita income, industrialization), Puerto Rico has become today the exemplar of the less salutary side effects of such programs (crime, a service economy, federal aid dependency, a nonexistent gross national product, high debt, and extreme social inequality). In the 1950s, the heyday of future promise, established urban elites and newly urban rural laborers were to forge a new society, side by side, across class disparities and racial differences. Upward class mobility was believed to be achievable, and race and class distinctions were thought to be nonexistent. The story of housing in Puerto Rico, in particular that of housing for the poor, showcases the island's unfulfilled expectations and downward spiral toward walled segregation. Experiments of integration, of upward mobility, of a common civic pact, of an integrated city, much like the promises of cities throughout the world, failed. The failure is exceedingly perceptible in Puerto Rico's gated landscape. The collapse is obvious in the experiences, frustrations, and disparate worlds of local communities.

Community gates multiplied across Puerto Rico in private and public housing from the 1980s onward. In Ponce, an example of how gates throughout the world distribute inequality, how they come about, how they are managed and perceived, and how they shape life chances is evident. In the center of Ponce, two public and two private communities illustrate the power of gates for reshaping community life by locking in or locking out. From a bird's-eye view, the four communities fit into a vertical trapezoid of about 1.5 square miles; to the north lies Dr. Manuel A. de la Pila, better known as Dr. Pila, a 906-unit public housing unit gated by authorities in 1993. (See Figure 1.) Immediately to the south is the private residential community of Urbanización La Alhambra, with approximately 111 single-family homes; it was one of the first elite suburban residential developments in Ponce. Just southwest of La Alhambra is a small private community of about 50 single-family homes called Extensión Alhambra, whose neighborhood association received permission to gate its community. South of all three is the public housing site José E. Gándara, better known as Gándara, consisting of 270 housing units; its presumed low-crime incidence allowed it to avoid gating by city authorities. Thus, elite housing is bound to the north and south by public housing.

The four communities, and their histories, unequal class statuses, and gates, are closely examined in Chapter 2, in the context of the New Deal reform movement of the 1940s and 1950s that was responsible for two distinct housing types—public housing and private subdivisions—with very distinct social reputations. Built next to each other as a purposeful integration policy, the proximity laid the groundwork for the emergence of the gated community in the 1990s. The four communities—two public, two private, one of each gated—showcase how inequality was erected through housing and the gate. It is in this chapter that the ways in which urban policy and planning affect everyday lives start to become clear. In the face of growing inequality and beliefs of social distinction, the promise of integration collapses and the fence emerges as a mechanism to segregate and to effectively navigate an increasingly complex city.

In Chapter 3, I show that the properties and operation of the gates are

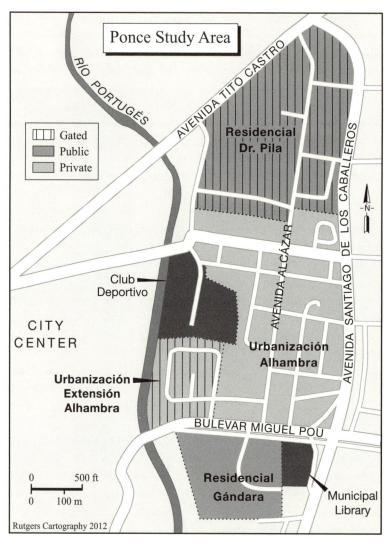

Figure 1. Four adjacent yet unequal communities: the public housing sites of Dr. Pila and Gándara and the private housing sites of Alhambra and Extensión Alhambra. Map by Michael Siegel.

important. Two dimensions of the gate, in tandem, manage the power in, and exerted through, the gate: One is a camouflage of the other. The first dimension is the electronic apparatus that aesthetics conceals in the housing for the elite; this is sophisticated technology that admits members of the same society or their servants and it locks out unsummoned others. Such gates employ a diverse set of technologies; I call them "beeper gates" and "garrison gates": They admit someone who can dial the correct numbers or use electronic devices. All give residents or security staff complete authority over who can enter. The second dimension is the aesthetics of color, design, and architecture that reflect status; bold color and beauty are reserved for the rich. Gated entryways into private neighborhoods of affluence are tastefully designed and perfectly manicured. They range from cement fortresses that circumscribe entire neighborhoods to locked iron gates that blockade streets or individual homes. The gates of public housing, in contrast, are generic and lack adornment and individuality. They form a drab grid of iron bars interspersed with concrete guardhouses (some with one, others with more), each manned by a Puerto Rico police officer behind a one-way mirror. Both distribute power: one by affording more or less control of the technology to specific bodies, the other by credentialing specific bodies and signaling social worth and threat as to who is redeemable and who is not.

In distributing power and making concrete social distinctions, in Chapter 4 I examine how gates reconfigure ideas of community and democracy. While gates expand the range of influence of private communities, they severely limit the political efficacy and self-determination of public housing residents. Public housing residents in turn express apathy over the political process and their influence, and they engage in small acts of resistance like cutting holes in the fences and speaking with impunity of government overseers. These acts reinscribe them as lawless and uncontrollable and force new ideas of a segmented urban democracy.

That the gates' symbolic aspects are as important as their physical contours is the focus of Chapter 5. I refer to the constant mention of gardens among residents as symbolic representations of the unequal lifestyles and community-making practices being secured and protected behind the gates. While gardens have become a way to beautify and improve city spaces, to make communities more equitable, healthier, and safer, they have also become a mechanism for exclusion. For the privileged of Ponce, gardens threatened by urban complexity and proximity to public housing and fear of crime are recovered and protected behind gates, symbolic of a lifestyle of privilege,

security, and order. In contrast, the poor in multifamily gated public housing are funneled to regulated community centers or the renewed city's urban
public spaces with private and public overseers, the axis of a regulated community life where residents are disciplined and monitored. As gardens are
purported to be an extension of life, and urban renewal projects are deemed
to make life in the city better, they can also segregate communities behind
perverted symbols of beauty and order.

Chapter 6 discusses how gates produce and reify exclusion. They, I argue,
freeze class, race, and gender by making opportunities for contact and mobility close to futile, and even undesirable. The gates administer women of affluence, delineating safe and inhabitable city spaces. Poor women, in contrast,
face clashing demands. They are considered inept at tending for their children and are simultaneously expected to be self-sufficient and to earn a living
outside the gates. The gates also solidify and simultaneously mask ideals of
race and practices of racism. Gated housing can spatially script acceptable
bodies, supporting racial privilege and identities of whiteness in private communities, while condemning a racialized poverty that restricts the movement
and opportunity of public housing residents. Throughout, social class and
race are embodied and masked in the gates.

Urban space is a site in which to articulate, negotiate, reframe, and con-
solidate important social identities.[82] Embedded in a history of spatial politics, residential gates emulate the Spanish colonial fortresses, the cages for
urban slaves, the prisons of a former century. Today in Ponce, as in Puerto
Rico overall, public housing developments are shunned by a large segment of
society, and private communities want little to do with their neighbors. Polar
representations and imaginaries of "good" and "bad," "safe" and "dangerous,"
"desirable" and "undesirable," are imprinted in private communities as well as
in public housing.[83] Gates and fences prompt these imaginaries of difference,
and they enforce race and class segregation.

Gates have transformed daily routines of the communities and their
residents, reshaping the experience of community and rerouting movement
across the city. The community gates guard the affluent with barbed wire and
spikes camouflaged by flowers; sentry gates restrain the poor from going in
and out. Gates create a safe and beautiful sanctuary for the elite; for the poor,
they create an aggressive, often barren of beauty, space controlled by government regulations, its monitoring now outsourced to private businesses. They
are modern-day versions of regulatory panoptic structures of the past. The
gates award privilege to the rich and deny it to the poor.

When gates divide and segment a city, the purpose of a city has been lost; encounters between classes are limited to employer and servant, policemen and the policed. Neighbors seldom encounter the street or each other. The house, not the city, becomes the locus of social life and the family, the central unit. The lifestyle of Ponce is a contradiction in terms—nonurban isolation amid ultra-urban complexity. It has not led to social integration. Residents of La Alhambra accuse residents of Dr. Pila and Gándara of stealing their mangoes and throwing stones over their walls. Dr. Pila's children are isolated in a school of their own and have to share a basketball court behind the single entry and exit gate. The gate has created an artificial community, one no longer serving the principal purpose of "gates," which is to identify by landscaping and welcoming. The gate is now used principally like a wall, to protect and confine, choosing whom to welcome and whom to deny. Social control is exerted at an increasingly small scale; both the overarching nation and city have become less and less vital, and thus less real. Division is fostered and contact broken or prevented across class and race.

Ubiquitous and inescapable, gates proliferate in Ponce, inside and out, in commercial locales, in housing (there are also interior walls, separating housing units), within government buildings, within schools and prisons, in gas stations, in parking lots, even in churches. The residential gates rearrange relations between communities and force city navigators to recalculate the social orientation of space. Gates have a psychological function, one of them being to make people feel safer.[84] Another is to create "legible" reminders of social organization, those of race and class.[85]

To move about in Puerto Rico is to confront a landscape composed of gates, the ability of which to control who can move within them play a role in the city's power arrangements. The gates are allegorical creations of a vision of "harmony" in which concepts of the cosmopolitan related to egalitarianism, contact, and acceptance have disappeared.[86] Puerto Rico's people live in secluded worlds, in a posturban modern island society of islands within an island.

Chapter 2

Cachet for the Rich and Casheríos for the Poor: An Experiment in Class Integration

> Yo tengo ya la casita, que tanto te prometí. Tan llena de margaritas para ti, para mí. Será un refugio de amores. Será una cosa ideal. Y entre romances y flores formaremos nuestro hogar. (I finally have the house I had promised. Full of margaritas for you, for me. It will be a refuge of love. It will be an ideal thing. And between romance and flowers we'll form our home.)
>
> —Rafael Hernández, "Ahora Seremos Felices"

In Ponce, like the rest of the island, in the mid-1980s, *urbanizaciones* (subdivisions) and private communities of the affluent and upper middle class organized neighborhood associations, collected dues, and pushed municipalities to establish the necessary infrastructure. In 1993, Extensión Alhambra was the first to bid successfully for controlled access. Many communities were successful in gating; by 1997, Ivelisse Rivera-Bonilla estimates that "over a hundred once-open middle-class and upper middle-class San Juan neighborhoods [had] totally or partially closed off their streets with gates."[1] Others were not successful; Alhambra, a Ponce community of affluence, located between the public housing projects Dr. Pila and Gándara, was denied permission to gate itself on the grounds that it would block access to a principal municipal street. Despite petitions and many alternative plans, including one for temporary blockades to remain open by day and closed at night, Alhambra was still unsuccessful. In a counter plan over which the city had no control, each Alhambra mansion gated itself. Alhambrans settled in behind private walls, many with spikes along the top. But, for members of other elite communities, the Closing Law of 1987, which permitted the gating of neighborhoods, offered a welcome remedy: to take possession of their own streets and shut the poor out. The New Deal vision and the 1950s ideal of a socially integrated society (though of sequestered areas within it) had failed. What resulted was a contradiction in terms.

"Mano Dura Contra El Crimen"

In 1992, the Puerto Rican governor Pedro Rosselló and his appointed superintendent of police, Pedro Toledo, suggested incorporating the National Guard with local police in a militaristic battle against crime. Operation Centurion, popularly known as "Mano Dura Contra El Crimen," was the result. To the Puerto Rico Public Housing Authority Secretary, Carlos Vivoni, Operation Centurion was an opportunity to continue "a social rebuilding model" already under way in the privatization of public housing communities.[2] On May 2, 1992, a "Project for the Privatization and Administration of Public Housing" was approved by both U.S. and Puerto Rican governments. Its goal was to "stimulate" participation of the private sector in administration and management of public housing projects, its reasoning to use "nuevos métodos y sistemas dirigidos a mejorar la calidad de vida, fomentar la actividad comunitaria, y el desarrollo personal y familiar de sus residentes, hace indispensable la intervención de ambos sectores, constituyendo una labor de equipo en el desarrollo de nuevas metas en favor de los puertorriqueños" (new methods and systems to improve the quality of life, to foster community activity, and encourage personal and familial development of residents, making intervention by both sectors [public and private] indispensable, a team effort in the development of new goals for Puerto Ricans).[3] Mano Dura conformed to U.S. federally approved legislation of new methods to fight crime and drug trafficking in public spaces and the fiscal reorganization of public housing management. It was an ambitious plan, aggressive and punitive in its approach to crime reduction, employing raids on property and in homes and climaxing with occupation of the projects by a police force and construction of monitored gates and high fences.

The first Mano Dura raid occurred on June 5, 1993, in a San Juan 500-unit public housing site, Villa España. The governor himself joined in the first raid.[4] This was the battle plan, as it was carried out in three phases:

Phase 1, *Rescue*: The National Guard raided the public housing sites,
a perimeter gate was erected, the National Guard withdrew, and a
police force remained;

Phase 2, *Restore*: Basic infrastructure services were restored and repaired, and basic services were reactivated;

Phase 3, *Re-empower*: Government agencies provided job counseling
and other services to residents.[5]

Over the course of four years, eighty-two sites, nearly a quarter of a total of
337 public housing sites in Puerto Rico, were "rescued" or "occupied" in the
same manner.[6]

In 2002, the then administrator of the Puerto Rico Public Housing Authority told me that the *escogidos* (chosen ones) had been those with "*más
alto nivel, problema de criminalidad*" (the highest crime rate and problem).[7]
But there was no confirming evidence. Size, especially in the super-block Le
Corbusian distribution typical of U.S. federal midcentury public housing, became a proxy. Thus, larger public housing communities, which are deemed to
be more dangerous, socially disorganized, and harder to control, became the
targets.[8] In the continental United States, the same Hope VI funding partly
used for Mano Dura was reshaping and demolishing the largest and most
infamous or, as the Housing and Urban Development Department (HUD)
referred to them, the "severely distressed" projects like Cabrini Green in Chicago, to relocate residents into scattered-site or smaller mixed-income low-
rise housing developments.[9] By then, projects that were smaller in size and
lower in scale were understood to be safer and more manageable. However,
the assumed relationship between public housing and criminality did not
hold in Puerto Rico. In San Juan, for example, an analysis of crime in police
sectors revealed higher incidences of crime in sectors without public housing
than in sectors with public housing.[10] And in Ponce, smaller projects were on
the top of the murder list between 1994 and 2001: Pedro J. Rosaly, with 238
units, had nine murders; Santiago Iglesias, with 280 units, had eight murders;
and La Ceiba, with 300 units, had seven murders. (See Table 1.) In the same
seven-year period, the largest public housing project in Ponce, Dr. Pila, had
only two murder victims.[11]

Following an unverified logic, on November 8, 1993, three helicopters
descended on Dr. Pila. With 906 units, Dr. Pila, the largest public housing
project in Ponce, was occupied at dawn by the National Guard and the Puerto
Rican police, a fate that evaded the nearby smaller project José N. Gándara,

and other smaller projects like Rosaly, Tibes, and Santiago Iglesias.[12] For another year, Dr. Pila would remain the largest occupied public housing community on the island. A newspaper reported on the event:

> Alrededor de 450 efectivos de la Policía y la Guardia Nacional ocuparon en la madrugada de ayer el residencial Doctor Pila en Ponce donde se incautó mariguana, cocaína, dinero en efectivo y se arrestó a 17 personas. Este operativo es el primero que se realizó en la zona sur de la Isla y, junto al efectuado en Vista Hermosa en Río Piedras, ha sido el más grande en término de recursos policiales.
>
> Para la incursión de ayer, en la que se utilizaron tres helicópteros, se diligenciaron nueve órdenes de arresto, pero se logró detener a otras 3 personas por posesión de sustancias controladas y por conducir vehículos reportados como robados o cuyas piezas no le pertenecen. . . . [E]se complejo de vivienda pública es uno muy activo en el tráfico de drogas, además de ser muy violento. . . . el residencial Doctor Pila es quizás el más conflictivo . . .

> (Around 450 officers from the police and the National Guard occupied in the dawn hours yesterday the public housing project Dr. Pila in Ponce where marijuana, cocaine, and cash money were confiscated and seventeen persons were arrested. This operation is the first in the southern zone of the island and, next to the one implemented in Vista Hermosa in Río Piedras, has been the largest in terms of police resources.
>
> For yesterday's incursion, where three helicopters were utilized, nine arrest orders were carried out, three persons were detained for possession of controlled substances and for driving vehicles reported as stolen or whose parts did not belong to the vehicle. . . . That public housing complex is very active in drug trafficking, on top of being very violent. . . . The Dr. Pila public housing project may be the most conflictive . . .)[13]

A resident described the incident at Dr. Pila as a "show." After the helicopters landed, a perimeter fence was erected. For the next three years, a police precinct was set up inside the walls with guards watching at initially two access points, then just one. A handful of residents and many officials recall the event as a celebration—the police had liberated residents from the drug lord, so they claimed. Other residents recall feeling not liberated but confined. Dr. Pila would be the first of six public housing communities gated in Ponce over the next six years.

By November 1996, the Autoridad de Vivienda Pública (AVP) or Puerto Rico Public Housing Authority (PRPHA) had transferred administration of the modernization programs to three private management firms to regulate costs and security and "coordinate service delivery" as instructed by the Quality of Life Congress.[14] The government considered its intervention "service." Agencies like Sports and Recreation, Social Services, Labor and Human Resources, the Right to Work Administration, the Office of Youth Affairs, the Office of Elderly Affairs, the Women Affairs Commission, and so on were instructed to join in a participatory enterprise with the residents. Residents in turn were to express concerns to the private management staff, who would intervene, decide, and execute remedies. Thus, Mano Dura would coordinate crime prevention with social policies, and private management companies would implement them. It was an alliance for (not by) the people.[15]

The upbeat titles of the stages of Operation Centurion—"Rescue," "Restore," "Re-empower"—were a charade. Residents had not sought "rescue." Nothing had been "restored." There was no empowerment of the poor, let alone "reempowerment." Indeed, when the National Guard and the police force occupied Dr. Pila and other similar projects the areas were stigmatized as sites of criminality. Thereafter, a public housing community, like Residencial José N. Gándara, which had been spared from a paramilitary raid, sought to avoid a similar severe stigma, but it, too, thereafter, was to be controlled by a private management firm not by the people who lived there. Gándara, too, thus, would also be effectively controlled by an invisible fence that afforded its people a better reputation than Dr. Pila, but it nonetheless circumscribed their lives inside the project.

In fact, public housing, all of it, had been imprinted with stigma for decades predating the gates' appearance.[16] In the 1950s and 1960s, the Puerto Rican government had sought to "*mejorar la imagen de los residentes de las urbanizaciones públicas*" (improve the image of public housing residents) by employing more courteous terms like *residenciales* (literally, group of residences) or *caseríos* (literally, hamlets, country houses), rather than a blunt "*público*" (public), thus seeking to promote a "*clima de comprensión y entendimiento*" (a climate of empathy and understanding).[17] A policy of integration was introduced to avoid "the creation of ghettos or 'social zoning' "; public housing was deliberately sited adjacent to higher-income communities to foster "human equality" and inhibit "social barriers."[18] Instead, integration had fostered social resentment.

The gates of Mano Dura erected at Dr. Pila and other public housing sites accentuated class resentment and contravened integration. "The only difference between a low-income and a high-income development," Oscar Newman wrote of housing in 1972, "is the presence of fences and guards in the upper-income project, or a doorman provided for each of its buildings."[19] "These slight but expensive additions, however, are what make the one a workable habitat and the other not. The same urban high-rise residential developments for low- and middle-income families, devoid of the doormen, guards, and resident superintendents, become pasturelands for criminals."[20] Newman had not foreseen that gates and guards would be used to set the poor apart as inferior persons. In the 1990s, Henry G. Cisneros, the secretary of HUD, advocated Newman's "defensible space" interventions for public housing.[21] In 1993, in Ponce, Mano Dura further insulated the well-to-do and isolated the poor. Both had gates but for different purposes. In public housing, gatekeepers, armed police sentries, managers, and social workers took over. Visible gates for the larger and most feared projects, and invisible fences in the smaller and "unrescued" public housing, enforced social separation and conjured images of poverty, a large community size, and criminality.

A New Deal Vision of a New Society of Justice and Social Integration

In the 1930s a song by Rafael Hernández reflected the century's push toward homeownership—everyone wants and needs a home "between romances and flowers," a "refuge," an "ideal thing."[22] Used in a twenty-first-century commercial for the Banco Popular of Puerto Rico's Internet-accessible mortgage program, this song conveyed images of white-clad families in spacious kitchens and living rooms, but the families behind Puerto Rico's gates of the poor did not live "between romance and flowers." Yet, ironically, the gated urban society came about in Ponce and in other Puerto Rican cities, not by intent, certainly not by overt intent. The New Deal government's purposes were, to the contrary, benevolent in concept and in policy, the hope of a unified society. This public ideal is symbolized today in what seems anomalous to a visitor and even to a resident: the fact that the gated communities of rich and poor in Ponce are closely adjacent to one another. The rich live in an enclave in between enclaves of the poor.

With "hopeful rhetoric" and government policies and programs, the New Deal had sought to create a new society.[23] The economic distress of the Great Depression had inspired programs whose prime goals were to establish a new social contract, to provide security, to deal with poverty and unemployment, and to "cultivate . . . farmers, workers, homeowners."[24] Housing—its construction and provision—was to be a prime means to distribute aid and lift all classes up.[25] An extension of the 1937 Wagner-Steagall Housing Act establishing the United States Housing Authority, Law #126 of May 1938, also created the Puerto Rico Housing Authority. Social integration was to be engineered by addressing, as Frances Fox Piven and Richard Cloward described the mission of the New Deal, "the old inequalities: the overprivileged [who] had not been weeded out or the underprivileged [who had not been] effectively lifted up."[26] Yet class divisions were consolidated through housing, ironically, by the very New Deal policies whose aim was to improve the lot of the poor and promote integration.[27] As the poor were shuffled into multiple-dwelling *caseríos* (public housing projects), and as upward mobility and privilege were confined to single-family home *urbanizaciones*, each was located next to one another in Puerto Rican cities to promote New Deal ideals of integration. The consequence was that class was cemented and configured into polar, and, eventually, exclusive, yet adjacent, housing types: "caché" for the rich, and "casheríos" for the poor.[28]

The concept of class integration through housing was not new to Puerto Rico. In 1923, a law known as Hogar Seguro de Puerto Rico (Secure Home of Puerto Rico) created a Homestead Commission,[29] and its mission was to guide urban development and ensure an orderly process of adequate housing for urban workers. The Homestead Commission built three urban worker districts, fittingly named *barrios obreros* (laborer barrios), to house together artisans, public employees, and other urban workers. The towns of Arecibo (183 units), Santurce (491 units), and Salinas provided detached two-bedroom concrete-and-frame dwellings that could be sold or rented.[30] Today, these barrios obreros house low-income communities, with many of their residents being Dominican immigrants. By 1934, the New Deal had created the Puerto Rico Emergency Relief Administration (PRERA), which, in 1935, became the Puerto Rico Reconstruction Administration (PRRA),[31] with a mission to rehabilitate rural areas after the hurricanes of 1928 and 1932 and to acquire urban land or property to develop or improve housing infrastructure.[32] Between 1935 and 1938, the PRRA put up six urban housing projects, with 1,460 units in Caguas, Ponce, San Juan, and Santurce: Barriada Hoare, Eleanor Roosevelt, Mirapalmeras, La Granja, Morrell Campos, and Tenement Group Project A (El Falansterio). In 1938, city housing authorities were established in five cities: Ponce, San Juan, Mayagüez, Arecibo, and Río Piedras, and $14 million was allocated, with 3,793 dwelling units built in Ponce, Mayagüez, and San Juan.[33] By the 1940s, there were 6,697 dwelling units. With the exception of New York, Massachusetts, and several other mainland states, Puerto Rico had received more federal government per capita investments in public housing than any state had.[34]

Of the six PRRA projects, Barriada Hoare, in Santurce, had 250 detached-frame dwellings, rented at no cost to qualifying families from a slum, but, by 1950, they were considered to have "degenerated" into a slum little different than the families' earlier homes.[35] Eleanor Roosevelt, three miles outside of San Juan, by 1950, had 635 concrete dwelling units "based on an orthogonal grid interrupted by four diagonal streets that connected the center of the complex with its most distant corners," for families of La Perla and of the Miranda slum.[36] The axial form of Eleanor Roosevelt followed the City Beautiful movement, with cross-cutting straight lines like the garden cities or the greenbelt towns.[37] The straight-line design shortened distances between places and thus made them more walkable. The architecture of units varied, with five single-family housing designs, three duplex house designs, and a rowhouse of two or three bedrooms, plus one bathroom, and a balcony. There was no design for car garages, again emphasizing walkability, and, no doubt, poverty. In the center of the complex were a school, church, and a two-story community building (for a police station, a fire station, a jail, a post office, a telephone office, a telegraph office, and an infirmary on the first floor, with administrative offices and a court on the second, although the fire station, jail, court, and infirmary were never built). A central plaza was to serve as a community space for informal socializing, with commercial spaces around the plaza, as with the Eleanor Roosevelt units. Like other PRRA projects—Mirapalmeras, La Granja, and Morrell Campos in Ponce—units were sold to tenants who had more than five years' residence on a twenty-year amortization plan with all rent paid credited for purchase; after the five-year initial payment, a tenant could pay the balance in cash, with a 30 percent discount.[38]

The first multiple-dwelling housing project, Mirapalmeras in Santurce, was a "joint effort" between the Division of Homes of the Public Works Administration (PWA), as designers, and the PRRA, its design resembling U.S.

projects built at the time, with no interior streets or parks, all units with a balcony, with living room, kitchen, and bathroom on the exterior and reached via the balcony, and a garden on lots with front and rear yards.[39] There were no closets, with the poor perhaps expected to have few belongings. "In this context," the architectural historian Luz Marie Rodríguez noted, "the façades lack any architectural character, and are reduced to solids and voids that exist simply because they are necessary to ventilate the spaces. The buildings remind us of the rowhouses that stood in many of the workers' neighborhoods in Puerta de Tierra and Santurce, only this time they are interpreted in reinforced concrete."[40]

Tenants, selected according to the George Healy Act, were "from workers' families that had their own means of economic sustenance and that lived in inferior conditions."[41] Income eligibility was limited to five times the rent of the unit. All adult tenants in a unit had to be kin; the only exceptions were persons who could prove a stable relationship. Tenants could not rent rooms to others. The second multiple-dwelling project, La Granja in Caguas, had 78 concrete dwelling units; a third, Tenement Group Project A, later renamed El Falansterio, of 216 units, was built in a lot on the grounds of the Miranda slum in San Juan on land "ceded by the people of Puerto Rico to the Federal government," although the PRRA objected to its multilevel plan, according to Rodríguez, because "Puerto Rican families cannot live together because their excessive individualism leads them to fight among themselves."[42] The criteria for tenancy were (1) U.S. citizenship; (2) good health with no contagious diseases; (3) no conviction for a serious crime; (4) a monthly pay salary of four times the rent; and (5) a family that contained no more than seven members. Married couples had preference. In the provisions and housing plans were the seeds of inequality: personal health and behavior credentials, limits on family size, lack of architectural details, shared behavior, scarcity of gardens.

With the 1941 appointment of the New Dealer Rexford Tugwell as Puerto Rico's last U.S.-appointed governor, the housing focus became slum eradication and multiple-dwelling public housing. Puerto Ricans resorted to the media to oppose the design of Tenement Group Project A, in Puerta de Tierra just outside San Juan, as communist-style beehives that would lead to overcrowded, unhygienic, and immoral and secular living conditions.[43] The urban scholar Dolores Hayden cites not only Bentham's panopticon structure and Robert Owen's parallelogram but also Charles Fourier's phalanstery (organized communal housing designed by the French philosopher in the seventeenth century) as collective housing antecedents of similar U.S. urban apartment houses. [44] In that debate appeared the first public awareness of a dichotomy in Puerto Rico's housing landscape. Multiple-dwelling projects, and their residents, were mostly seen as malignant; single, detached developments were seen as benevolent, as symbols of democracy and upward mobility. Over the next decades, this architecture would effectively stigmatize the poor residents of subsidized housing and idealize affluent residents of single-family homes.

In 1945, Puerto Rican legislators drafted legislation to remove and rehabilitate slum areas.[45] According to Rafael Picó, the Puerto Rico Planning Board was the first in the United States "to prohibit . . . permanent development in slum districts until a plan for the improvement of those districts as a whole could be put into effect." The Federal Housing Act of 1949's Title I emphasized "slum clearance and community development and redevelopment."[46] By 1950, there were so many razed areas that Puerto Rico planned 30,000 units of public housing to be built within six years, to replace the demolished dwellings.[47]

The first federal public housing project in Puerto Rico, Juan Ponce de León, opened in the southern city of Ponce in 1941, like other New Deal buildings on the western outskirts of the urban center.[48] Its multiple-dwelling structure of three hundred units, with thirty two-story buildings of one-, two-, and three-bedroom units, was designed as a high-density super-block, with buildings arranged on parallel lines with green spaces in between.[49] Few vehicular streets crossed the site. Like earlier New Deal communities, there were centralized services and public spaces: a community center, recreational areas of parks and basketball courts, and an administrative center.

Many slum dwellers had resisted the move to new and sanitized "American" public housing.[50] Some scholars believe the resistance was a protest against destruction and displacement of an organic community.[51] The anthropologist Helen Safa believes that, as an alternative, shantytowns or slums could have been developed into a more Puerto Rican landscape than any of the government's housing projects and could have become "substantial working class neighborhoods," that is, if the government had provided "public services such as paved roads, water, electricity, and the like," with the residents "absorbed into the city as part of the overall process of urban growth."[52] Safa found one slum community in San Juan to be a "live, viable, community."[53] Instead, "Most shantytowns are eradicated by an ambitious urban renewal program that clears these areas for other residential, commercial, or public purposes and relocates a large percentage of shantytown families in public housing."[54] In public housing, Safa noted, many tenants felt isolated, with spontaneous socializing among men curtailed by replacement of familiar streets, local bars, and stores with a community center "not conducive to informal meetings between friends who just want to chat a while."[55] The multiple-dwelling architecture of public housing also led to arguments about the "jurisdiction and responsibility" of shared stairways and entryways that served between six and eight apartments. In Oscar Lewis's 1965 study of Puerto Ricans, *La Vida*, a young woman who was compelled to move to public housing said, "This place isn't like La Esmeralda, you know, where there's so much liveliness and noise and something is always going on. Here you never see any movement on the street, not one little domino or card game or anything. The place is dead. People act as if they're angry or in mourning. Either they don't know how to live or they're afraid to. And yet it's full of shameless good-for-nothings. It's true what the proverb says, 'May God deliver me from quiet places; I can defend myself in the wild ones.' "[56]

The government tried to respond to protests and discontent. Residential cooperatives would be allowed to build low-cost homes.[57] Some families would be permitted to choose among housing options and families could relocate from slums to public housing or choose to have their home rehabilitated and transferred to an available lot elsewhere. Rural neighbors could help each other build homes with materials the government provided. But it was public housing that received the biggest investment from the Federal Housing Program in Puerto Rico, as in the United States. By the late twentieth century the Puerto Rico Housing Authority had the second largest number of public housing units in the entire federal system.[58] The opportunity for choice was, by then, in effect, an empty choice.

By the 1950s, *urbanizaciones* (single-family home subdivisions) had become the model for private housing, the standard housing of the upper class and for working people who aspired to upward mobility. The first large private, detached-unit development in Puerto Rico, built by a North Carolina developer, Leonard Darlington Long, was purported to be one of the largest in the world. It was certainly the largest of its kind in Puerto Rico.[59] It provided several construction designs, a front and a back lawn for each, with paved streets and recreation areas. Built just outside of San Juan in Puerto Nuevo, it marked the beginning of a sprawling single-family, suburban residential design.[60] The *urbanizaciones* fulfilled two important ideals: single-family homes and homeownership.[61]

Luis Muñoz Marín, who, in 1949, became Puerto Rico's first elected governor, envisioned land policy and housing made possible with federal funds as a principal instrument to bring about an integrated and just society where equality and understanding reigned. The program was Operation Bootstrap, under way by 1952.[62]

La localización de proyectos de vivienda para familias de ingresos bajos y moderados contiguos o como parte de proyectos de vivienda para familias de más altos ingresos ayuda a mantener y ahondar el sentido de igualdad humana. La concentración de proyectos de vivienda para familias de un mismo nivel económico tiende a establecer una barrera social.

(The location of housing projects for families with low and moderate income next to or as part of projects for families with high incomes helps maintain and deepen the sentiment of human equality. The concentration of housing for families of the same socioeconomic level creates a social barrier.)[63]

The government sought to enlist more privileged residents in its crusade to integrate public housing ex-slum dwellers into civilized urban life. Before construction of a public housing site, "intensive orientation work was done with the neighbouring families, to enlist their aid in promoting good will towards the less fortunate who would become their neighbours."[64] But a "not-in-my-backyard" attitude (NIMBY-ism) was apparent. When residents from bona fide (private) *urbanizaciones* complained, Governor Muñoz Marín sent a personal letter to a resident of Urbanización Dos Pinos in Río Piedras (within the San Juan metro area):

Me escribes que cometí un error porque ayudé a que se construyera un Caserío en terrenos adyacentes a la Urbanización Dos Pinos ... Precisamente la proximidad del Caserío a la Urbanización Dos Pinos, donde viven maestros, funcionarios públicos, personas que han tenido ventajas de la educación, podría servir para mejorar el entendimiento de los que en el Caserío no lo tengan claro. ... Tú y todos los demás amigos de la Urbanización Dos Pinos pueden ayudarles mucho con su ejemplo de Buena conducta y con el interés que se tomen en igualar las oportunidades a los menos afortunados ...

podrían estimular la organización de clubes de vecinos en el Caserío y en Dos Pinos. . . . Confío en que después de leer esta carta y de pensar detenidamente sobre lo que en ella te digo, estarás convencida de que no cometí error alguno. . . . El beneficio a la larga será todo el pueblo de Puerto Rico.

(You write that I committed an error because I helped build a public housing development in land that is adjacent to the Neighborhood Dos Pinos. . . . It is precisely the proximity of the public housing to the residential development, where teachers, public officials, and persons that have had educational privileges live that could serve to better the understanding of those in the public housing that are lost. . . . You and all the friends of the Residential Development Dos Pinos could help a lot by providing examples of good conduct through your interest in equalizing the opportunities with the less fortunate . . . you could stimulate the organization of neighborhood associations in the public housing and in Dos Pinos. . . . I have confidence that after reading this letter and after thinking carefully about what I've said in it, that you will be convinced that I did not commit any error. . . . The long-term beneficiary will be the people of Puerto Rico.)[65]

The government worked hard to integrate multiple dwellings for slum dwellers, government officials, and the general public. The solution it arrived at was to present public housing units as transitory, as a stepping-stone toward single-family homeownership.[66] To address the stigma of multiple-dwelling public housing, debates about language led the Corporación de Renovación Urbana y Vivienda and the Planning Board to remove the world *público* (public) from *caseríos* (projects) and to rename them *residenciales* (residential complexes), *viviendas* (housing), and *urbanizaciones*.[67] In a handwritten note of 1954, Muñoz Marín thanked Telésforo Carrero, the chief of the Urban Development Division of the Puerto Rico Planning Board, for reminding him to avoid the term *"caserío"* when referring to public housing: "El estar alerta a esos valores es una de las cualidades que le dan, y deben cada día darle más, excelencia a nuestra democracia" (Being alert to those values is a characteristic that will continue to make our democracy more exemplary).[68] A campaign to reduce the stigma of public housing promoted the use of the term *urbanización pública* (public subdivision) for public housing: "Entre los proyectos que nos proponemos desarrollar figura una campaña

de orientación para mejorar la imagen de los residentes de las urbanizaciones públicas ante el resto de la comunidad y lograr un efectivo intercambio
de ideas y recomendaciones, a la vez que el clima de comprensión y entendimiento más adecuado en todos los aspectos de nuestra labor" (Among the
projects that we want to develop, is an orientation campaign to improve the
image of public housing residents among the rest of the community and to
encourage an effective exchange of ideas and recommendations, and an environment of care and understanding for all aspects of our labor).[69]

The program's plan to remove the stigma of public housing by placing it
next to neighborhoods of the middle and upper classes backfired by angering
those in private housing who feared the stigma would simply spread to them.
Today some of Alhambra's mansions are empty, their windows boarded up,
the properties apparently abandoned because they border the Dr. Pila housing project for the poor. *Urbanizaciones* and *caseríos* reflect differences between, not the integration of, rich and poor in Puerto Rico. The dramatically
contrasting housing defines community and individual identity, and it guides
movement in, and control over, the public sphere. As some residents of Dr.
Pila said to me: "Eso [urbanización] es caché. Gente de caché. Nosotros no.
Somos de casherío" (That is cachet. People with cachet. Not us. We are from
casherío). "*Caché*," Spanish for "cachet," captures favorable status: prestige,
high class, reputation, worldliness, and even being fashionable, having good
taste, and being current. "Cache" without the accent mark, "cache" in English,
captures other meanings of the play on the word: a hoard, accumulation, an
amassing, collection, or storage.[70] The resulting "casherío" wittily expresses
the deep running distinctions between public and private neighborhoods. As
a cognitive map for Puerto Ricans, caché is "distinction" and "elegance," its
socio-racial profiles (White, educated, professional, businessowner), its physical profile (sprawling single-family home, controlled access, silent streets).
Caseríos represent violence, chaos, insecurity, poverty, lack of education, lack
of control, and blackness.[71]

Adjacent Public and Private Housing in Ponce

Ponce, the second largest city in Puerto Rico, had always been in the van-
guard of urban and social development. Puerto Rico's first two public
housing developments—Juan Ponce de León and Santiago Iglesias—had a
combined total of 446 units and were constructed in Ponce.[72] The city was

in the lead in eliminating slums and in constructing public and low-cost private housing substitutes. In the 1950s and 1960s, communities in Ponce considered the worst and largest slums, again recycling the assumed relationship between size and social disorganization, were targeted for razing or development: Machuelito and Cichamba. Public housing projects built throughout the city included José N. Gándara (1951) and Dr. Manuel de la Pila (built in three parts in 1954, 1958, and 1974), both communities within my own core study. Ponce's two private *urbanizaciones*, La Alhambra (1919–30) and Extensión Alhambra (the 1970s), also part of my core study, were an outgrowth of this development. These four communities, on the fringes of the city center—two public housing, two private housing—are tightly clustered in a trapezoid. Nearby is a members-only social club, Club Deportivo, a small commercial strip, a fire station and transportation hub, and a new municipal library. The communities sit in the Barrio Machuelo Ponce sector, bounded by an intermunicipal highway to the north, Santiago de los Caballeros or Malecón Highway to the east, and the canalized Portugués River to the west. (See Figure 1.)

Although adjacent, the four communities are unique and representative of others throughout the island. (See Tables 2 and 3 for details on their size and demographics.) In the north is Doctor Manuel A. De la Pila, known as Dr. Pila, with 906 units of public housing, gated in 1993 by Mano Dura; to the south is a private residential community of gated individual homes, Urbanización La Alhambra, the first elite suburban residential development in Ponce. Southwest of La Alhambra is Extensión Alhambra, a small gated private community of about fifty single-family homes. South of all three, within the trapezoid, is José N. Gándara, better known as Gándara, an ungated public housing site of 270 housing units. Alhambra, Extensión Alhambra, Dr. Pila, and Gándara exist side by side, their clustering not accidental, but an intentional result of the policies of social integration propagated by Rexford Tugwell, Muñoz Marín, and their colleagues and successors, as an integral part of the New Deal program of benevolent purpose. However, the opposite of integration has been the result.

Urbanización La Alhambra was built between 1919 and 1930 in an area that was "once the domain of sugar cane [but] became, practically from dusk to dawn, the home of hundreds of people."[73] It was the first suburban neighborhood (that is, outside of the city center hub) with private homes for the wealthy, connected to the city by the Guadalupe bridge, which was expressly built for the residents.[74] Its large turn-of-the-century cement colonial homes, "isolated buildings with ample gardens all around," were built on "extensive" 600-meter lots carved out of sugarcane fields.[75] A municipal street, Avenida Alcázar, a major thoroughfare, links northern Ponce to the city center. Because of that thoroughfare, Alhambra has been denied the right to barricade the street that separates it from the poor in Dr. Pila. The street names— Fuente, Obispado, Generalife, Gándara—and the surrounding architecture resemble Spanish castles like the Moorish one that gives the community its name. Occupied by some of the most "prestigious families" of Ponce, the homes are passed down to sons, daughters, and their offspring, but, with economic fluctuations in the city and the closing of a petrochemical plant west of Ponce, a downturn in the neighborhood has led to the abandonment of some Alhambra homes and the decline of others into disrepair, especially on the border with Dr. Pila. With urban expansion and the explosion of modern middle- and upper-middle-class suburban *urbanizaciones* in the northern part of Ponce, Alhambra is now positioned in a less desirable city-center location, although older residents remain, and new families restore old mansions, housing stock unparalleled in Ponce.[76] Denied the right to gate the neighborhood, all because of the municipal street that runs through it, residents have resorted to the next best thing: spiked high walls and fences around each individual home.

The private neighborhood of Extensión Alhambra, also known as Alhambrita, a small private community of single-family homes, was built in the mid-1960s as a suburban *urbanización,* just southwest of Alhambra. It was allowed to retrofit its own infrastructure of controlled access. It has become the standard form of Puerto Rico's private subdivisions. A road that loops around the square community ends in the center of the square in a cul-de-sac, providing a shape that separates, protects, and identifies. Originally built with open access, it no longer is open; in early 1993, in the wake of Mano Dura, its professional families organized to request and finance a system that restricts entry to residents of the neighborhood and their visitors, and, in March 1994, they received municipal approval to close off its street. Its modern one-level houses, built en masse in cement, typify Puerto Rico's late-century trend. Intended as an exclusive community for middle- and upper-middle-income families, it bears a name that reflects its aspirations to the prestige and class status of La Alhambra itself, although its dwellings are far less grand.

Ironically, the municipal street that prevented Alhambra from becoming a unified gated community is shared by the low-prestige, gated public

Figure 2. Barricades blocking passage to Dr. Pila. Photo by author.

housing of Dr. Pila, a government gate not considered a barrier to the municipal street. In the north border of the trapezoid, Dr. Pila, the fifth public housing site to be built and the largest in Ponce, has three sections of fifty-eight buildings geometrically arranged, the two- to four-story buildings (four to ten apartments per floor) separated by small roadways, parking spaces, and paved areas.[77] There are a community center, a baseball park, basketball and volleyball courts, a Hope Project center for the elderly, small parks, and offices for its Resident Council and its private managers (hired by the government). An elementary school inside the gates serves the children of Dr. Pila and other nearby public housing. Seventy-five percent of the households, as of 2004, were headed by females relying on public assistance, and the majority of them paid less than $25 a month for rent. It is a diverse community, according to residents, of "all types of people," "good and bad."

On the southern boundary of the trapezoid is Dr. José N. Gándara, an ungated public housing community built between 1951 and 1953 immediately north of the official entrance to Ponce's city center. As of 2004 53 percent of its households relied on public assistance and 65 percent paid a monthly

Figure 3. A row of fences faces the empty sidewalk and street of Alhambra. Photo by author.

rent of $25 or less. Its fifteen two- and three-story buildings are geometri-
cally arranged in a square lot, its services areas inside the square duplicating
Dr. Pila's. There are community volleyball and basketball teams. Considered
small and hence more manageable than Dr. Pila, it has never been gated, but,
like all public housing, its management, in 1992, was outsourced to a private
business.

Figure 4. Fortressed colonial mansions in Alhambra. Photo by author.

Figure 5. An abandoned Alhambra home immediately adjacent to the Dr. Pila community. Photo by author.

Dr. Pila and Gándara are similar in important respects. They were both built in the early 1950s: Gándara was completed in 1953 and Dr. Pila in 1954. They were built adjacent to privileged communities, and the designs of the concrete buildings resemble each other. The main difference between the two communities—their size—developed gradually. Although now seen by outsiders as one large community, Dr. Pila was built in stages, as three clustered smaller projects. Originally a 586-unit project, an extension of 120 units was added in 1958, followed by a second extension of 120 units almost two decades later, in 1975. The resulting community retained some formal separations, each with different managing staff and different resident councils. Yet to outsiders, and eventually even to residents, Dr. Pila was perceived as being one large project, much larger in size than Gándara. Although associations of criminality and disorder pervaded with Dr. Pila, Dr. Pila and Gándara both suffered from the stigma attributed to public housing sites, even if only one saw physical fences erected.

Figure 6. A gated entrance to Extensión Alhambra. Photo by author.

Housing the "Good Civilization"

By the end of the decade, in 1958, at the conclusion of his second term, Governor Luis Muñoz Marín had begun to fear that Puerto Rico's aggressive urbanization and economic development would turn it into a "stone city" (*ciudad de piedra*) and that competitive urban consumerism would replace the good-natured social cooperation that, in his view, preceded it.[78] Muñoz Marín's public addresses begun to reveal a disappointment, a "disgust," notes Sepúlveda Rivera.

> Los cambios acelerados en los hábitos de consumo de una sociedad que añoraba sin necesidades extremas, pero sin lujos innecesarios, le hacían insistir en las bondades de la buena civilización, asentada en valores que no eran otra cosa que la moderación y la serenidad. "En la falta de valores se habría desvirtuado la trivial motivación de imitarse los vecinos unos a otros en cuanto a posesiones sin gran significado. Mientras esta motivación no sea hondamente sustituida por otra de más originalidad, de mejor semejanza, a la parte creadora del espíritu del hombre, no tendremos plenamente lo que podemos llamar buena civilización."

> (The changes and consumerism in a society that had desires, but without great need, or unnecessary luxuries, made him insist on the merits of a good civilization, based on the values of moderation and serenity. "The loss of good values leads to the trivial motivation of neighbors to imitate each other, in order to attain possessions of little significance. As long as this motivation is not substituted for another of more originality, of more importance to the spirit of man, we won't have what can be referred to as a good civilization.")[79]

"The home is the best place to get physical and spiritual rest. It provides security against the elements and security in the future."[80] So reads a 1960s document detailing the housing philosophy of the government of Puerto Rico, the culmination of two decades of aggressive urban planning and housing programs on the island. Muñoz Marín had called for refocusing social justice aims: "El ritmo de desarrollo no es sencillamente, ni siempre, que los lujos de ayer conviertan en las necesidades de hoy ni los lujos de hoy en las necesidades de mañana" (The rhythm of development is not simply, nor

Table 1. Murders in Ponce Public Housing Projects by Project Size and Mano Dura Interventions, 1994–2001

Project Name	Units	Mano Dura	Murders 1994–2001
Pedro J. Rosaly	238	No	9
Ponce de Leon	300	No	5
Rafael Lopez Nussa	404	Yes	3
Los Claveles		No	2
Aristides Chavier	480	Yes	3
Ponce Housing	131	No	4
La Ceiba	300	No	7
Tibes		No	9
Ramos Antonini	350	No	3
Brisas del Caribe	116	No	2
Los Lirios		No	4
Dr. Manuel de la Pila	906	Yes	2
Santiago Iglesias	280	No	8
Lirios del Sur	400	Yes	4
Los Rosales	180	No	4
Laureles		No	1
Miramar Housing		No	1
Villas del Río		No	1
Dr. José N. Gándara	270	No	1
Villa Elena	100	No	2
Hogares Portugues	152	Yes	
Brisas del Sur		No	1
Kennedy		No	1
José Tormos Diego	168	No	
Perla de Bucana	50		
Perla del Caribe	272	Yes	
Las Delicias	11		
Canas Housing	96		
Golden View	50		
Cooper View	50		
Silver Valley	50		
Total	5,354		77

Sources: Westbrook Management Company; Puerto Rico Police; Puerto Rico Housing Authority; U.S. Department of Housing and Urban Development.

Table 2. Community Demographics by Census Tract

	Dr. Pila	Alhambra/ Extensión Alhambra	Gándara
Census tract	704	705.03	719
Total population	3,289	4,317	5,729
Total occupied housing units/total households	1,010	1,674	1,875
Owner-occupied housing units	129	1,108	696
Percentage of owner-occupied units	12.8	66.2	37.1
Renter-occupied housing units	881	566	1,179
Average household size	3.26	2.58	3.06
Total housing units	1,053	1,869	2,004
Median rooms	3.8	5.0	3.9
Percentage of one-unit detached or attached residences	14.3	58.2	47.9
In buildings with more than ten units	52.3	28.9	40.7
Percentage that lack plumbing	12.7	0.3	21.8
Percentage that lack complete kitchens	2.5	0.2	3.2
Percentage of structures built from 1990 to March 2000	2.6	23.2	5.3
Percentage of structures built in 1939 or earlier	5.3	2.0	3.7
Median value of owned unit	48,900	145,600	62,800
Median contract rent for renters	Unavailable	210	126
Household median income in dollars	4,540	25,558	7,170
Family median income in dollars	4,981	34,583	8,609
Percentage of population with 1999 incomes below poverty	79.5	28.8	69.2
Percentage of families with 1999 incomes below poverty	79.6	24.0	67.7
Percentage of households with sixteen-year-olds and over in labor force	37.9	46.5	37.0
Percentage of unemployed individuals in civilian labor force	46.4	14.1	38.2
Percentage of units with no vehicles available	67.5	20.5	52.9
Percentage of units with no telephone service	51.2	7.3	37.8
Percentage of units with three or more bedrooms	33.9	60.4	36.0
Percentage of households with children under eighteen	50.7	31.2	45.6
Percentage of married-couple families	28.8	53.8	35.2
Percentage of female householders without husbands	46.5	16.1	37.7
Percentage of management, professional, and related occupations	8.8	52.7	25.2

	Dr. Pila	Alhambra/ Extensión Alhambra	Gándara
Percentage of service occupations	26.5	5.1	16.3
Percentage of sales and office occupations	24.5	31.7	35.5
Percentage of farming, fishing, and forestry occupations	0	1.2	0.7
Percentage of construction, extraction, and maintenance occupations	18.2	3.2	10.5
Percentage of production, transportation, and material moving occupations	22.0	6.1	11.8
Percentage of agriculture, forestry, fishing, and hunting occupations	0	2.0	0
Percentage of manufacturing occupations	14.6	14.1	10.9

Source: 2000 U.S. Census.

always, that the luxuries of yesteryears become the needs of today, or that the luxuries of today become the needs of tomorrow).[81] But the housing programs he counted on to lead the way to "good citizenship" would instead take the island on a detour away from progressing to social integration, neighborliness, and equality, for with class and racial integration came suspicion and contempt among many of the rich, apathy among many of the poor, and divisions by class and, to some extent, race.

The political scientist Iris Marion Young writes that "group segregation is produced by aversive perceptions that deprecate some groups, defining them as entirely other, to be shunned and avoided."[82] The progressive policies of the New Deal and of Governor Muñoz Marín that sought social integration, moderation, and serenity led to "aversive" perceptions reflected in structures that mask but foster inequality.[83] Through controlled access, the homes of the affluent have been effectively secured for "physical and spiritual rest" and "against the elements."[84] The poor, envisioned as capable of being socialized into homeowners,[85] have been moved from decaying but organic slum communities to planned micromanaged housing adjacent to the rich, regulated by a government-business alliance. The New Deal philosophies that sought to train the poor and integrate them with the middle class and rich, ironically, contributed to continued stigma and reinforcing strategies. By the last quarter of the century, public housing projects like Dr. Pila had become what the writer Edgardo Rodríguez Juliá referred to as "the legendary symbol of all the criminality on the face of our Beauteous Puerto Rico . . . [an] antiutopia."[86]

Table 3. Community Demographics by Census Block Group

	Dr. Pila	Dr. Pila	Alhambra and Extensión Alhambra	Gándara
Census block group	1	2	1	1
Census tract	704	704	705.03	719
Total population	1,731	1,558	760	No data
Median age	24.8	18.9	47.9	No data
Total households	599	411	319	No data
Average household size	2.89	3.79	2.38	No data
Total family units	457	350	214	No data
Average family size	3.42	4.17	2.96	No data
Housing units	620	433	360	No data
Occupied housing units	599	411	319	No data
Vacant housing units	21	22	41	No data
Average household size for owner-occupied units	2.81	3.6	2.51	No data
Average household size for renter-occupied units	2.91	3.79	2.02	No data

Source: 2000 U.S. Census.

Chapter 3

"Precaution: Security Knives in the Gates"

> He has an important job: Protect the yard. Sometimes people come
> in and out. . . . Most of the time, they are good people and he
> doesn't bother them. He doesn't know why they are good people.
> He just knows it. Sometimes they are bad people, and he has to do
> bad things to them to make them go away.
>
> —Neil Stephenson, *Snow Crash*

Ramiro explained to me on the phone how I was to get inside his house in
the affluent gated community of Extensión Alhambra in order to interview
him. His instructions were precise and seemed practiced: You drive to the
gate. The community is in the shape of a U. You come in one gate and leave
through the other. When you get to the gate, you will find a dial pad. You
have to dial my number. Here is the number. . . . Wait for me to answer. I will
ask you who you are. You will tell me. Once you talk to me, I will push the
button to open the gate and let you in. The gate will open. You will be allowed
in. You will drive to my house. I will be outside waiting for you. Ramiro was,
indeed, waiting outside his home and greeted me warmly. But, once inside,
he proceeded to interview *me* to confirm whether I was, in fact, from where
I said I was. He interrogated me about whom I knew, where I was going, and
why. He, like others elsewhere, asked about where I said I had been perhaps
to see if he could catch me in a lie. Would I name the streets around Harvard Yard? What was my lineage? Distrust was constant: my legitimacy not
assumed. Where had I lived in Ponce? Who had graduated with me from
the Caribbean School? I tried to think of those whom I knew from upper-
class social circles who might "vouch" for me. The multiple aspects of my

identity—*una negrita,* black/brown-skinned—confused other residents of Ponce's private housing, most of whom identified themselves as "white," regardless of their own shade of skin. My color, youth, and demeanor seemed, to some, to contradict who I said I was. It took carefully cultivated contacts, phone conversations, and prearranged meetings to gain admission through the gates. Admitting me required overriding a presumed customary denial of entry.

Before my appointment with Ramiro, I had driven by the looming front gate of the private community of Extensión Alhambra several times but had not mustered up the nerve to drive in and circle around to get a sense of the layout. More than once, I could have followed another vehicle that was driving in, thus avoiding the electronic gate's safety-stop mechanism. I had also considered parking outside and approaching on foot, in order to appear less forbidden or, rather, more vulnerable. I had decided against both. But in another elite private community, Alhambra, walls provided no such options. In that community, where the street itself is not gated, each house or mansion was encased behind a private cage of cement and iron. I did not consider approaching any house without prior phone contact, a formal invitation, and instructions of how to get inside. The gates with ten-foot iron poles encompassing the Dr. Pila public housing project, on the other hand, were not the only barrier; there was also an armed security guard whose supervision was as formidable as the iron fences, if invisible behind a one-way mirror. In my head echoed the voices of family, friends, and the media urging me to stay away: ¿Y tú te vas a meter ahí? Ten cuidado, eso está caliente. Para en el guardia. Te van a asaltar (Are you going to go in there? Be careful. Stop at the guard. You're going to get mugged).

In Neil Stephenson's science-fiction novel *Snow Crash,* about a city of monitored spaces and technological checkpoints, no one could enter without a visa. Puerto Rico's gated communities resemble that city; technologies and an aesthetic of exclusion are embodied in its gates. An omniscient-all-powerful "He" decides who can enter and who cannot. There are "bad people" to whom "bad things" are done "to make them go away"; there are "good people" whom no one bothers. How does "He" know the difference? The housing gates of Ponce and other Puerto Rican cities range from cement fortresses that circumscribe entire neighborhoods to locked iron gates blockading streets, to fences guarding individual homes from contact with the street and its users. Many middle- and upper-middle-class neighborhoods, too, have been retrofitted with gates to control access and to set a boundary outsiders may not cross. In many, a single entrance/exit allows vehicular traffic, and sometimes there may be a single shared pedestrian access point.

"Discipline," Michel Foucault contends, "may be identified neither with an institution nor with an apparatus; it is a type of power, a modality for its exercise, comprising a whole set of instruments, techniques, procedures, levels of application, targets; it is a 'physics' or an 'anatomy' of power, a technology."[1] Gates are instruments of power supported and shored up by the discipline of techniques and procedures. Gates lock in and lock out. Two dimensions, in tandem, manage the power exerted through the gate, one a camouflage of the other; the functional apparatus and technology lock out or admit. The aesthetics of color, design, and architecture welcome or forbid. The function of the gate complements its design, aesthetics, and technology and combines all three to signal inside and outside; the gates mediate who will and will not be allowed in, symbolizing, and enforcing, the power to control.

Instruments of Control: Urban Aesthetics and Design

A sense of threat can cause one to erect, design, and plan a gate, but a gate's aesthetics and design are also a threat. Which comes first? In the community of the poor the danger is considered to be inside; in the communities of the rich the danger is seen as outside. But "raw iron" separates and confines them both.[2] Gated entryways into private neighborhoods of affluence are tastefully designed and manicured with bright colors and landscaping, and the iron bars are softened with decorative elements and signage. Helen, a resident of the privileged gated community of Extensión Alhambra, told me that the gates "can be pretty but also suffocating."

Extensión Alhambra, the subdivision of fifty single-family homes where Ramiro and Helen live, originally provided open access. But, in the early 1990s, after the Closing Law of 1987, which sanctioned private communities' building of a controlled access infrastructure, Extensión Alhambra residents organized a neighborhood association and built an electronic gate to restrict access to residents and designated visitors. Now, vehicles move in a one-way direction (in-to-out) through its single, looping arterial road around the community. In complementary sunny hues of yellow, a symmetrical cement wall extends between square pillars topped with cement spheres. A bushy flower bed displays green and red and the front of the wall is stamped with matching green letters announcing "Ext. Alhambra." Forest-green iron bars are topped

Figure 7. A sign on the Extensión Alhambra gate. It says, "Caution: Security Knives in the Gates." Photo by author.

by circular adornments and figurative arrowheads. But, in the gates are two discrete strands of braided barbed wire, visible only up close. A large white wooden sign hangs on the gate: "Precaution: Security Knives in the Gate."

To enter the gated home in another private elite community, Alhambra, in contrast, is to leave an unprotected outside street and to enter a seemingly tranquil Eden of single-family homes, porches, and lush gardens, with some newer condominium complexes. Fortresslike towers and layers of brightly colored iron fences enhance each privately owned stately mansion and its walkways, doors, and windows. Seamless rows of pastel iron bars and cement walls form a strict boundary between life inside and the sidewalk thorough-fare outside. Red clay-thatched rooftops and verandas and windows with de-tailed looping ironwork and modernist-style single-level homes are barely visible from the street and recall Mediterranean or modernist architecture. Verdant trees and bushes are visible through and above the gates, resisting Ponce's arid heat by their frequent watering. Strategic signs warning of private security surveillance and alarm systems hang on the gates. Many houses have separated vehicular from pedestrian access in their entranceways, but vehicular access is the norm. Only the poor walk in Puerto Rico (except for exercise).

The aesthetic of the *caserío* (public housing) gates, on the other hand, tends to be generic—"ugly," as many residents said to me. These gates lack adornment or individuality; the gate is made of tall iron bars, between six and ten feet high, that are connected by horizontal bars at top or bottom, some fences free-standing, some grounded by a cement base. An opened gate marks the official entry, at its center, a *caseta,* a guardhouse resembling a geometric concrete box. Each *caserío* retrofitted with gates after the National Guard helicopter raid of Mano Dura typically had one access point for a smaller project; there were several for a larger project, with additional pedestrian gates at coordinates of the perimeter gate. A second cycle of interior fences inside the outside gates segregates sets of buildings and parking spaces from each other, into what some Dr. Pila residents call "jail modules." Individual apartments are fortified with tall cement walls and fenced-in balconies.

The raid and occupation of Dr. Pila in 1992 by the Puerto Rico Police and National Guard were accompanied by construction of the present inner and outer fences, a hierarchy of barriers. Two points of vehicular access were

Figure 8. Interior fences in Dr. Pila. Photo by Dr. Pila Staff.

built—one in the north end, and the other to the west—but after the western gate was disabled in 1998 it was available only to pedestrians. An additional pedestrian gate to the east provides access to a school across a highway.[3] Inside the perimeter gate, Dr. Pila is divided into cells of three or four buildings separated by an internal circumference of ten-foot-high fences, each with a single open vehicular (and, by default, pedestrian) entry point. The northern part of Avenida Alcázar, a north-to-south thoroughfare, which used to connect the northern suburbs to the city center, became the official entryway to Dr. Pila, divided by a centrally placed green concrete guardhouse, framed by yellow traffic guidepoles, in order to sort entering and exiting traffic. The street is an extension of the one outside the gated mansions of Alhambra. A one-way mirror in the guardhouse makes it impossible for someone entering to discern whether the guard is actually inside but surveillance is assumed. A speed bump in the entryway reduces drivers' speed. There is a public telephone in the entryway, several trees, and a light post. Dr. Pila's own elementary public school is near the gate. A short stretch of brick sidewalk frames the gate but a nonworking (when I was there) white traffic arm forces pedestrians to step down into the street. A yellow sign on the guardhouse reads "Zona residencial de acceso controlado. Residente sin identificación y visitante sin identificación también deben de identificarse a la entrada. Autos visitantes sujetos a registro. Administración de Vivienda" (Residential zone with controlled access. Any resident or visitor without identification must identify himself at the entry. Visiting cars are subject to search. Housing Authority). The sign is a reminder that entering public housing, government property, requires becoming vulnerable to unexplained and spontaneous searches, even if there is no apparent reason for suspicion.[4]

Avenida Alcázar, the single-access road that enters and exits from Dr. Pila, used to be a principal north-south thoroughfare to "connect all of Ponce." With Dr. Pila's gates blocking the avenue, public transportation routes were detoured, with the only traffic on this part of Avenida Alcázar now by residents of, or visitors to, Dr. Pila. At the two pedestrian entryways—one on the east, one at the west—the gates are opened and closed at scheduled times of the day. There is no access gate to the south, no doubt intentionally because the private community of Alhambra is located there and the lack of a gate keeps Dr. Pila residents away. A southern access would, actually, be the most useful of all for Dr. Pila residents because it leads to *el pueblo* (the city center). Therefore, blocked off now from the south, some residents resort to stealth, removing bars of the fence to get in and out. Management checks the perimeter regularly; on several occasions when I visited, I learned that management company personnel had just fixed a bar someone had removed. The administrators and the residents were engaged in a back-and-forth game of control and resistance.

The gates in the upper-class Extensión Alhambra and Alhambra are voluntary, planned, and maintained by residents; the gates in Dr. Pila are involuntary: "por lo menos aquí no tiraron la cerca" (at least here they didn't throw the fence on us), one resident of ungated Gándara said.[5] Dr. Pila residents had had no part in decisions about where to place a gate or how many gates to allow. The design and arrangement that control their daily movements with webs of iron poles opening and closing at designated times dictate when and where residents can come and go. But there are also internal gates separating clusters of buildings. A resident explained to me that it would be important to remove those internal gates. "Si vas a casa de fulano hay que dar una vuelta para nada" (If you go to anybody's house, you have to go around for no reason). Rosa told me that the gates were intended "para cerrar el residencial y encerrarnos como si fuéramos animales. Aparte de que nos ponen La Grande [verja] afuera, nos dividen por dentro también. Animalitos dividos por secciones" (to close the public housing project and lock us up as if we were animals. Aside from putting the Big One [fence] outside, they divide us inside, too. Little animals divided by sections). Junior, a police officer in charge of Dr. Pila security, explained to me: "Si tú te fijas en Dr. Pila, tú vas a ver que mismo dentro del residencial hay como unas pequeñas verjas que dividen unas áreas de otras. . . . Esto se hizo . . . por tratar de reducir, tener más control" (If you pay attention to Dr. Pila, you are going to see that within the housing project are small gates that divide some areas from others. . . . This was done, well . . . to try to reduce, to have more control). To me, the internal fences suggested the site plans of a prison.

The fences at Gándara (the smaller public housing project sited south of Dr. Pila, Extensión Alhambra, and Alhambra) are metaphorical, not actual, but they are equally strict. Because Gándara was small and not considered a public danger at the time of Mano Dura, it was not regarded as in need of "rescue" and hence no fence or gate was ever erected there. Its residents want no fence; a gate like Dr. Pila's, would make Gándara appear "ugly" and in need of control.[6] A resident told me that if Gándara were to be gated, the neighborhood would be considered "dangerous," its people considered in need of confinement to protect people outside.[7]

In the private gated communities of affluence, on the other hand, residents and sanctioned visitors are welcomed as into an oasis in a protected retreat. Colorful fences welcome the privileged and their employees and a sign at the entry gate reminds strangers or intruders sternly not to trespass. The symmetrical, tidy, color-coordinated design denotes a sense of quiet order. To enter Extensión Alhambra, for example, is to enter a planned, well-integrated, peaceful community with formal indicators of "civilized" cooperation. A neighborhood association agrees on rules and on neighborhood fees to pay the private guard and maintenance workers. Inside Dr. Pila, however, as in other *caseríos*, the aesthetics suggest a militaristic, hyper-controlled society structure of a sort designed to deal with anticipated lawlessness. The government-controlled public housing not only limits and monitors movement by fences and gates but also supplements and reinforces them by regulations that restrict behavior and daily routines.

Instruments of Control: Technology

The gates' technologies, like their design, distribute power unequally, their mechanisms concealed by aesthetics in the communities of the elite and the middle class. Residents in private neighborhoods rely on modern technologies to provide swift and efficient crossings for those sanctioned to enter and to bar enemies. In public housing neighborhoods, gates work against the residents, betraying the assumed purpose of a gate, which is to protect but also to welcome. Instead, they act to protect citizens outside, and act as barriers against those inside.

The private gated neighborhoods use two common types of gating technologies: (1) "beeper" gates and (2) what I call "garrison" gates. Beeper gates are controlled by remotes distributed to bona fide residents and require minimal intervention to enter but only to visitors approved in advance, effectively making social relationships more formal. Garrison gates require contact with the private security company that is securing residents from a watchtower at a distance (communicating through an intercom system or by direct contact between a guard and those seeking entry). There are garrison gates, too, in public housing but these are not electronically controlled: a watchtower and a sentry monitor them, but the overseer is not the obedient private gatekeeper of affluent housing but a state police officer.

In Extensión Alhambra, the gates identify who belongs to the community, and they determine and control the residents' social network.

Residents get in and out of gates with private beepers. Outsiders get in by dialing an access code to open the gate after the resident has confirmed a visitor's identity. Once in the community space, a visitor must be met at the door or know someone on the premises to get into a residence. The entire community of affluence is, in effect, "home" to its residents. As I did with Ramiro, a visitor finds a keypad hanging at the gate, locates the appropriate name from a posted list, notes the extension number, and then dials the pound key and relevant digits to reach the intercom of the host. The beeper distinguishes insider from outsider. Those let in are those considered familiar and safe. "*El que viene aquí es porque es de aquí*" (Whoever comes here is from here).[8]

The gates in affluent Alhambra, on the other hand, are beeper gates with intricate layers of security technologies: "tall fences, . . . more gates, more gates on the window, alarm systems, and surveillance rounds," in addition to "motion light detectors, spikes on the roofs and pipes, and secure doors."[9] In Alhambra, a vehicular gate opens in response to a signal from each entering private car. Those who haven't erected gates around their homes are urged by their neighbors to do so, because the street has not been allowed to be gated. When Aurora noticed workers across the street near a neighbor's home, she applauded, "¡*Ah mira, están poniendo verja, qué bueno!*" (Oh, look, they're building a fence! Good!).[10] Cars drive past. Visitors and trespassers are the only pedestrians. Residents who signaled to let me in opened a compound of gates controlled by keys in locks, beepers, or codes. Marta, who told me she "has to have the fence and all that security system," said she feels unprotected when she visits her daughter's home in North Carolina, where there were no protective fences: "*Me sacas de mi hábitat y no funciono*" (You take me away from my habitat and I can't function).[11]

According to those who live in Extensión Alhambra and Alhambra, beeper gates work well in creating havens for residents and sanctioned visitors. They work because they allow residents to control the credentialing process:

> [D]ificulta un poco cuando la gente nos visita porque tiene que pasar por un mecanismo de hacer unas llamadas y nosotros a través del teléfono accesar abriéndoles el portón de entrada. En ese sentido hace que las personas que nos visiten pasen un poco de trabajo pero a lo largo es una cosa extraordinaria y nos brinda seguridad tanto a ellos como a nosotros que estamos aquí adentro.

(It makes it harder for people who visit us because they have to go through a mechanism of making calls; we open the gate via the phone. Our visitors go to some trouble but in the long run it is great and provides security not only to them but to us who are inside.)[12]

The garrison gates of upper-class gated communities work in a similar fashion, except that residents have transferred control of admission and exclusion to a hired private security guard company. Visitors and residents identify themselves to the guard, orally or through a distributed identification system, an intercom system. A series of steps may be necessary to gain admission: using a car sticker, showing an official photo ID, identifying who or what property is being visited, or providing a license plate number. A guard may decide on his own whom to send away or when to call for approval. Residents pay for, approve the design of, and establish the machinery, the criteria, and the process. Public housing residents recognize the power of these self-determined technologies: "Ellos tienen *sus* casas, *sus* accesos [controlados] para entrar a *sus* casas" (They have *their* houses, *their* controlled access, to enter *their* homes).[13]

In a technological hierarchy, beeper gates are preferred over garrison guards (just as private guards are considered better than public guards). But neither is foolproof. When the electrical power is out, the gates in Extensión Alhambra cannot close and have to remain open. At these times, what the urban planner Kevin Lynch calls the "imageability" of the gate—the powerful structured images created by the gate's qualities (shape, color, arrangement)—grants or blocks admission. When gates, on occasion, fail to respond to beepers, Alhambra residents must get out of their protective cars and go into the unprotected street to lock and unlock gates manually, exposing them, they fear, to holdups at gunpoint. A newer resident of Alhambra told me about the insecurity of her former residence in a gated walk-up apartment complex:

En el walk-up que nosotros vivíamos teníamos un guardia. A mi esposo lo asaltaron dentro y [los asaltantes] salieron caminando por al frente del guardia. El guardia no hizo nada, no vio nada. Eso nos dice que el pillo o era familiar de uno que vive allí, o logró acceso por el mismo guardia. [Mi esposo] estaba seguro que no le iba a pasar nada [porque] estaba adentro de los perímetros [de la verja].

(In the walk-up apartment where we lived we had a guard. My husband was mugged inside and [the assailants] left on foot in front of the guard. The guard did nothing and saw nothing. That told us that the mugger was related to someone who lives inside, who gained access from the guard. [My husband] was sure that nothing would happen to him because he was inside the perimeter [of the gate].)[14]

In Dr. Pila the generic public housing gate is manned by a virtual "phantom officer," an officer of the local police precinct who sits in the guardhouse behind his one-way mirror, with full discretion to be seen or to remain covert. The officers are meant to control all access to the neighborhood, but they don't. Junior, the security manager for Dr. Pila, explained to me that "los oficiales comenzaron a utilizar a los policías para otros servicios, y empezó a menguar la vigilancia" (the officials began to use the police officers for other services, and the monitoring, and vigilance, began to diminish).[15] The residents themselves referred to the guard as "faceless," as a "phantom" who hides behind a one-way mirror in an air-conditioned cabin. Seen or not seen, everyone assumes a guard is there, in eight-hour shifts, twenty-four hours a day. There is "presión psicológica . . . dicen vamos a controlar esto y no controlan

Figure 9. A rollback fence at a home in Alhambra. Photo by author.

nada" (psychological pressure . . . they say they are going to control and they do not control), one resident said.[16] Residents believe the officer is there not to protect them or to provide them with security but, more likely, to harass residents as they cross the gates and to turn a blind eye to entering nonresidents. Residents mentioned to me confrontations with the gate guard, whose often invisible presence was an inescapable reminder of who controlled the community. The two elements of power, according to Foucault—visibility and unverifiability—are formalized in Dr. Pila's guardhouse.[17] On my own trips to Dr. Pila, both driving and on foot, I never saw the guard and was never stopped or questioned.

Figure 10. The sentry gate to Dr. Pila. Photo by author.

To Public Housing Authority and other government officials, the gates are a necessary intervention that has improved the lives of public housing's residents. A Puerto Rico Housing and Urban Development official told me of a warm response of public housing communities themselves to the gates as a sign that residents had gained a marker of luxury.[18] To him, the gate was class-equalizing. Perhaps, for such reasons, after Mano Dura, Operation

Centurion's Stage 3 (see Chapter 2) was labeled "Re-empower."[19] But to the public housing residents I spoke to, the gates were a means of control, though, in fact, they were disappointed not to have the technological gates of private housing communities. The gates "don't work in public housing," residents say. For gates "to work," by their definition, each resident needs a "beeper" he or she could control, "an intercom in each house so every time someone visits . . . I would say 'Who are you looking for? Where are you going?' Like the private places" (un intercom en cada casa y cada vez que venga alguien no abrieran el portón, y le dijera "a quién usted busca, para dónde usted va?" Como los sitios privados).[20] Personal control meant freedom.

It was also, to residents, not only a matter of appearances ("Se ve más bonito el portón privado. Allá es privado, acá es controlado" [The private gates look more attractive. There it is private, here it is controlled]) but also a matter of a lack of freedom because they themselves were not the decision makers.[21] Electric gates make communities private, a public housing resident said to me of Extensión Alhambra: "Sí, ellos cerraron eso allí. Eso antes no estaba cerrado . . . ahora eso es privado ahí. Ahora tienen portón eléctrico" (Yes, they closed. It wasn't closed before . . . now it is private there. They have an electric gate).[22] Another public housing resident noted, "Los controles de acceso que tienen permiten entrar al que vive en esa área. Ellos tienen policía privado" (The controlled accesses permit entry to those who live in that area. They have private police).[23] Beepers or private security guards were providing "privacy" for the housing of the rich. The Puerto Rican police of public housing provided exposure, not privacy, to housing of the poor. Privacy evokes individual "control"; "public" meant being under the "control" of others, in this case a national police force. Public housing residents wanted private control; with the gates others managed they felt disempowered.

The monitored gates of public housing resemble Foucault's panopticon: "prison-machines with a cell of visibility in which the inmate will find himself caught as 'in the glass house . . . ' [and] . . . a permanent gaze may control."[24] Indeed, some public housing residents refer to themselves as "inmates," required to follow regulations they did not choose.[25] To me they used language like this: "We are in a prison"; "We are isolated, like inmates"; "I have fences like I'm in Las Cucharas [detention center], even the kitchen has bars"; "We are locked in with gates everywhere."[26] Residents reported that, sometimes, when rebulús (problems) occurred, the gates were locked and they were not permitted to leave.[27] Like the lives of true Foucaultian "delinquents," their lives are monitored. Residents spoke to me of the rules, the increased surveillance.[28] Adela said, of the apartment, that if one tried to repaint, a can of paint in the original shade would be sent over from the office to cover the new color up.

Technology and aesthetics complement each other, both selective in the awarding or the withholding of power. To Dr. Pila's public housing residents, the electronic gates of private housing meant prestige and resident control. They envy the private housing security: some wanted a similar identification sticker or a beeper: "El control de acceso cambiarlo. Que sea por beeper. Que el residente tenga un beeper y le den acceso" (Change the controlled access. Have a beeper, so the resident has a beeper and gains access).[29] An electric gate would destigmatize the community. As for private housing residents, they welcome the police-powered gates of public housing as protective "control" and as signaling separation and "distance" from themselves. A resident of the Alhambra private neighborhood, adjacent to Dr. Pila, said to me, "Me gusta que lo hayan cerrado [a Dr. Pila], porque pone un poquito más de distancia" (I am glad they have closed it, because it provides a little bit more distance).[30] To another resident, a sense of distance was insufficient: "Sí, pero ellos [residentes de Dr. Pila] rompen las rejas y se salen, pero como quiera hay un poco más de control" (Yes, but [residents of Dr. Pila] break the gates and come out. Still there is a little bit more control).[31]

Keeping Certain People Out: Credentialing

The private-gate systems have been programmed to keep certain people—people that looked like me or "people from public housing"—out. The message was as clear to me as it was to public housing residents: the undesirable strangers, the "bad" people Neil Stephenson's novel refers to, the "wolf-man" that Giorgio Agamben refers to, were themselves.[32] A resident of Dr. Pila explained to me: "Los controles de acceso que tiene [Extensión Alhambra] permiten entrar al que vive en esa área. . . . Ellos entienden que por ser un residencial las personas de un residencial van a ir a robar allá. Para ellos somos la lacra de la sociedad" (The controlled access in [Extensión Alhambra] allows people from that area to enter. . . . They think people from public housing, because they are from public housing, want to go there to rob. For them, we are society's scum).[33] Another Dr. Pila resident agreed: "Cuando ellos [en Extensión Alhambra] mandaron a hacer ese portón fue para . . . que la gente del residencial no cojan para allá . . . que no entre la chusma" (When they [in Extensión Alhambra] erected that gate, it was . . . so that the people from public housing would not go there . . . the vermin would not enter).[34] Entry, always presumed to be by car, marked pedestrians as trespassers, further identifying as intruders any public housing residents seeking to pass through the gates (most have to walk because they do not have a car for errands). A proper credential required not only a car but also the right driver, a *gente de bien* (a good person) as many Extensión Alhambra residents described their own community, friends, and family.[35]

To gain entry into Alhambra myself, I had to have direct contact with a resident—the sole controller of the gates—because in that community each house has a separate gate and all walls face an empty public street. As a visitor, I had to expose myself to the dangers, whatever they might be, of the street to seek entrance by ringing a bell at the gate or giving my name over the phone. Sometimes I was accompanied by a sponsor who vouched for me—a referral or a community member who might have known me from my days at the Caribbean School, the college preparatory school I had attended for fourteen years in Ponce. If unaccompanied, I made sure to announce my name, loud and clear, hoping my voice would upgrade my appearance, that is, the color of my skin. On one occasion, Aurora, who had lived in Alhambra for more than twenty years, walked with me along the street to her neighbor's home, four houses down—a big yellow and white colonial house—then called out to her neighbor from the sidewalk across the three-foot-high yellow and white iron fence that enclosed the front lawn (other fences in the neighborhood were much taller). She called out the last name "Pérez! Pérez!," apologizing to me for not remembering her neighbor's first name.[36] A white aluminum window on the top floor opened slightly and a woman's voice emerged; she would be "down soon." The window closed and Aurora and I waited on the sidewalk until Marisa, a chubby white woman of middle age, opened her front door and motioned us to cross through the now-unlocked gate. A second gate fully enclosed her front porch; Marisa opened this one, too, and we crossed over and through the door. Aurora's introductions stemmed the credentialing questioning I had become accustomed to in Ramiro's Extensión Alhambra community, where elaborate routines had tested my identity before I could approach a house for an appointment.

When I ventured into Dr. Pila, however, the experience of crossing was quite different. To enter a space outsiders consider a source of crime, I had, first, to cope with my own fear of violence and with the fear expressed by my family and friends. As a child, accompanied by my parents, I had gone to basketball games in public housing communities, and, as a teenager I had visited friends there despite what I was told, that public housing was to be avoided. I did this as much from my sense of justice and equality as from my own discomfort in an elite society that rejected people like me because of my skin color. With my youthful public housing friends, I was not only "normal" but I could also be "beautiful." But, later on, when I returned from graduate school in Michigan and prepared to undertake research, unclear about the realities of public housing and cognizant only of rumors, my own family's fears, and media reports, I was, at first, hesitant to enter. A member of the Dr. Pila community subsequently told me, to my chagrin and embarrassment, that she sensed I was nervous when we met with members of Dr. Pila's elected Resident Council.

When, for the first time, as an adult researcher, I passed by the guardhouse of Dr. Pila alone, I did not know whether to stop or whether I was being watched through that one-way guardhouse mirror. The yellow sign on the gate, demanding that I identify myself and warning that my car might be subject to a search, communicated only unfriendly messages. I drove slowly over the speed bump, looked toward the closed door of the guardhouse, and then saw that, ahead, some men who were standing about were observing me. I was being watched but didn't know by whom or when someone would let me know whether I had been granted entry. But, contrary to my experience at Extensión Alhambra, my skin color here seemed to have a soothing effect, both on me and on the observers inside, or so I thought and I entered the space with less suspicion.

Residents of both private and public communities had previously told me that a race credential was required for someone to enter community spaces. An Alhambra resident said that her whiteness kept her from responding to her priest's pleas to go to Dr. Pila to proselytize: "A mi me daría pánico, porque yo me siento distinta hasta físicamente . . . una rubia! . . . no encuentro cómo pasar desapercibida" (I would be in a panic, because I feel different even physically . . . a blonde woman! . . . I wouldn't know how to go unnoticed).[37] Appearance—the aesthetics of race, not only the aesthetics of architecture—matters in the experience of crossing through the gate to the other side.

Although I was never stopped at the Dr. Pila gate, some do get stopped. It is hard to know why. Public housing residents told me it was they, not visitors, who were under scrutiny at the gate: "A mí me han parado . . . me han preguntado para qué bloque voy, qué voy a hacer. . . . La cara de maleante que me ven" (I have been stopped . . . and asked what building I am going to, what am I going to do. . . . They see the face of a *crook* in me).[38] It is true that residents of Dr. Pila, in days of violence, encouraged me to leave for my own safety but the "crook" is the villain at all gates, public and private, whether coming in from outside, among approaching visitors, or living inside. I was also never stopped in my visits to Gándara, the ungated public housing community, ungated because the government of Mano Dura years ago did not believe crime festered there. Yet no outsider enters Gándara's premises unobserved, as I learned myself when I first ventured there: I had to receive a formal introduction from a resident to drug-dealing youths lounging at the front of the project in order to enter. Such youths are metaphorical gates or monitors who decide whom to admit. When I drove to Gándara later in an unidentified new rental car, I made sure that my face was clearly visible to the teenage monitors. Contrary to private housing gate crossings, where cars (and especially new late-model cars) have credentialing power, I found walking into Gándara and other public housing an easier way in. My plainly visible (dark) face was, or so I felt, a passport inside. Once inside public housing, people seemed excited to talk with me. I was questioned, as in private gated communities, but less formally and, often, this time timidly. Was I once a public housing resident of whom they could be proud? Or was I actually an undercover police officer? My admittance had to be confirmed and justified. Crossing private and public gates requires different credentials from out to in and back out. But it was clear to me that to go inside the gated *caserío* (public housing) was, as one resident said, to "not move freely," to be controlled, isolated, and actively barred from freedom of contact both inside and outside. Residents' movements were restricted; so were mine. Visitors were signaled to stay out or tread carefully. To be a resident of a private community, on the other hand, or an expectant visitor, was to be welcomed into a safe haven protected from outside perils. Welcome depends on who is seeking entry and who is doing the credentialing: in private housing it is the residents; in public housing, the government.

Gated Discipline

There has been significant research on the emergence of the gate as a central feature of cities across the globe but most research is about gates protecting the privileged, not about gates used as a barrier between the poor and the city. Most studies have focused on the rise of the gated communities of the rich as a demonstration of "fear" and of a quest for security from urban crime and the fear of crime and from declining property values outside, or simply to reinforce an atmosphere of acknowledged privilege and prestige. The gate is presented as standard in form, function, and meaning, an exclusive feature of privileged communities.[39] The role of gates as controllers of unprivileged others has not been examined. Technological and aesthetic variations of gates, their interplay of art and the science of engineering, employed together strengthen each other and also discipline and reinforce inequality. As Foucault suggests, they set "the intelligence of discipline in stone."[40] Some research shows that, in modern society, public space is becoming increasingly privatized by interventions that seek to "control" and "secure" the environment.[41]

Public housing communities, portrayed as dystopias by their gates and fences, are not a mirror image of the private gates of the rich, though both types of gates lead to isolation. Private gates are products of a security

Figure 11. A warning sign on the Alhambra gate. Photo by author.

construction industry that promotes gating as providing privileged utopias and of an architecture that reinforces exclusivity and autonomy within a city. The intercoms, telephones, and technologies of voice communication that monitor potential entrants offer impersonal connections in voice, tone, and language between residents, guarded sentries, and potential visitors or transgressors from the street. In the communities of the rich, gates are self-imposed; in the communities of the poor, gates are imposed from the outside. Video technology, although still rare in Puerto Rico, supports screening further, introducing a newer and more fortified means of credentialing profile by appearance. I myself might have found it more difficult to cross the gate in Extensión Alhambra if it had had video surveillance. The questions posed to me in living rooms might have been posed at the gate, introducing an additional barrier against entry. After Aníbal Acevedo Vilá took office on January 2005 as Puerto Rico's governor, he discussed the potential of video technology for the controlled access infrastructure of Puerto Rican public housing. His suggestion was hotly debated as an additional surveillance mechanism to supervise public housing residents. Public housing in the United States has already incorporated video technology as a security measure. Security guards, in private housing, and police officers, in public housing communities, as agents of power, can screen faces, hear voice inflections, digest information, and put it together into an algorithm that leads to "entry" or "non-entry." The absence of gates may significantly change the way cameras work and how they are perceived by residents. Video surveillance is used more and more in public spaces, with national security cited as the necessary cause. Scholars like Mike Davis have noted that such public supervision significantly changes the character of urban life itself. Questions raised about whether comprehensive surveillance impinges on individuals' Fourth Amendment rights to privacy tend to be ignored.

The city, historically, has been seen as a site where socially heterogeneous individuals frequently come into contact, in parks, in libraries, in streets, in churches, in theaters, in restaurants, on buses or subways, and in other public spaces, all residents enriched thereby, even though contacts are secondary, not primary, as in families. Urban enclaves' quests for sameness, the political scientist Iris Marion Young argues, result in strategies that defeat the democratic virtues of the city. She mourns the processes of segregation and exclusion: "One of the most disturbing aspects of contemporary urban life is the depth and frequency of aversive behavior which occurs within it. Group segregation is produced by aversive perceptions that deprecate some groups, defining them as entirely other, to be shunned and avoided."[42] Community gates in Puerto Rico narrow the concept of community and of individual through decisions about group social worth and social threat, about who is redeemable and who is dispensable, about who is "good" and allowable, and about who is "bad" and made to "go away."

Chapter 4

Community: Where Rights Begin and End

No quiero vivir en una ciudad con tanques de guerra. Yo vivo en una democracia y la democracia se respeta. (I don't want to live in a city full of war tanks. I live in a democracy and and democracy is to be respected.)

—Nelly, Extensión Alhambra resident

When I interviewed Nelly at the upper-middle-class gated community of Extensión Alhambra, I knew I could not waste time. Nelly was very busy with civic endeavors. Her IKEA-like modern multipurpose den–family room–office served as a work headquarters. She was used to questions; her posture and articulate answers had a political flavor. What about the Mano Dura gating policies, I asked, "¿Qué piensa sobre la política de Mano Dura contra el crimen y cuáles son sus elementos?" (What do you think of the Mano Dura policies and the strategies to combat crime?). Nelly offered slogans, making her way through contradictory points about political ideology, principles of self-responsibility, and philosophies about justice and democracy:

Tienes que buscar por qué el por ciento de criminalidad ha aumentado. Si esto es en la familia, en la escuela, darle clases a los muchachos de civismo. El derecho mío empieza donde termina el tuyo. Tienes que respetar y conservar lo que tienes para poder ayudar a otro. Si quieres progresar va a depender de ti y de lo que puedas hacer por otro y de que puedas crecer y de tener unos valores, unos principios. Esa ética se le debe enseñar a todo el mundo. Creo en La Mano Dura porque el que comete algo lo comete teniendo justa y causa. Lo que hizo lo hizo porque quiso o porque quería más. Mano Dura contra el pobre y el rico. . . . No debes tener un policía con una pistola en mi casa al salir. Porque si no, entra la policía y me arresta porque hice algo malo. Si conozco la ley, áreas de civismo, de humanismo, como mejorar el ambiente y me educo para progresar, no creo que haya necesidad [de Mano Dura]. [Que] se preparen leyes para traer justicia social a todo el mundo, no a unos sí y otros no.

(You have to find the reasons why the crime rate has increased. Is it because of the family and schooling? Should kids be given civic classes? My rights begin where yours end. You have to be able to respect and take care of yourself and your things to be able to help others. Progress depends on you, what you can do for others, whether you can grow and cultivate good values and principles. Everyone should be taught ethics. I believe in Mano Dura because a person who commits a crime is fully aware of what he does. He wanted to do it or wanted to accumulate more. I believe in Mano Dura against both the poor and rich. The rich also rob and hurt others. . . . I shouldn't need a police officer with a gun at the exit of my house. If so, the police officer would enter my house and arrest me because I did something wrong. If I know the law, civics, humanism, how to improve the environment, and I educate myself to get better, I don't think there is necessity [for Mano Dura]. Laws should be made to bring justice to all, not for some but not for others.)

Nelly concluded: "No quiero vivir en una ciudad con tanques de guerra. Yo vivo en una democracia y la democracia se respeta" (I don't want to live in a city with war tanks. I live in a democracy and democracy is to be respected).

But, what, exactly, is *her* democracy, the democracy that needs to be respected? Does it consist of rights and privileges for all, or of enforced boundaries and vigilance for the undeserving, those who fail to "progress," those who lack ethics? What democracy do Mano Dura and the gates protect? The community gates for public and private housing in Puerto Rico have reconfigured democracy. In a democracy, rights and privileges are to be equally distributed; Jean-Jacques Rousseau saw democracy as embodying the social will, responsive to the preference of its citizens.[1] History exposes democracy's failure to fulfill needs equally and the often exclusionary character of the democratic process, clarifying for whom it is designed, who can voice an opinion, who counts. In Ponce, the devolution process empowered the rich and disempowered the poor. With the gates and via the government, the rich controlled and privatized the city and their own communities and homes, and they gained a position of entitlement, a sense of "competence."[2] The poor, with increased public supervision, experienced civic apathy, what Bourdieu refers to as a "sense of impotence and objective and subjective exclusion."[3] Their limited recourse for participation and influence, outside of the electoral vote, has been to rebel, but they rebel symbolically and indirectly with small acts of sabotage that seldom have a visible actor. Those who cause too much trouble can lose their housing.

The Self-Governing Elite

In the gated enclaves of the rich, gates confirm oligarchy, effectively demarcating the boundary where, as Nelly says, "my rights begin and yours end." In the gated elite communities the rules, regulations, and "government" are their own, to "act for their own protection," as the Closing Law of 1987 provides.

With autonomy comes citizen responsibility; the two are necessarily related. When Extensión Alhambra organized a neighborhood association and built a gate in 1994, the community came alive with meetings, activities, and parties. Neighbors designed a governance to manage, fund, and operate gates. It was a community, as one resident said, "*que se rige por una directiva*" (governed by a directive). To be under a "directive" meant (1) a process and structure for community action, (2) a designated body for complaints, and (3) an identifiable space and group structure for planning community events. The "directive" identifies certain behaviors and home practices as acceptable and others as unacceptable. The association collects dues, maintains the gates, organizes neighborhood events, and attends to other community matters. It sponsors Halloween trick-or-treating, Christmas parties, and Valentine's Day get-togethers; invitations go out and expectant conversations abound. During the time of my interviews there, community members talked of an upcoming Valentine's Day party and the neighborhood association president, Rebecca, displayed the red invitation she had personally designed. One resident excitedly described the association as serving *la comunidad* (the community).

The gate afforded Extensión Alhambra residents a clear identity of community membership and a structured system for processing disagreements.[4]

Nelly explained to me: "Ese grupo que dirige los residentes presentan sus querellas, sus incomodidades, sus preocupaciones. . . . Por esto también hay actividades familiares que se hacen. . . . hay una comunidad que se rige por una directiva (The group that is directed by residents allows complaints to be filed, discomforts and worries to be voiced. . . . They organize family activities. . . . a community subject to a board of directors).[5] A resident explained the sense of family: "Es más íntimo. Hay contacto más con el vecino que es tu familiar más cercano" (It is more intimate. There is more contact with the neighbor, your closest family member).

But for all the benefits of intimacy and "family" that the neighborhood association bolstered by gates provides, there is a sense of surveillance, both welcomed and resisted. The day-to-day lives in the community are known to all. "Aquí sabemos cuando se va fulano, cuando se va el de al lado, sabemos lo que pasa a diario" (Here, we know when everybody leaves, when our next-door neighbor leaves; we know the daily happenings).[6] Ramiro told me of monitoring neighbors' behavior not sanctioned in their social circles:

> Dos o tres familias . . . han venido aquí cuyos hijos han traído droga a la urbanización y eso ha hecho que vengan elementos no deseables. Nos ha puesto en nivel de estar vigilando a estas personas, a los hijos de estas familias porque sabemos el peligro que engendra a los otros muchachos jóvenes en la urbanización. La familia que sabe que esto ocurre velan por sus hijos para que no se mezclen y entablen amistad con esa familia.

> (Two or three families . . . have come here whose children have brought drugs into the neighborhood, bringing in undesirables. It has forced us to monitor these persons and the children of these families, because of the danger they represent for other youth in the community. Families who know this is happening look out that their children do not mix with, or begin friendships, with those others.)[7]

The democracy behind the Extensión Alhambra gates imposes rules of comportment and propriety, and it creates maps of contact. The neighborhood's democracy is cultivated but restrictive.

Helen feels left out of the Extensión Alhambra's social contract. She is not Puerto Rican although she has lived in Puerto Rico for more than three decades and, at the time I interviewed her, she had been in Extensión Alhambra for five years. To Helen, the association and its rules provide liberties for only a few. As she described it, it was "the most unfriendly neighborhood I've ever lived in my life." She saw Extensión Alhambra and its association as hypocrites who bend regulations to their own benefit. Rebecca, the president, she said, "takes [being President] like an ego problem. . . . The regulations state that there should be no loose dog in this gated community [but] she was feeding all these stray dogs, sometimes ten at a time. There's an empty lot at the . . . entrance. She would keep the stray dogs there and throw food at them. . . . It would bring dogs, not very nice dogs. So, me, being a good citizen, I would walk my dog by the leash and these dogs would attack. And I made a formal complaint to the association. They simply didn't care." Helen, who was white and studied law, was concerned with the "rule of law." The neighborhood association, she said, applied its regulations unequally; she did not think she was treated as an equal citizen because she objected.

In my interview with Rebecca, the president of Extensión Alhambra's neighborhood association, a lively middle-aged white woman, it became evident that she was, wanted to be, or wanted to demonstrate that she was busy. One of the "causes" she espoused was the "animal protection society," which explains the neighborhood association's response to Helen's complaints. When I arrived at Rebecca's home for the interview, she was standing on the front porch with her husband. After the routine questioning to which I had become accustomed, and up-and-down stares, she called two neighbors over to join in our interview. She never stepped out of her role as "president," interrupting numerous times to answer phone calls and stepping away to attend to other community matters. She was directing or trying to direct the interview. For me, the process itself was a revealing part of it. That Helen's complaint was ignored by the neighborhood association was as much a result of the president's own posture toward stray dogs as it was indicative of an exclusive culture of "neighborliness."

Race and ethnicity were codified in Extensión Alhambra's sense of a family neighborhood. One resident proudly reported that they were all Puerto Ricans and *Caucásicos* (Caucasians), not foreigners as in other communities. Helen remarked that Puerto Ricans were "racist." Helen, a foreigner herself, white but not Puerto Rican, had little contact with neighbors, who, Nelly had said, were supposed to be the community's "closest family members." Helen felt a xenophobic sense of community. I had been keenly aware of an intersection of race, class, and immigration myself because my parents had come to Puerto Rico from the Dominican Republic; Dominicans, the largest ethnic minority on the island, were commonly excluded in Puerto Rico from the formulation of community identities.[8]

Helen had a sense of elitism of her own, describing the community as composed of people who lived beyond their means and who could not afford to maintain their homes. In her eyes, and contrary to her neighbors' views, the neighborhood was in disrepair. Neighbors unwilling to hear her pleas tolerated the clamor of their next-door neighbor, the elite Club Deportivo (a social club). Helen complained to me of the club that "those people make so much noise with their music. . . . I complained. . . . But a lot of high[-status] people are a member [*sic*] . . . doctors, lawyers, whatnot, [and] the police won't do anything. Right now I've taken them to the Junta de Calidad Ambiental . . . the local environmental quality board and I pressed charges. . . . It's a private nuisance. They [say], 'Ay Bendito, it's been going on for more than thirty years that noise'. . . . The people don't like [the fact that] I complained about it . . . and the club, very cowardly, has been giving free membership to lots of people here as long as they do not complain. I can't be bought." Residents were subjected to rules, but rules could be bent. The gates made some feel protected and empowered, but it made others feel disempowered.

For Alhambra, the elite community that had individual but no community gates, democracy is configured in a different place, at the crossroads of the street and individual homes. Residents have worked for many years for permission to establish a community-exclusive gate, but, because of the municipal street that runs through it, they have been denied. The influence of class has not overcome the transit map of the city. They see the absence of a gate as constricting their own liberties and contrary to their sense of entitlement: "[Alhambra] debe tener acceso controlado. Estamos todo el tiempo como que atacados por estas personas que pasan sin ningún respeto hacia las propiedades de nosotros. Entran y salen de la urbanización como si fuera todo esto de ellos ([Alhambra] should have controlled access. We are always constantly attacked by people who go by without respect for our properties. They enter and exit the community as if it was theirs).[9] Because the street is municipal, of course, the street is, indeed, theirs but not theirs alone.

With no community gate, Alhambra residents have gated each home, retreating behind wall and fences to mansions without neighbors but each with a sense that next door, behind a wall, is one like themselves. They see each wall as a sign of respect for others. Democracy is a matter of guarding one's "own things."

Lo más que me gusta es . . . el respeto de los vecinos. Cada cual vive en sus casas y ocupado en sus cosas. Cuando nos vemos nos saludamos y si algo pasa pues nos enteramos. A veces no nos enteramos y nos preocupan algún daño pero ese es el estilo de vida que llevamos aquí. Yo creo que la mayoría de las personas están a gusto en eso.

(What I like the most is . . . the respect that neighbors have. Each lives in their homes and is occupied with his or her own things. When we see each other, we say hello, and if something happens, well, we find out about it. Sometimes we don't find out about it and we worry about any harm caused but that is the lifestyle we lead. These people feel good about it.) [10]

At the center of life is the individual family. "La vida que uno lleva lo concentra a uno a estar con la familia. A veces no tienes tiempo ni para saludar al vecino de al frente porque estás en el ajetreo diario" (The type of life we have leads to concentrating on the family. Sometimes the daily grind doesn't even allow time for saying hello to the neighbor right across the street).[11] In Alhambra, the scale of democracy has shifted from community to the atomic, individual family.[12] New residents may try to foster a wider community. "Estoy recién mudada; lo que llevo es un mes . . . un saludo cordial. Estamos tratando de reunirnos, tratar de levantar eso en la comunidad. La calle que nos conozcamos, que cada cual sepa quién es quién" (I moved here just a month ago . . . a cordial greeting. We are trying to get together, trying to get that going in the community, to know each other on the street, to know each other).[13] Alhambra residents meet in Ponce's social clubs for the elite, creating a community of class not because of place or their exclusive work environments: their community identity transcends their house and street and encompasses the higher levels of Ponce itself, a transcendent garden and playground.

The Governed Poor

For public housing residents, the gates and their operators represent external governing structures and limit their rights. Public housing is not a democracy or a representative republic. The price of housing (beyond the rent) is surrender of governance to the police and to the company to which the city has subcontracted its responsibility for management and security and to the city government itself. Increasingly prohibitive regulations require good conduct letters, strict rental agreements and eviction proceedings, and welfare policies. The autocracy is camouflaged symbolically by the residents' election of a Resident Council, whose president holds the physical key to the community center but not absolute power to schedule activities within the center.

With the gates of public housing came the *privatizadores* (private management companies) with their intervention strategies. On May 2, 1992, just before the implementation of Mano Dura and the gates, a "Project for the Privatization and Administration of Public Housing" was approved by the Puerto Rican and U.S. federal government. Its goal was to "stimulate" participation in the administration and management of public housing projects of the private sector, considered to be a more effective manager of federal funds, a sector able to introduce needed innovation: "Los privatizadores son uno de los puntales en la estrategia de intervención en los residenciales" (The private management companies are central to the public housing intervention strategy).[14] On April 12, 1996, a memo from the Department of Housing and Urban Development (HUD) in Washington, D.C., to public housing authorities outlined a new federal mandate:

> The Clinton Administration has implemented the most far-reaching transformation of public housing since its inception to improve the safety and quality of life in public housing. HUD has enabled cities to demolish dozens of blighted vacant, high-rise projects and replace them with garden-style, economically integrated developments. HUD is changing the social dynamic in public housing by instilling positive incentives, rewarding working families, and setting tougher expectations on personal responsibility so that families can achieve self-sufficiency. We have initiated a national crackdown on gangs and violence called Operation Safe Home that has resulted in thousands of arrests and confiscation of assault weapons and drugs.
>
> As one important step in this larger, comprehensive strategy to improve the quality, safety and well-being of public housing communities, HUD recommends that PHAs [public housing authorities] design and implement "One Strike and You're Out" (One Strike) policies. . . . PHAs have broad authority to screen applicants and are required to state clearly in their leases that illegal drug use and other criminal activities that threaten the well-being of residents are

grounds for eviction. A new law, the Housing Opportunity Program Extension Act of 1996 (Extension Act), also gives PHAs new authority and obligations to deny occupancy on the basis of illegal drug-related activity and alcohol abuse.[15]

Puerto Rico's Housing Authority followed suit, affirming its mission to

ofrecer un ambiente comunitario que promueva la seguridad y el desarrollo humano de sus residentes, limitará la asignación de vivienda a aquellas familias cuyos miembros no participen o cooperen con la manufactura, venta, distribución, uso o posesión de drogas ilegales y la actividad criminal violenta.

(provide a community environment that promotes security and human development for its residents, will limit housing to families whose members do not participate or support the manufacture, sale, distribution, use, or possession of illicit drugs and violent criminal activity.)[16]

In Puerto Rico's public housing, the stringent regulations came with a new cadre of overseers and enforcers. The distant Asociación de Vivienda Pública (AVP, Public Housing Authority) managers in a large and inefficient bureaucracy were replaced by private company management (of housing and, in some instances, of other institutions like prisons).[17] The management of Dr. Pila and Gándara had been transferred from the Puerto Rico Housing Authority to Park Management Company in 1992 and, in 1995, to Westbrook Management Company, which, in turn, appointed one *administradora* (a woman) for Gándara and three *administradores* (two women, one man) for Dr. Pila, one per section of the project, and each with supporting staff that included one or two social workers and groundkeepers.[18] One Gándara resident said, "La privatización lleva a cambios y la gente . . . le tienen miedo al cambio" (Privatization leads to changes and people . . . fear change). "Antes nos sentíamos más libres porque antes no hostigaban tanto" (Before we felt freer because we were less harassed). Another in Dr. Pila said, "Ellos como privatizadores tienen derechos, pero nosotros también" (As private management, they have rights, but so do we). For residents of public housing, privatization has put their own rights in play.

The managers, backed by federal legislation and local housing policies, imposed more regulations. Unemployed adult residents now had to work for their housing, and residents who did not obtain a letter of good conduct from the police department or who failed to pay their rent on time would face eviction. Programs were set up to monitor the community, and monitoring, in turn, led to ranking of the community's perceived problems. Dr. Pila's profile as a violent and ruthless community was affirmed by a manager ranking drug use and drug business at the top of the list, alcohol use next, then unemployment, and, toward the bottom, illiteracy, school dropouts, domestic violence, and child abuse. In Gándara, managers ranked unemployment ahead of substance abuse and drug trafficking; next came single motherhood, child abuse, school desertion, alcohol abuse, domestic violence, and illiteracy. The regulations have brought a more aggressive surveillance of residents' lives. No one ranks or lists the problems that must exist in Alhambra and Extensión Alhambra.

Privatization, as Dr. Pila and Gándara residents described it to me, both gave and took away. It gave more investments—more money, more efficiency, more technicians, more maintenance of the physical grounds, reduced waiting periods for services, a petitioning process, more order. It took away more privacy and imposed more regulations: "Esto es privado entre comillas. . . . Esto no es privado. Cuando era Vivienda que corría esto, habían más beneficios. Mejor que ahora" (Public housing is better. This is "private" in quotation marks. . . . This is not private. When the Public Housing Authority was running this, there were more benefits. Better than now). Private management staffers themselves see only virtues in privatization—innovation, efficiency, order, and responsibility. Yvette, the representative of Westbrook Management who introduced me and provided access to Dr. Pila and Gándara, saw private enterprise as a model of capitalist enterprise: "Lamentablemente cuando mencionan empleados de gobierno se recuestan mucho. La agencia privada es producción y hay que cumplir. . . . y hay que trabajar, hay que producir" (Unfortunately government employees are lackadaisical, they are too dependent. A private agency is about production; you have to have something to show for. . . . We have to work, we have to produce).

Private management is not autonomous. The links between government and business are readily visible, said a resident of Dr. Pila: "Esto es privatizado y es como si no lo fuera. Las leyes de privatización son las de Vivienda Pública o sea que Vivienda. . . . Esas reglas no las imponen el privatizador. Esa son reglas que vienen de allá (This is privatized and it's as if it wasn't. The laws of privatization are the same as the Public Housing Authority. . . . Those rules are not imposed by the privatizing company. The rules come from over there).[19] The residents themselves are now two steps removed from democratic participation, their lives governed by a public bureaucracy and by the outsourced private management.

The privatizadores have supplanted and disassembled organic community associations and events. Residents spoke to me of yesteryears when the community was buzzing, when children could take a plate of food to a neighbor's apartment, or take part in field days they themselves had organized:

> Antes había mucho deporte, ahora no hay tantos. Para sacar un grupo de deporte ahora está raro. Antes todas nosotras nos movíamos. La privatización tiene que ver con eso. Es difícil motivarlos. Antes era más facil motivarlos. Antes iban a las casas y los apuntaban en las cosas. Antes para todo había actividad. Para Thanksgiving hacían la carrera del pavo y eso. Para Navidades, para todo hacían una actividad.

> (Before, there were more sports. Now, there aren't so many. It is hard to form a group for a sport. Before, we were all active. Privatization now deals with that. It is hard to get people motivated, before, it was easier. Before, neighbors would go to the houses and sign people up. Before, there was an activity for everything, for Thanksgiving, the turkey race, for Christmas, for everything an activity.)

The once spontaneous or community-directed events are now the purview of the management group. Social workers hired by government and private management companies organize sporting leagues and form interest groups, such as sewing classes. Fewer residents take part now that the programs are no longer their own creation. A job fair I attended at Dr. Pila drew only a few residents, most required to be there because they were unemployed.

The projects have a skeletal structure of democracy; although residents elect the members of the Resident Council, a sure sign that democracy is understood to be a camouflage—participation at council meetings is low and the tasks members perform are considered of little consequence. Dr. Pila has three elected Resident Councils (one for each section) each with a president, a vice president, a secretary, a treasurer, and *vocales* (elected members at large).[20] Gándara, which is small, has one Resident Council. The Resident Council members did seem to be lively and fully embedded in the communities—in Dr. Pila, they edited the wording of my recruitment flyers, and they helped with recruiting residents for interviews, with varying degrees of success. An example of the recruitment flyers is the following:

RESIDENTES DE DR. PILA, 1ERA Y 2DA EXTENSIONES
CON 18 AÑOS O MÁS

Te invitamos a participar en una encuesta para conocer el perfil de la comunidad.

La encuesta la está haciendo una estudiante de doctorado de la Universidad de Michigan de Estados Unidos para satisfacer los requisitos de su tésis doctoral. Sólo tienes que participar en una entrevista de grupo que durará entre 1 y 2 horas. Por favor comunícate con la estudiante Zaire Dinzey al [phone number removed] para participar.

¡Gracias!

INFORMACIÓN SOBRE ESTUDIO DE COMUNIDAD:

¿Quien está haciendo esta encuesta y cuál es el propósito? Zaire Dinzey es la investigadora principal de este estudio. Ella es una estudiante de doctorado de la Universidad de Michigan y está haciendo esta encuesta para su tésis doctoral.

¿De qué trata la encuesta? Esta encuesta es sobre la calidad de vida comunitaria de algunas comunidades en Puerto Rico. La encuesta intentará determinar como la arquitectura de las comunidades residenciales afectan algunas dinámicas sociales. Nos interesa entender como los cambios físicos que han tenido las comunidades en Puerto Rico durante los pasados 10 años afectan la vida y satisfacción de sus residentes, así como la vida comunitaria con miembros dentro y fuera de su comunidad.

¿Cuáles son los requisitos para participar? Para participar en este estudio usted tiene que ser residente de la comunidad y tener por lo menos 18 años de edad.

¿Qué tengo que hacer para participar en esta encuesta? Para participar en el estudio, le pediremos a los residentes de las comuniades que participen en una entrevista de grupo que durará no más de 2 horas. Las entrevistas serán por citas y no incluirán más de 6 personas por entrevista. El horario de la entrevista será flexible y podremos ajustarlas para que facilite la participación de esos que deseen.

Qué recibe el residente y la comunidad a cambio de su participación: En agradecimiento, cada participante será compensado **$10** por su participación al completar la entrevista. Además, la investigadora está dispuesta a proveerle los resultados de la encuesta a aquellos que estén interesados.

(RESIDENTS OF DR. PILA, 1ST AND 2ND EXTENSIONS
OF 18 YEARS OF AGE OR OLDER

We invite you to participate in a survey about the community's profile.

The survey is being conducted by a doctoral student from the University of Michigan, from the United States, to satisfy the requirements for her doctoral dissertation. You only have to participate in a group interview that will last between 1 and 2 hours. To participate, please get in touch with the student Zaire Dinzey at [phone number removed].

Thank you!

INFORMATION ABOUT COMMUNITY STUDY:

Who is doing the survey and what is its purpose? Zaire Dinzey is the principal investigator of this study. She is a doctoral student at the University of Michigan and she is doing a survey for her dissertation.

What is the survey about? This survey is about the quality of life in some communities in Puerto Rico. The survey will try to determine how the architecture of the residential communities affects some social dynamics. We are interested in understanding how the physical changes that have occured in communities in Puerto Rico over the past 10 years affect the life and satisfaction of its residents, as well as how they affect comunity life with members of its community and residents outside the community.

What are the requirements for participating? To participate in this study you have to be a resident of the community and be at least 18 years old.

What do I have to do to participate in the survey? To participate in the survey, we will ask community residents to be a part of a group interview that will last no longer than 2 hours. The interviews will be by appointment and will include no more than 6 persons per interview. The time to conduct interviews will be flexible and we can adjust the time to make it convenient for those who would like to participate.

What does the community resident receive for their participation? In thanks for their participation, each participant will be compensated with **$10** upon completion of the interview. Furthermore, the researcher is willing to share the results of the survey with those who are interested in seeing them.)

Still, the range of influence for the Resident Council members was narrow, limited by private managers. An administrator in Dr. Pila pointed out to me a poster that offered residents one of three similar colors of paint for their buildings. Renovations of the physical plant seemed to be the primary agenda. Resident Councils seem to act more as passive participants or mediators in the processes of governance, the process itself directed by government through its private interlocutors. Yvette, the Westbrook representative, indicated the top-down process:

> Lo de modernización, eso [la Administración de] Vivienda [Pública] determina, por el tiempo que lleva el residencial, por tantas órdenes de servicio que se generan, el deterioro que tenga la planta física. Pues Vivienda determina qué proyecto puede irse a modernización y cuál no. Ellos hacen un plan de cinco años que lo discuten todos los años con los Presidentes de consejo o la comunidad con unas Vistas Públicas. Y entonces les informan qué Vivienda tiene para planes de cinco años, quién ha solicitado, qué piensan hacer, y entonces el procedimiento. . . . Ejemplo, entendemos que Gándara necesita modernización. Cada año le dicen a los consejos o representante de la comunidad en las Vistas Públicas en qué proceso está ese proyecto para irse a modernización, hasta que llega el momento que vienen los fondos y se puede comenzar con el trabajo y en las facetas que está el pedido de modernización del proyecto que sea.
>
> (Modernization is determined by the Puerto Rico Public Housing Authority [PRPHA], depending on the age of the public housing project, how many service orders have been generated, the deterioration of the physical plant. So the PRPHA determines which project can go to modernization and which can't. They formulate a five-year plan to be discussed every year with the Presidents of the community councils or the community, in public hearings. . . . For example, we understand that Gándara needs modernization. Every year they tell the councils or representative of the community in the public hearings where this project is in the process for "modernization," until the moment comes when the funds arrive and the work can begin.)

Residents hear about plans for modernization but do not determine the plans or the process or choose the preselected paint-color tabs. Yvette explained that Gándara's location in a historic zone makes its selection of paint color subject to municipal codes: "Inclusivo los colores que vayan a la par con la zona histórica. . . . No podemos perder de vista que está en zona histórica" (Everything, including the colors, has to be on par with the historical zone. . . . We cannot lose sight that it is in a historical zone).

Residents are not fooled by the top-down process. They see the renovations as merely cosmetic, as excluding more vital problems like the aged sewer system, the leaking roofs, the lack of hot water, the banning of ceiling fans, and the substitution of vinyl tiles for ceramic tiles over their bare cement floors. Residents I talked to were well aware of the community's needs and desires, like the lack of sufficient recreation spaces, the removal of the once-green stretches, and the paving over of yards for parking. Residents of Dr. Pila mourned the loss:

> *Miriam*: Había patio antes. (There was a patio before.)
> *Teresa*: Cerraron el balcón completo atrás. (Now they completely closed the balcony.)
> *Minerva*: Antes podías salir por las partes de atrás. Había gente que tenía un jardín, tenía su privacidad. (Before, you could exit through the back. There were people who had a garden, had their privacy.)[21]

In gated Dr. Pila, one resident protested the loss of autonomy and discouragement of individual expression: "Uno decoraba la entrada de uno a su manera y de la oficina mandan pintura para que uno le quite el color que uno le puso. Te digo porque la entrada de la casa de mi mamá le pasó eso. La pintaron amarillito y le mandaron pintura para quitárselo. Tiene que ser lo que *ellos* digan" (You used to decorate the entrance of your own home your own way, then they sent paint from the office to replace it; you would have to paint over it. When my mother had the entrance to her house painted yellow, they sent other paint to cover up. It has to be what *they* say).[22]

Between Apathy and Resistance

In the everyday, resistance can come in many forms, from apathy to protest to subversion. It can, to use James Scott's words, be "prosaic" and "ordinary" or abrupt.[23] Residents behind gates of the poor devise creative ways to have their voices heard in small and irreverent acts or in bolder statements: they paint entryways, deal in illicit commerce, cut a hole in the fence, burn down a guardhouse, confront a sentry guard or an administrator, or engage in illegal activities nearby authority figures.

Some acts of resistance are purposely overlooked. On an afternoon walk with Lydia, Gándara's lively Resident Council president, I saw many residents sitting on their balconies conversing with others or playing dominoes on small tables they had carted to the dirt patches. She pointed out building entryways where residents had imposed a design of their own: a row of off-white ceramic tiles circling an entryway wall, a brighter color paint risking discovery in another. Residents were claiming their homes in the process. Lydia explained that managers punished some trespasses and accepted others. Lydia drew my attention to a small shack of painted wood with a zinc roof on a patch between two residential buildings. It was a *tiendita* (store), selling candy, cookies, snacks, and drinks. It was illicit, but the managers had ignored its presence. On this particular afternoon, it was not yet "open for business," but a few adults stood around because it was an impromptu meeting place. Although Gándara and Dr. Pila have prescribed community spaces

Figure 12. A decorated entrance and a garden in Gándara. Photo by author.

officially sanctioned for activities at designated times—a community center, a baseball field, a basketball and a volleyball court—natural places to hang around in do not exist, except for Gándara's illicit candy store. The firmly packed dirt and some folding chairs there were a clear sign that those who lived in Gándara had asserted a measure of autonomy and self-determination in their tightly planned and scheduled community.

But some acts of resistance challenge the system itself and are not accepted or tolerated. Early one morning when I arrived to interview the administrator of Dr. Pila, she was too busy and I learned she had to take care of a security breach. Someone had removed a set of bars from the fence. Two men were hovering nearby over a map, noticing openings to the south and west, where the fence had barred Dr. Pila residents from crossing to the elite neighborhood of Alhambra or to a direct, and shorter, route to a middle school, the city center, or the mall. I expressed a surprise I did not really feel. Residents had already told me of tearing down bars to create a space to squeeze through:

Zaire: Desde que pusieron el acceso controlado y la verja, ¿ha cambiado alguno de los lugares donde ustedes van o cómo llegan allá? (Have the places you visit or the routes you use to get there changed since the gates were set up?)

Lilah: Digo, si la gente por ahí no rompen las dos o tres varillas para salir al shopping se le hace difícil porque hay que dar toda la vuelta. Cierran y vuelven y la rompen. (Well, if people don't break two or three bars to get out to the shopping center, it is very hard because we would have to go around. They close the opening but people remove the poles again.)

Zaire: ¿Por dónde tú usualmente vas a los sitios? (What route do you usually take to get to places?)

Palma: Si no hay el portoncito hay que dar toda la vuelta. (If there isn't an opening, we have to go all the way around.)

Mia: Si no hacen el portoncito ahí ponen los tubos de nuevo y uno tiene que dar toda la vuelta entonces hay que buscar cómo volverlo a romper. Los mismos residentes tenemos que romper para poder pasar. (If they don't open a hole, they put the poles again and we have to go all the way around. So we have to find a way to break the poles again. We ourselves have to break them to be able to cross.)

Zenia: Uno rompe una varilla de esa porque no tiene donde meterse.

(We break one of those bars, because we don't have any place to get through.)

Lilah: La rompen y ya la están volviendo a poner a las malas. (We break the bars and they insist and replace them right away.)[24]

In other interviews, the necessity to create openings was revealed in residents' views:

Berta: Seguro por los boquetes que se hacen. Voy de shopping, me meto en un boquetito ahí atrás. (Now we go through fences that have been cut open. When I go shopping, I go through a hole back there.)

Zaire: ¿La mayoría de la gente usa eso? (Do most of you use the holes?)

Berta: ¡Todo el mundo! (Everyone!)

Eladia: Uno se mete en uno de esos rotos para poder caminar. Imagínate caminar tan lejos. (We go through the holes to be able to walk. Imagine walking so far.)

Berta: Con todo y cogiendo el boquete uno sale explotao. (Even if we go through the hole, it is exhausting to get around.)[25]

Removing bars are small everyday acts of resistance in order to walk shorter distances, to get to appointments on time, to accompany a child to school, to reach public transportation. The acts are subversive. In speaking of the breaks in the fence, residents spoke vaguely so that responsibility is displaced, the actors unnamed and invisible, the mechanics of opening a hole unmentioned, the tools used unknown. I got the sense that I shouldn't ask for more facts than were volunteered. Protection was a matter of tone and universality. One resident of Dr. Pila exclaimed, "*Si me dejan cojo un marrón y la rompo todas*" (If they let me, I would take a club and break them all).[26]

But some acts of resistance are loud and obvious, even if they go unmentioned. Residents themselves didn't reveal one of the most aggressive expressions of resistance: the burning down of a guardhouse. It was Lucy, a staff person from the management company, who told me about Dr. Pila residents setting the guardhouse on fire.[27] In her mind, she explained, the guardhouse was set on fire precisely because the residents were opposed to the gates. These acts are not unheard of in public housing communities, where residents are deemed occupants, not residents or owners of the government-owned

Figure 13. Patched-up holes in fencing at the Dr. Pila complex. Photo by author.

properties they inhabit. In 2005, a newspaper report discussed how the residents of a San Juan public housing unit painted a mural against repression in their communities for "*el largo y forma de su pelo o su color de piel*" (the length and style of their hair and their skin color). In response, Carlos Laboy, the director of Puerto Rico's AVP, reminded residents and the public that this housing did not belong to the residents but to the government: "La norma general es que no se pinte nada en las paredes de un residencial. 'Las paredes de los edificios no son tablones de expresión pública. Recuerda que estas son propiedades que se reglamentan por disposición federal'" (The general norm is that nothing gets painted on the walls of the public housing project. "The walls of the buildings are not posters for public expression. Remember that they are properties under federal law").[28]

In other mundane acts or expressions of resistance, some persons confront the sentry guards. One ridiculed a guard for hiding behind the guardhouse whenever something was "going down." Many spoke of the administrator as useless; one young man accused her (not to her face) of favoritism; others also critiqued the administrators with impunity, if only to each other. Some youth engaged in illicit activities near the guards—drug trade was obvious; the hidden guards did not intervene if, that is, they were aware of it. But even minor trespasses, complaints, as well as nonovert rebellion feed a perception of public housing as lawless, recycling the rationale for the gates. People in Extensión Alhambra who complain about Dr. Pila residents think it would be worse without fences, although they "rompen las rejas y se salen, pero como quiera hay un poco más de control" (break the gates and get out, even so there is a little more control).[29] The sense of urgency I saw on the morning when a broken gate had to be fixed made clear how important the manager thought it, because the gate was an essential instrument in social control.

Scholarly literature on offenses that require detention and on the timing of when, if ever, incarcerated individuals should be released from prison has studied the buffer factors that act to deter offenders from absconding and recidivating: community ties, monetary pressure (e.g., a court-set bond), gravity of offense, and the offender's "self-responsibility."[30] In public housing that confines persons distrusted by the outside community, relocking a broken fence symbolizes a punitive lack of trust or an assumption of irresponsibility of those who live behind it. It reflects a punitive, paternal relationship between the manager and managed. Is a resident, in fact, an inmate? To government and to outsourced managers, public housing is seen as a beneficial service for which the poor should be grateful enough to behave. Some see children this way, requiring rules until they are civilized enough to be on their own. But the poor are seen, primarily, as unable ever to be responsible for themselves. Nearby residents from Alhambra and Extensión Alhambra describe the residents of Dr. Pila as rowdy and untameable, unable to control themselves, damaging the means of access, of exit, essentially dysfunctional: "*Ellos mismos [en Dr. Pila] hace[n] del acceso controlado lo que ellos crean*" (Those [in Dr. Pila] make of the controlled access whatever they want)[31] Aggression is a contradictory trope to that which describes the poor's assumed inability to overcome their poverty. The contest between administrator and the residents exemplifies the paradox of the images of the poor as, on the one hand, lazy or incapable or, on the other hand, as impulsive and destructive.

A middle-aged empty-nester in Extensión Alhambra notes another form of devious logic of the poor, impulsive but purposive: "Ahí [en Gándara] no se van a robar nada. Si van a robar algo se las desquitan ellos. Ellos mismos se roban y se entregan las cosas. Si se van a robar algo ellos mismos allí no lo hacen porque saben que ellos allí tienen sus leyes" ([In Gándara public housing], nothing really gets stolen because if something is stolen, the victim takes revenge. They rob and give what they get to each other. If somebody wants to steal, he doesn't because they have their own laws there)[32] In Kingston, Jamaica, poor communities plagued by crime are considered to be "garrison communities" in that they self-administer laws dictating appropriate behavior.[33] The "culture of poverty" thesis, promulgated by Oscar Lewis, speaks of Puerto Ricans' adaptation to the urban environment as a self-sustaining subculture perpetuated by the structure of poverty, a culture of its own that is inconsistent with middle-class values and aspirations and that inhibits upward mobility.[34] Thus, illicit economies, an aversion to work, broken homes, out-of-wedlock birth, and criminal activity are all both causes and consequences in an unending cycle.[35] Most important, the culture of poverty is seen as an utter lack of self-control, disorganization, abandonment, and an inability to progress. Such sentiments were expressed by Francisco, a staff person of a management company:

> Hablo de una subcultura, hábitat del residencial público que hace a las personas dependientes . . . una residente, en particular, la cual estudió, se superó, pero sigue viviendo en Residencial Gándara. Y sus hijas salieron preñadas y siguen viviendo en Gándara. La vida la siguen viviendo ahí mismo . . . en ese hábitat.

> (I'm talking about a subculture, a habitat of public housing that creates dependency . . . for example there is one resident in particular that got an education, improved herself, but continues to live in Gándara. And her daughters got pregnant and continue to live in Gándara. They continue to live right there . . . in that habitat.)[36]

The gates of public housing affirm mainstream society's concept of a culture of poverty, of the poor as unable to rule themselves and, hence, in need of being ruled; and of rowdy beings capable of revolt, up to no good, on both grounds requiring restraint from those wiser and more effective than themselves. They elide what Gerald Suttles recognized as the internal order of poor neighborhoods, mandating "discipline and self-restraint in the same way as do the moral dictates of the wider community."[37]

Blame, Responsibility, and the Right to Speak

Conversations with the poor about the politics and policy of housing usually yielded neutral responses except when the question dealt directly with their own community. A few in Dr. Pila discouraged my asking questions about other communities: "No, eso los deciden ellos [en Extensión Alhambra] allá. . . . Nosotros hablamos por lo de nosotros. . . . Nosotros no sabemos la problemática y no sabemos lo que ellos necesitan" (No, they [who live in Extensión Alhambra] decide. . . . We talk about our own business. . . . We do not know their issues and don't know what they need).[38] But, even so, few if any believed their thoughts about their own concerns would be heard. Pierre Bourdieu has suggested that "the propensity to speak politically, even in the most rudimentary way . . . is strictly proportionate to the sense of having the right to speak."[39] The right to speak "is correlated with competence in the sense of a socially recognized capacity, ascribed by and ascribing status—the opposite of which is both impotence and objective and subjective exclusion ('That is none of my business'; 'That doesn't interest me')."[40] The "don't know's," "*yo no me meto*" (I don't meddle), of the poor reflect their sense of, and actual, status, a low sense of legitimacy, let alone of influence in political matters.

Conversely, among the privileged, conversations about policy were ample. The well-off felt free and competent to comment on any aspect of urban life and public policy. They assumed special expertise in discussing the poor and the communities of the poor. Even though few had actual contact with the poor (except in hierarchical service relations), they spoke as if they knew them well or, at least, knew how to fix their problems. In Alhambra and Extensión Alhambra, I got "ready talk," as in the comments of Gretchen from Extensión Alhambra:

> Le deberíamos dar más atención y más ayuda. Creo que hay mucha gente buena que no tiene cómo salir de ese entorno en que viven. A lo que se habitúan a ese tipo de vida y no ven más allá. No tienen aspiraciones a adquirir su posición. Se vuelven uno más de ese sistema. . . . Trataría . . . [que] hubiera más vida en comunidad y que ellos pudieran participar de esas actividades. Los muchachos llegaran a su casa y tuvieran que más hacer, no nada más ahí. . . . Los niños que cuando salgan de la escuela tengan otras cosas que hacer además de estudiar. Que pueden jugar volleyball . . . baile . . . , cosas que los niños puedan ir disfrutando.

(We should pay more attention, give them more help. I think there are a lot of good people who have no way to come out of the environment they live in. They get used to that type of life and can't see beyond that. They have no aspirations. They become part of the system. . . . I would try . . . to give them more of a community life and to get them to participate in activities, so the youth would have something to do at home, not just there. . . . When the children get out of school they could play volleyball . . . dance . . . , things children can enjoy.)[41]

One discussion among Alhambra residents about public housing, to my surprise, carried over, post-interview, to cheesecake and sangria on the back veranda. Gimena, the host, said, "Mira, es interesante, porque hablamos de mudar las barriadas pero no hablamos de mudar nuestra comunidad. O sea, trasplantar nuestras casas" (It is interesting that we talk about moving public housing but not our own community. In other words, transplant our own homes).[42] Discomfort was apparent among the others. The comment reflected a redirected gaze, a look back toward herself. Few others I talked with in Extensión Alhambra and Alhambra did the same.

The well-off discussed how to solve the problems of poverty: move public housing, gate public housing, control those who live there, teach them how to behave, offer them jobs, educate them, and so on. Most placed responsibility on the poor themselves or on those who managed them. Somebody other than the affluent was responsible; somebody else should change things. The gates afforded an island from which an expansive reach was possible, but it was one that displaced responsibility and blamed the victim.

Although I had to pull teeth to get public housing residents to discuss those in private enclaves, at the end many thanked me for the interviews, saying something like "take this to the government . . . so that they know what we think and feel."[43] For many, the interview seemed to be the first time he or she had a voice. The only other opportunity of having a voice in the polling booth seemed irrelevant.

Democracy is often measured through electoral politics, because voting is used to measure democratic participation.[44] But community participation, where "neighbors talk to each other about politics," beyond the "solitary act" of voting, is increasingly understood as a more telling measure of democracy and "real citizenship."[45] In Puerto Rico, participation in national elections is high and community participation low.[46] As neoliberal policies devolve power to municipalities and private institutions, it is at the community scale that

participation may be more vital. The residents of private and public housing
vote in political elections, often side by side. Doña Aurora, an elderly resident
of Gándara, came to our interview ready to converse in English and to boast
of raising her son to become a police officer. An election, she explained, presented one of the few times she encountered her "neighbors" from Alhambra
and Extensión Alhambra, at the community scale, the site of the everyday.

The range of influence, "efficacy," as political scientists would call it, of
the rich compared to the poor, is partly a matter of ownership, of capital—in
this case, houses.[47] Raquel, a resident of Alhambra, echoes a finding that is
prevalent among scholars that the lack of homeownership in public housing
is responsible for its ineffectiveness in creating "good citizens." Ownership is
equated with sacrifice and caring.

> No cuidan lo que no es de ellos. No tienen sentido de pertenencia.
> Nosotros como es difícil adquirir una casa y tienes que sacrificarte
> pues tú lo ves como tu residencia. Tú lo cuidas. Lo proteges. Ellos
> no tienen ese tipo de pertenencia y muchas veces no lo cuidan ni lo
> protegen.
>
> (They don't take care of what is not theirs. They don't have a sense
> of ownership. For us it is hard to acquire a house, we have to make
> sacrifices, and so we see it as our home. We take care of it. We protect
> it. They don't have that type of ownership and many times don't take
> care of it or protect it.)[48]

To own has been seen as an important factor in community viability, ris-
ing property values, and a sense of community. The logic is that nonowners
(renters) care less about the property and hence decrease its value and also
that renters are transitory and thus do little to sustain a sense of community.[49] The discussion is even more aggressive when it comes to public housing. Much of the scholarly debate, especially in the United States, has focused
on public housing's failure as a direct result of a welfare program that gave
tenants cheap housing with little responsibility for its care.[50] Programs proposed to induce a sense of "home" or "community" have been seen as critical
in twentieth-century planning. A sense of "ownership, " either financial or
psychological, in the four communities of Ponce I studied—two for the poor,
two for the rich—is mediated by the presence of gates.

In Extensión Alhambra, a neighborhood association represents an audible majority. Its gates and its management have made the community a governing entity—self-ruling in many ways. The residents are private owners of previously public streets, and they dictate codes of behavior and comportment, not only for physical grounds but also for social mores and values. They have created their own utopia, if sterile and confined, behind their walls. Their class and status, complemented by the gate, have provided an illusory sense of an expansive reach of democracy. It is perhaps no coincidence that a resident of Extensión Alhambra became the mayor of Ponce.

In Alhambra residents disallowed a gated street, the democratic reach is established by class status and gated homes; each is independent of the other and buffers the assumed chaos and anarchy of the street with their *jefes de casa* (home chiefs). Alhambra residents access a more expansive democracy behind their private walls via their class and social positions, expecting public influence in wider spheres of sports and with gates and as guards at their own city, in social clubs, and in social networks of public influence.

Gándara's public housing status, despite the lack of a community gate, affords selective freedoms with some violations tolerated but with lives conditioned by government and its private management agents. Residents of the immense gated Dr. Pila had little choice except to complain in private or to sneak through rapidly patched-up openings they made in the fences. They had little or nothing to say about policies of the city or the island. It is as if the peripheral fences turned their gaze inside, upon themselves.

Chapter 5

The Secret Gardens

I've stolen a garden. . . . It isn't mine. It isn't anybody's.

—Frances Hodgson Burnett, *The Secret Garden*

Rexford Tugwell, the last American governor appointed for the island of Puerto Rico, a fervent New Dealer, wrote of the upscale area of Condado in the city of San Juan and its private gardens: "I thought it might be hard to leave so beautiful a neighborhood. . . . This, I could see, was the right side of the railroad tracks; . . . semi-palaces buried in the most resplendent foliage: palms, bitter almonds, flamboyanes, casuarinas, for trees; hibiscus, oleander, crotons, gardenias for shrubs; and trinitaria (or bougainvillea), allamonda (or canario), coralita (or bellisima) for vines; all furnishing year-round color, pinks, purples, reds and yellows, to shine upon and through the basic liquid greens."[1] The Condado semipalaces buried in gardens that Tugwell described are similar to those in Alhambra, Extensión Alhambra, and many upscale gated communities in Ponce and Puerto Rico. Locked inside cement and iron fortresses, private cloistered gardens provide glimpses to outsiders, daring, almost demanding, to be seen. These gardens, on "the right side of the railroad tracks," reclaim and privatize nature for the exclusive enjoyment of the rich.

Gradual Greening

The landscape writer J. B. Jackson noted that "garden comes from an Indo European word, *gher*, which appears . . . for apparently such disparate things as farmyard, pasture, sown field, hedge, house, fence, enclosure, stable, girder, fortified place—and garden. All these words clearly imply enclosure or an enclosed place."[2] Gardens, in Ponce, are enclosed places, so that the lifestyles of the privileged are contained and realized behind walls and fences. These Edens threatened by urban complexity, proximity to public housing, and fear of crime are recovered and protected behind gated walls. Although residents raved about their gardens in Ponce's upper-middle-class community of Extensión Alhambra, residents of upscale Alhambra, unable to close off their street, complained that public housing intruders snatch fruit from their trees and go off with plants and orchids. Casandra, of Alhambra, saw her own and her neighbors' gardens, properties, and families as under siege: "todo el tiempo como que atacados por estas personas que pasan sin ningún respeto hacia las propiedades de uno" (constantly under assault by persons who come through without respecting our properties).[3] Affluent inhabitants of Alhambra magnified this concern:

> *Resident 1*: Yo te diría que aquí el caso de los robos pequeños y
> me refiero a robos *pequeños*. Yo vine de Navidad y me había
> ido para la playa y resulta que . . . en el frente mío, queda
> como medio escondidito, y ahí yo tengo unas orquídeas y se
> las llevaron. Eso fue el recibimiento de Reyes. Y después me
> enteré con [Josefina], que es otra que vive en mi misma calle, le
> habían hecho lo mismo. Y si tú dejas la manguera se la llevan.
> Las bombillas de Navidad, si las pones pegadas a la verja, se las
> llevan. Después si tienes un perrito de raza y es pequeñito, si lo
> dejas afuera también se lo llevan. O sea que es una majadería
> continua. (I would tell you that, here, the robberies involve
> small things. I mean small thefts. After being away at the beach,
> I came after Christmas, and . . . in front, it's a bit hidden, I had
> some orchids and they took them. That was my welcome for
> Three Kings Day/Epiphany. I found out from [Josefina], who
> lives on my street, that the same thing was done to her. If you
> leave the hose, they'll take it. The Christmas lights, if you place
> them by the fence, they'll take them. And if you have a purebred
> dog and it's small, if it's outside, they'll take it. So it's a constant
> nuisance.)
> *Resident 2*: Se meten a tu patio a llevarse los limones, mangós,
> aguacates. Y tienen esa libertad de entrar al patio. (They go in

your backyard to steal the lemons, mangos, avocados. And they feel such liberty to go into your backyard.)

Resident 1: Entonces con una tranquilidad porque tu vienes y les gritas y te dice 'Es mi hija. Ay Señora usted la deja que coja un mangoíto?' Y luego te dice que la señora del lado le dio permiso. (And with such tranquility. You yell at them and they tell you, "It's my daughter. Oh madam, can you let her take a mango?" They say that the neighbor gave them permission.)[4]

Orchids have a special place:

Resident 1: Déjame decirte que no nos debemos quejar porque, ¿qué es lo que se roban? Una manguera, un zafacón, un sillón que yo tenia ahí. (We shouldn't complain because what is it they steal? A hose, a garbage can, a chair.)

Resident 2: No, a mí me robaron mucho. A mí se me metieron. (They stole a lot from me. They got inside.)

Resident 3: A mí al mes de mudarme me robaron las orquídeas. (One month after I moved here they stole my orchids.)

Zaire: Las orquídeas son populares. (Orchids seem to be popular.)

Resident 4: Y los zafacones. Un día los saqué por la mañana y a las cinco de la tarde ya no los vi. ¡Estando yo allí! (And the garbage cans. One day I took them out in the morning and by five I didn't see them anymore. And I was home!)

Resident 5: El zafacón yo lo tengo en el balcón. (I keep the garbage can on the porch.)

Resident 4: Yo compraba uno todos los meses, porque me tenían loca. (I had to buy a can every month. They were driving me crazy.)[5]

Residents' minifortresses, with security mechanisms, protect their land-scaped gardens and garden lifestyles. They and their gardens became retreats behind fences, into homes, away from the streets. Alhambra residents envied the liberated gardens of gated communities like Extensión Alhambra, whose children could play and socialize on their streets. One Alhambra resident re-sented the ten-foot fence around her house that hid her gardens:

No es atractivo tú tener que poner una verja altísima y vivir como en una prisión. . . . Esto era un área bien bonita y todos tenían jardines preciosos. Pero éramos el playground de los muchachos que tenían caballos de Gándara. Los caballos amanecían en las gramas de aquí haciendo número uno y número dos por ahí. Tú no le podías decir nada. Pues tuvimos que cerrar. Por eso y por los robos, las mangueras, patinetas. A la vecina le robaron dos tiestos de al frente con la matita. Eso no hace el lugar atractivo.

(It is not good to have to put up a real high fence and live like in a prison. . . . This was a lovely area with a lot of beautiful gardens. But we became a playground for the Gándara youth and their horses. At dawn, the horses would be in our lawns doing number one and number two, and we couldn't say anything. So we had to close. The hoses, skateboards, the neighbor's pots were stolen. That doesn't make a place appealing.)[6]

In their private gardens, the rich block the other side of the tracks and avoid the poor who were forced on them as neighbors in the New Deal's plan of social integration of neighborhoods. The rich have replicated the gardens, expanding them from gated home to gated street, to gated clubs, to gated island, gradually greening the city to form a protected network of sequestered private gardens that segregate them as well. Fenced homes, streets, and social and recreation clubs protect the garden lifestyles and provide spaces to build a community for the rich, effectively escaping the New Deal vision and outwitting its ideal of integration.

In contrast, public housing communities are denied secluded areas or virtually any gardens of their own. In an exchange between Gándara residents, they lamented the many constraints to having gardens of their own:

Xenia: Yo quisiera poner una palma ó un arbolito pero sé que me
lo van a destruir, que no lo van a respetar. Una cerca son 20
pesos más. La esquina está llena de muchachos y juegan ahí y
hay que llamarles la atención. (I would like to plant a palm tree
or another type of tree, but I know that it would be destroyed.
It wouldn't be respected. A fence is twenty dollars. There are
children playing there who have to be disciplined.)
Abdul: Tenía tres framboyanes que los sembré juntos: amarillo, azul,
y "orange." Y se los llevaron. Voy a sembrar un cactus. (I had
three breadfruit trees that I planted together: yellow, blue, and
"orange." And they took them. I'm going to plant a cactus.)

Evi: Aquí no quieren nada que tenga espinas. (Here they don't want
    anything with thorns.)[7]

In place of beauty and retreat, the poor have symbols of control by others of
themselves. Originally there had been gardens in front of the Dr. Pila apartments but, when Mano Dura's gating scheme took hold, the gardens were
paved over. Residents had hoped for private patios so they could grow flowers, fruits, and vegetables of their own. But a community center designated
by managers became their only "secret garden." In that hall, kept locked when
not in use, social workers and administrators, outsourced from a private firm
hired by the city, sponsor planned activities. The key to the hall, that symbolic garden, is held and wielded by the elected head of the Resident Council.
This key provides symbolic power to a tenant but no real authority. Public
housing communities have no private gardens; residents cannot cultivate
their own style of home and family life. As private gardens are eliminated,
urban renewal projects assign public city spaces for recreational use by the
poor. Home gardens have been usurped with community spaces in an urban
complex. One Dr. Pila resident joked, but with an edge of bitterness, that she
called her neighborhood "Dr. Pila Gardens."[8] Public housing residents are
aligned between government-controlled neighborhood facilities and renovated public spaces. They have no genuinely private outdoor spaces. Public
zones provide generic gardens—government-controlled spaces with regulations of comportment—so, for example, when the municipal band plays
in the central plaza, children at play are stared down and shushed, and La
Guancha boardwalk visitors are warned not to throw food to the water below.

Home Edens and Cement Gardens

I first became aware of the gardens protected by the gates in an interview with
Rebecca, a community leader and member of Extensión Alhambra's neighborhood association. Rebecca loved gardens. Her ceramic-tiled front terrace
was surrounded by every palette color for green foliage and vivid flowers.
Before the interview began, she proudly displayed photos of her plants and
flowers to two admiring neighbors and to me. The flowers and plants—
distributed throughout her home and backyard—were one of the most precious jewels protected by Extensión Alhambra's beeper-powered gate. In this
and other interviews, surrounded by gardens in beautiful porches and patios,

I came to understand that botanical Edens and elite lifestyles were interdependent and that both depended on the fences and the walls. The gardens are literal, but, more than that, their flowers and fruits are symbolic of a lifestyle of privilege painstakingly cultivated and defended behind gates. The protected lifestyle—tranquil, aesthetically pleasing, leisurely—is the setting for private social occasions and sanctioned community events that complement family and home.

That Alhambra residents would protect their gardens is not surprising; gardens have always been a marker of prestige, and gardens are at the heart of the concept of the privacy of home and family. Ponce residents, both in public and private housing, echo the association between garden and privacy. Public housing residents also dream of living in houses with yards: "*la casa de uno que uno siembra y hace de todo*" (my own home where I can plant and do anything); "*una casa propia de uno . . . [donde] tú tienes tu patio*" (my own home . . . [where] you have a yard) for children to play in.

J. B. Jackson has noted that "the concept of garden was, in early days, closely involved with the concepts of family or household, of property, of defense, and even of community layout."[9] Fences and hedges provided "an effective barrier . . . discouraging any trespassing or theft . . . there could be no garden, legally speaking, without a hedge or wall or fence; there could be no legal protection for the life and property of the family unless it built such a hedge or fence or wall; there could be no guarantee of privacy, no self-rule by the family unless that boundary was established, made visible, and carefully maintained."[10] Gardens have been inseparable from the concept of defense and protection of the home, and of an increasingly insular and exclusionary private family life and community life.[11] Gardens around, and within, suburban homes, in particular, are meant to cultivate the family unit.[12] For an Extensión Alhambra resident, the garden duplicated the suburb: "*Esto es como un suburbio pero dentro del pueblo*" (This is like a suburb but inside the city).[13] With vegetable plants and flowers, common indoor and outdoor spaces contained intimacy and, in the words of Lewis Mumford, "creat[e] an urban environment favorable to the health and nurture of children . . . a parklike setting for the family dwelling house; and for all the domestic activities associated with it. . . . In the kitchen, the garden, the workshop, activities that had once been necessities of country life could now be carried on as a relief from the grim, monotonous, imprisoned collective routine of the city." In the suburb, the family was at the center of the convergence of house and nature, and, as Mumford declares, "achieved a new form, more congenial to family life in all its stages of development."[14]

Andrew Jackson Downing wrote that "when smiling lawns and tasteful cottages begin to embellish a country, we know that order and culture are established."[15] "Pleasure gardens," for example, emerging in baroque palaces throughout Europe in the seventeenth to early nineteenth centuries, "kept in constant view the aristocratic concept of space and verdure, as an essential part of urban life."[16] To have a garden was essential to aristocratic life as a symbol of status and access and civility. But, in Ponce, the people and animals of the nearby public housing threaten the access to beauty and civility that the private gardens of Alhambra promise. "Yo tuve una fiesta en mi casa y me entraron a pedradas de la barriada. Estaba la gente de la Alianza Francesa reunida y había una ponchera de copas en una mesa y ahí mismo cayó una piedra que salpicó. Y ahí mismo se acabó la fiesta" (I had a party in my house and the barriada started throwing rocks at us. The French Alliance people were there and there was a punch bowl with glasses in a table and a rock splashed in the bowl. The party ended right there and then).[17]

The advent of the fenced backyard in the United States, according to the landscape architect Christopher Grampp, came as the home expanded to include an inhabitable outdoor living room, only achievable if it was private; "privacy meant fences."[18] Alhambra and Extensión Alhambra residents have made sure that their outdoor living rooms are somewhat habitable by locking them behind home fences. The poor can glimpse the garden blooms behind the gate of Extensión Alhambra: what they imagine is apparent in an exchange with Gándara residents:

> *Zaire*: Y Extensión La Alhambra piensan que es bonito? [And Extensión Alhambra, do you think it is beautiful?]
>
> *Woman 1*: Es bonito, de mi casa se ve. Es bonito pero es bien aburrido. (It is beautiful. You can see it from my house. It is beautiful but very boring.)
>
> *Zaire*: ¿Por qué piensan que es bonito? (Why do you think it is beautiful?)
>
> *Woman 1*: Está en un sitio bien tranquilo. (It is in a very tranquil place.)
>
> *Woman 2*: Las casas son bien bonitas ahí. (The houses are very beautiful.)
>
> *Woman 3*: Esa son gente que tienen dinero y se pasan trancao ahí. De la calle para su casa. (Those people have money and keep themselves locked in. From the street to their house.)

Woman 3: Vi los otros días un señor en unos pantalones con unas
   gafas cogiendo sol. Se creerá que está en el Holiday Inn. El
   señor con unas gafas, y unas de esto de playa allí al frente de la
   casa. Es bien chévere. Nadie lo molesta, y él ahí. (The other day
   I saw a man with shorts and sunglasses sunning. He must have
   thought he was at the Holiday Inn, the man with his sunglasses
   and beach chair in front of his house. It was very "cool." He sat
   there, and nobody bothered him.)[19]

In Dr. Pila, a locked community center—a large room with chairs and
tables that can be randomly arranged, not a garden—is the axis of a regulated
community. It is meant to serve as the center of community life: "el escenario
para la realización de actividades deportivas, culturales y sociales . . . para
celebrar toda aquella actividad que complemente la formación integral de
nuestra juventud y que sirva de vínculo entre escuela y comunidad" (the stage
for all sporting, cultural, and social activities . . . to celebrate all activities that

Figure 14. Trees and a cement wall hide this Alhambra home. Photo by
author.

aid the development of our youth and that serve as a tie between school and community).[20] But, in reality, the refurbished locked room offers only symbolic power to the residents through a key held, and wielded, by the elected head of the Resident Council. When I visited, Roxana, a vocal and feisty resident, held the key in Dr. Pila, yet she did not "possess" it or hold it with authority. She seemed aware of the limited control it represented. It was in this space only that I was permitted to conduct interviews, not in private apartments. Once, finding the door locked, I went to the administrator's office next door, and she waved me off; residents must open the door, she said, and grant me admission to the hall. I went out to find Roxana. She scoffed at the administrator's refusal to open the door for me, and she came with the key to let me in. Key or not, Roxana did not have full authority to schedule meetings and programs held in that room. Only the managerial staff, whom residents did not employ, had the authority to do that. Social workers, outsourced from the private management firm, sponsored planned activities, such as job fairs, resident council-manager meetings, and other community events.

The community center was one of a number of facilities at Dr. Pila that had been renovated after the Mano Dura raid and the gating. Actually the renovations had begun a few years before Mano Dura. In 1991, the baseball park in Dr. Pila was restored and inaugurated by the municipal government: "Se techaron las gradas, se construyeron dos baños y dos kioskos y se reparó totalmente la verja" (We put a canopy over the bleachers, built two bathrooms and two kiosks, and repaired the fence).[21] Other improvements had been undertaken—new kitchen tiles were installed, ceilings were sealed, buildings were painted. In Gándara, the office of the Resident Council, whose key is held by the president of the Council, was freshly painted. In its "Restore" phase, Mano Dura had promised several renovated community spaces. Managers, and some residents, boasted of the new midnight basketball games, the new zinc ceiling over the outdoor basketball court, the baseball leagues, all large group activities. But the garden lots that once existed in public housing were eliminated. In Dr. Pila, when Mano Dura erected fences, green spaces were dug up and small plots of land that residents had planted in front of first-floor balconies were paved over. With the gardens went the residents' already limited private space and their sense of order and beauty: "Había patio antes. . . . Había gente que tenía un jardín, tenía su privacidad" (There was a yard before. . . . There were people who had a garden, had their privacy).[22]

Opportunities to reflect residents' aesthetic tastes and to claim their home through plants and flowers have been increasingly curtailed by the managers' gates. Even a sense of security has been threatened, because paved-over gardens give priority to vehicular traffic rather than children's play. A Dr. Pila neighbor reported, in direct contradistinction of what private communities themselves have been able to achieve through their fences, "No hay seguridad para los residentes ni para los niños porque no hay áreas verdes para los niños" (There is no security for the residents nor for the children because there are no green spaces for the children). Residents complained about lack of improvements and elimination of safe community spaces. Community activities have become increasingly choreographed and spaces have become contested zones. Through urban improvement projects and calculated openings in access (e.g., the key), the facilities and amenities, like the community itself, have been appropriated and, increasingly managed by others. The surveilled community inhibits community contact inside the gates, as residents' access to nearby neighbors is inhibited by interior gates, the gates around their buildings funnel them to the community center, which provides not a green retreat but a regulated cement floor inside four walls, over which they have limited control.

Elite Botanical Clubs

For the rich, garden lifestyles are sought, protected, and realized not only in private homes but also in member-only social clubs. Carolyn Merchant, an environmental historian and scholar of "radical ecology," writes that Western culture has "tried to reclaim the lost Eden by reinventing the entire earth as a garden" and that "this story has propelled countless efforts by humans to recover Eden."[23] One such effort has been the upwardly mobiles' escape throughout the world from the increasingly complex, hard-to-manage, threatening city.[24] Elite residents of Ponce who have stayed in the city have taken refuge not only in gated family-home gardens but also in community gardens of gated streets and social clubs in the wider city.

Creating protected garden homes requires spaces for social exchange that transcend and expand family networks and social prestige. Residents within the elite communities of Ponce, as of many others in Puerto Rico and elsewhere, defend their status and position and expand their rights by forming and maintaining exclusive gated social spaces outside their own homes.[25] As Lewis Mumford noted in *The City in History*, "Pure air and weather, freedom from raucous human noises, open fields for riding, hunting, archery, rural strolling—these are qualities that the aristocracy everywhere has always valued; and they are responsible perhaps for their bodily fitness and self-confidence, which contrasts with the occupational disabilities and deformations of the specialized urban drudge, too long confined to the workshop, the counting house, the library."[26] For Extensión Alhambra, community gardens were granted and expanded by the 1987 Closing Law, but for Alhambra, whose bid for a community gate has been unsuccessful, elite botanical clubs in the larger city have become essential for the preservation of their lifestyles as places to mingle with people like themselves out of the reach of others.

Botanical clubs are social clubs that, like resorts, with increasing privatizing of resources once considered natural resources, provide a network of protected social spaces of what Merchant calls a "green veneer" for the elite. In what Mumford would label "playful emptiness and civic irresponsibility," Alhambra and Extensión Alhambra residents, like those of other communities of the rich in Ponce and elsewhere in Puerto Rico, but also throughout the world, get to "build a house in, join the Country Club, and make life center about your club, your home, and your children."[27] Ponce's premier yacht club, Club Náutico, one of a about a dozen on the island, and Club Deportivo de Ponce (the Sports Club of Ponce) provide garden lifestyles with access to nature (a beach, pool, garden), sport, and exercise. Both were built to be outside the city: one, in 1915, located across a river from the city center; the other, in 1938, was put on a separate island eventually bridged over by the club. Both clubs help the elite to segregate themselves, to enforce the boundaries between them and others, and to keep their gardens and lifestyles self-contained.

Club Deportivo, today adjacent to and west of both Dr. Pila and Alhambra, is a members-only "country club." [28] The city's first, it was built in "17 cuerdas de terreno aproximadamente cerrada por bosques de higueros y tamarindos sin puente de entrada sobre el Río Portugués" (17 hectares of land almost completely closed by forests of fig trees and tamarinds, without a bridge to enter over the Portugués River).[29] From the club began the northward middle- and upper-class suburban expansion of the city.[30] One of the founders, and the first president of the club (through 1932), was Dr. Manuel de la Pila Iglesias himself, the very person, ironically, for whom the Dr. Pila public housing project was later named.[31] In the first edition of the club's annual publication, Dr. de la Pila Iglesias explained that the club sought to revive sports in Ponce:

Conocido es el ambiente deportivo de nuestro querido Ponce.... Ese ambiente deportivo es el terreno fértil donde cualquier semilla fructifica fácilmente y ese grupo de deportistas es el árbol secular en él plantado semejante a esos almendros de las huertas levantinas que secos, al parecer muertos, bajo la nieve y escarcha del crudo invierno, se remozan y cubren de flores a las primeras bonanzas del tiempo.... La vida deportiva ponceña languidecía: El almendro bajo el hielo de la indiferencia; sin hojas y sin flores, parecía seco. Por eso unos aficionados del deporte futbolista constituyeron una asociación informal... y se instituyó la Asociación Deportiva de Ponce, organismo precursor de nuestro Club.

(Well known is the sportiness of our dear Ponce.... The sporting environment is fertile ground for planting and a group of sportsmen is the flowering tree which, like dried-up almond trees that look as though they are dead under the snow of a crude winter, flower again in the Spring.... Sports life in Ponce was dormant: The almond tree under the ice of indifference, without leaves and without flowers, appeared to be dead. Because of that, some soccer enthusiasts began an informal association ... and the Ponce Sporting Association was instituted, the precursor to our club.)[32]

And, indeed, Club Deportivo was a carefully cultivated garden. Between 1914 (when initial plans were drawn) and 1932, members lent their time and money and worked arduously to build the club; a member who held a position in government successfully advocated for the location and construction of the Guadalupe bridge near the club's entrance.[33] An attorney (José Angel Poventud) and an engineer (Alfredo Viechers) helped work through all the legal aspects of the club's incorporation as well as the construction of its facilities (both infrastructure and recreational), its soccer and baseball fields, tennis and cricket courts, and clubhouse and pergola. To complete the garden effect, "la siembra de flores, árboles ornamentales fue obra de un grupo de damas" (the planting of flowers and ornamental trees was done by a group of ladies).[34]

In the club's second publication, Dr. Manuel de la Pila Iglesias concluded his report by reminding the board of "el gran bien que a la humanidad estáis prestando al fomentar estas clases de asociaciones porque trabajáis, sin daros cuenta quizás, por la salud de nuestro pueblo" (the immense contribution you are making to humanity, by fomenting these types of associations, because you work, perhaps without knowing, for our people's health). But humanity is hardly a sufficient criterion for this secret garden. The club's gardens, and the social benefits they bring, are strictly for members. Member families participate in volleyball leagues, attend cotillion balls, host private carnivals, and throw wedding receptions; they compete in "Thanksgiving Bowl" tennis tournaments and celebrate a "*Navidad Ponceña*" (Ponce Christmas) with a private *bomba y plena* concert.[35] Club Deportivo's masonry fence recalls its early twentieth-century beginnings. Amid palm trees and flowering bushes, a simple guardhouse divides vehicular entry and exit, plastered with signs reminding members to show their membership identification, warning that cars are subject to security checks and that security cameras are stationed throughout the property.

Ponce's Club Náutico, founded in 1938, expands the private gardens of the elite to the sea; its mission is "el desarrollo y fomento entre sus asociados de la afición y desenvolvimiento de los deportes náuticos en general, así también como el deporte de pesca" (to develop and promote among its associates a liking for and involvement in nautical sports in general, as well as the sport of fishing).[36] The program was to organize regattas, sport competitions, recreational excursions, and the "celebración de fiestas sociales, reuniones de sus asociados y familiares; celebración de actos culturales en forma de conferencias y torneos; establecimiento de una biblioteca; organización de juegos lícitos y de mero pasatiempo y práctica de toda clase de deportes" (celebration of social parties, meetings of its members and families; celebration of cultural acts in the form of conferences and tournaments; a library; organizing lawful games for entertainment, and all types of sports).[37] It was built on Isla de Gata (Cat Island), off the coast of Ponce.[38] Members had to arrive by boat, but, today, the commodore boasts, the club has a "secure gated road access" via a bridge with a manned guard at the entrance.[39] The club's recreational activities were reduced during World War II; postwar "recreational boating activities moved to the fore and membership grew from 100 individuals in 1946 to 900 families in 2006."[40] Today, the club boasts a "gymnasium, two swimming pools, tennis courts, basketball court, small golf course, running track, children's playground and activity area, small beach, the Marlin Room activity area with cocktail lounge and food services, fully equipped fuel dock, a boat hauling yard, dry dock, and 168 ships [in a] marina across seven piers," and it hosts yearly "White Christmas" parties.[41]

Club Náutico's entrance is secluded, off the main road from La Guancha, hidden behind palm trees; it is close to an artificial rocky coast made of cement planks, with a sculpture of two crossed marlins facing the sea. At the entrance is a cement guardhouse, designed like a boat, and painted in bright colors; it stands at the middle of the road that opens to the bridged road to the island. A nautical sign of a boat's steering wheel with a flag, the club's logo, is affixed to the guardhouse. Iron gates and a mechanical arm on one side block access and sort vehicles coming in and out. Club Náutico's "barrera tipo cruce de tren . . . se mant[iene] bajada hasta que el guardia de turno haya inspeccionado las tarjetas de socios . . . y los invitados (si alguno) hayan firmado el Registro de Invitados" (a barrier like that at a train's crossing . . . remains down until the stationed guard has inspected all member identifications . . . and the guests have signed the Guest Registry).[42] Members must show credentials; a guest must be accompanied by a member or have written authorization.[43]

Both Club Deportivo and Club Náutico have a long tradition of exclusion. With slight variations based on rank and type of membership, to become a *socio*, or member of such a club, a person, or, more typically, a family, fills out an application and is reviewed for admission.[44] In Club Náutico, for example, to apply as a regular member, a person needs the endorsement of two current members.[45] Once the application is filed, it is displayed for ten days in a public area so all members can review it and any member can register an opinion whether the applicant should be admitted.[46] The club's board of directors then takes a secret vote; two negative votes, or three abstentions, deny admission. A new member pays an initial fee and monthly dues. If denied by negative votes, an applicant must wait a year to reapply; if denied by abstention, an applicant can reapply after thirty days. For some time, member friends joked about which picture should accompany my own family's application to Club Náutico. Prompted by Dominican families who had become our extended family in Puerto Rico and who successfully applied for membership, my parents submitted an application. Their friends recommended that, because of ethnic stereotypes—even though clubs like these saw themselves as part of a global elite, and so held exchanges with the elite in Dominican Republic—a Puerto Rican family should endorse and submit our application. We must have been rejected, because we never heard back.

Rejection created increasingly difficult situations for my siblings and for me; many of the parties, get-togethers, and other events of the recreational and social life of our private-school classmates were held behind the gates of these clubs. In years to come, I came to dread facing the gates of both

Club Náutico and Club Deportivo, as we considered attending summer camps, sports tournaments, or parties of our privileged classmates. The gated entrance—a private guarded road in Club Náutico and a gated sentry in Club Deportivo—sorted members and their guests from strangers and undesirables. Sometimes, even in the company of members, my siblings and I were denied admission. When I was about eleven and my sister and I went to a party at Club Deportivo with member and nonmember friends, the two of us were denied admission by the guard, even after the plea of the parent, a member, who had driven us, with our friends, to the event. The only difference between my sister and me and the others was that we were black. The parent drove us home. A complaint by the father of one of our friends, also a member, elicited a letter of apology from the club's president (addressed to us or to the member, I can't remember), offering us admission to the next party. On occasion, with an arsenal of verifiable evidence—printed invitations, and the like—we were admitted.

Just behind the Náutico guardhouse, a large sign announces the day's activities: *programa de tennis comienza* (tennis program begins), *torneo de pesca* (fishing tournament), *verbena* (fair), *asamblea de propietarios* (owner's meeting). As you enter the road to this exclusionary garden, framed by large pines, and cross to the island, you see small yachts and sailboats in the harbor. At the end of the road, the island opens up to a new world of tennis courts, a pool, a large clubhouse with pergola, and a car drop-off atrium. Here, residents of Alhambra and Extensión Alhambra, and other elite communities, can escape the noise and clatter of the city; families can swim, exercise, run, and enjoy safe play spaces for their children. Club Náutico advertises "plenty of activities ranging from dances, carnivals, and 'socials' for our club members as well as international fishing and sailing events."[47] Monthly calendars schedule parties, swimming lessons, aqua-aerobics, summer camps for children, golf classes for diverse age groups, and cocktail hours for adults.

The private clubs supplement or provide substitutes for the home neighborhoods of the elite. Earlier, a resident of Alhambra recalled:

> Aquí hubo una época que nosotras . . . corríamos bicicletas, nos sentábamos en la acera y conversábamos y hasta podíamos dejar las bicicletas un segundo. . . . Podíamos cruzar la calle con confianza . . . y había mucha tranquilidad. Pero ahora no estoy tranquila en ningún momento, porque pasan tecatos y drogadictos por ahí todo el tiempo.

(There was an era here that we . . . rode bikes, would sit on the sidewalk and talk, and we could even leave our bikes unattended for a second. . . . We could cross the street without much care . . . and it was very tranquil. But now, I am not at peace at any time, because drug addicts pass all the time.)[48]

In Alhambra, streets became prohibited for children's play. Rocío, a resident of Alhambra, told me that "los hijos míos nacieron en esta casa, se criaron ahí detrás [en El Deportivo], donde habían muchas actividades, desde campamentos, habían equipos de baloncesto, natación" (My children were born in this house, but they grew up back there [in El Deportivo], where they had many activities, from camps to basketball teams, to swimming).[49] Renata, of Alhambra, said, "Aquí . . . cada cual vive dentro de su casa y socializa en El Club Deportivo o en El Náutico. Tú no ves niños corriendo en las calles" (Here . . . everyone lives inside their homes and socializes in Club Deportivo or Náutico).[50] The club complements the home and provides a network of the elite of the city. To be "in" is to have access, to share a common exclusive lifestyle.

In my interview with Ramiro in Extensión Alhambra, he explained to me the centrality of the clubs in a position of privilege, what Pierre Bourdieu refers to as the "aesthetic disposition"[51] and the lack of necessity among the bourgeois, signaled by the focus on art and leisure, on "exercise for exercise's sake . . . walking and tourism, . . . movements without any other aim than physical exercise and the symbolic appropriation of a world reduced to the status of a landscape."[52] Ramiro described the parallel social lives of the home and club:

Soy muy diestro con las manos. . . . Tengo una buena colección de orquídeas que atiendo. Trabajo un poco en mi patio. Me gustan los deportes. Practico mucho deporte. Soy socio de varios clubes. . . . Me encantan las cosas del mar, la pesca, la pesca submarina, navegar como hasta las Islas Vírgenes Americanas y las Británicas. Nos quedábamos en hoteles y navegábamos y conocíamos las playas y hacíamos pesca, nadábamos. He practicado mucho deporte toda mi vida. . . . Soy socio del Club Náutico. Ahí se practican los deportes acuáticos, más todas las mañanas hago ejercicio de caminar en la pista que tienen. Me meto al gimnasio y practico pesas para mantener tonicidad muscular. Cuando el agua está templada suelo nadar una media milla todos los días. En el Club Deportivo de Ponce, otra institución privada, ahí es que practico el deporte de softball. . . . ¿Ya ves qué muchos trofeos me he ganado? . . . Bajo con frecuencia al teatro, al cine, salimos a cenar fuera con frecuencia. Me encanta viajar y viajamos mucho. En la semana visitamos nuestros hijos en sus casas. Nos reunimos en familia o nos visitan ellos. . . . hacemos una vida familiar.

(I am very good with my hands. . . . I have a nice collection of orchids that I take care of. I work a bit in my backyard. I like sports. I practice a lot of sports. I am a member of various clubs. . . . I love the things of the sea: fishing, submarine fishing, sailing to the U.S. and British Virgin Islands. We stay in hotels, sailing, visiting beaches, fishing, and swimming. I've practiced a lot of sports in my life. . . . I'm a member of the Yacht Club. There I practice aquatic sports. Every morning I walk their track. In the gym I lift weights to keep my muscular tone. When the water is warm, I swim about a half a mile every day. In the Club Deportivo de Ponce, another private institution, I practice softball. . . . You see how many trophies I've won? . . . We go on our boat with our children, wives, and grandkids. I go to the theater frequently, to the movies, and out to eat frequently. I love to travel and we travel a lot. During the week we visit our children's homes. We get together as a family or they visit us. . . . We build a family life.)[53]

These secret gardens in the neighborhood and the city, in the words of Pierre Bourdieu, reaffirm the "suspension and removal of economic necessity" and enforce "distance from practical urgencies, which is the basis of objective and subjective distance from groups subjected to those determinisms."[54] Inside the private lives of these clubs, "those determinisms," the race and class exclusionary character of the clubs, and the many ways in which they grant power and control to the elite, are more apparent. In these secret gardens, the mostly white elite retire from the city proper and escape from the dark poor. Said Lewis Mumford, "If one did not quit the city for good on one's own initiative, the doctor's orders would prompt one to take temporary quarters in a health resort, a bath or a spa or a seaside retreat."[55] Equating a neighbor with a friend had to be reclaimed through clubs outside the neighborhood of Alhambra:

Sus vecinos no eran sus amigos; eran sus vecinos. El término vecino como se supone que sea no existía. Te veían, te saludaban "Buenos días, buenas tardes" pero no había una relación de por ejemplo donde tú vives que todo el mundo se conoce, que tú eres sobrina de todo el mundo y todo el mundo es tu tío, entras y sales por la casa de cada cual con confianza. A los adultos eso a lo mejor no les afecta, pero a los niños creciendo sí.

(Their neighbors were not their friends; they were their neighbors. The term neighbor, how it's supposed to be did not exist. They would see you, they would say "Good morning, good afternoon" but there was no relationship of, for example, where you live that everybody knows each other, that you are everyone's niece and everyone is your uncle or aunt. You go in and out everyone's homes in confidence. Maybe adults are not affected by that, but children who are growing do feel it.)[56]

When inside these clubs, I felt much as I did during research interviews with residents of elite communities. I was questioned, examined, and observed, just as when I was fifteen attending a cotillion ball. I had been invited

Figure 15. A board announcing activities at Club Náutico (the Ponce Yacht and Fishing Club). Photo by author.

to the ball by a friend who was a debutante. I felt like one of the polka dots on my black-on-white polka-dot dress—a fly in a bowl of milk. I heard sneers and avoided stares; in a sea of white princess gowns, I was out of place.

In my interviews in Dr. Pila and Gándara, public housing, the topics of family, of creating more time and spaces for children to play, of having a thriving community were common. But, the poor, unlike the rich, lacked the exclusive home and community spaces to realize family life. They are, so one resident said, "weak and used" by those in power, shuffled between externally controlled public spaces.[57] Unable to buy a home of their own with a private yard, residents of Dr. Pila have only public spaces as the alternative to their hyper-controlled and contested home zones. Residents of Dr. Pila, as of Gándara, cultivate community life in between the monitored spaces of the *caseríos*, in which they and their loved ones live, or in the few still open common spaces in the city of Ponce—principally, the boardwalk of La Guancha, located in the southwestern coastal part of Ponce right outside of Club Náutico, and the city center's Spanish colonial plaza, the poor's alternative to the clubs of the elite.

A Renovated City for the Poor

As gates proliferated throughout Ponce's private and public residential areas, Ponce was in the midst of an aggressive urban renewal planning project, referred to as Ponce en Marcha (Ponce on the Move). Driven by a Ponce native (and later the governor), Rafael Hernández Colón, efforts had been made since 1961 to establish a historic zone in Ponce to guarantee the preservation of buildings in the city's center.[58] By 1976, a historical preservation district had been established.[59] On May 19, 1986, Hernández Colón signed an executive order to create Ponce en Marcha, allocating $600 million for public-private partnerships to *"revitalizar Ponce, como puntal económico en el país y rescatar el patrimonio histórico de la ciudad"* (revitalize Ponce as an important economic center of the country and rescue the historical patrimony of the city). [60] Public spaces were to be rehabilitated, new industries cultivated, and the entrance to the city beautified. By the end of 1991, 140 projects had been completed and more were in process, including a new judicial center; a new regional hospital; a renovated museum for music; a renovated historic casino building; seven new public schools; road improvements; a system of parks, plazas, and public art and sculpture projects at the entry to the city center; a

Figure 16. "Beautiful Debutantes of El Club Deportivo de Ponce." Source: La Perla del Sur, Archivo Municipal de Ponce. Photo by author.

new hotel; an arts school; a regional jail; a housing renovation program; and improvements to recreational facilities on an island off the coast of Ponce. More projects for beautification and renewal of the city and its public and private spaces were planned, among them a golf park, residential development at varying costs, a mall, an industrial park, renewal of the municipal track and field court, a baseball park and stadium, and a public boardwalk at La Guancha.[61]

La Guancha was once a functioning port opening up to the Caribbean Sea and a manufacturing site with factories. In the 1980s, the strip spontaneously became a nightlife site, with music blasting from street vendors who sold a panoply of local truck fare like *pinchos* (skewers), fried chicken, and pizza. In the 1990s, the beautifying effort made the area an official hangout; a boardwalk was erected with kiosks selling drinks and food. Hundreds of bright orange lights and palm trees spread along the straight-line boardwalk with thatched green kiosks that overlooked a Caribbean sea dotted with yachts. Just as elite housing was adjacent to housing for the poor because of the New Deal design intending to foster integration, so La Guancha is situated next to the exclusive yacht club, Club Náutico. On any weekend night, on the public boardwalk, visitors will find live music and spontaneous dancing. People of all types and ages walk on the boardwalk, sit on the benches, or patronize one of the kiosks. Its openness and lack of restriction makes it feel "free" but also dangerous. As I grew up I heard of incidents in La Guancha; I even remember being there when fights broke out. Monitored by guards and overseers, La Guancha does not feel like an Eden; it is a public space for the poor, just as public housing is.

The city center, a thriving urban commercial hub through the 1980s, has the "most extensive conglomerate of the Southern Puerto Rican style of buildings in the 18th and 19th century [*sic*]," including "Colonial, Criollo Residencial Plueberino, Criollo Ponceño, Europeo Neoclassico, Criollo Pueblerino, Criollo Neoclassico, and Neoclassico Superior."[62] By the late 1980s efforts at preservation and restoration had been reactivated for Ponce en Marcha, but a growing suburbanization led in the 1990s to empty storefronts lining desolate streets, businesses and streets migrating to air-conditioned malls and megastores; ironically, these changes were propelled by the very private economic development incentives that Ponce en Marcha created. Amid the decline, efforts to renew the city center continued, and a central plaza with gardens and fountains of lions (the city's mascot) spitting water continues to symbolize memorable public architecture. From the central plaza, streets have been converted into tiled pedestrian walkways. At night, the plaza hosts local and foreign tourists, who admire its nineteenth-century red-and-black wood firehouse and who line up to buy tropical fruit ice cream at Los Chinos, a Chinese-owned ice-cream shop. But although there have been, and continue to be, intermittent periods of active nightlife in the plaza, where one or two businesses still thrive, *el pueblo* (the city center) is rather dormant. However, it is still the destination for those with few private options for social life and recreation. In my last years in high school, and in my early years in college, I remember returning to the city center for nightlife. In 1992, at the heyday of Ponce en Marcha, I went to parties in clubs there and hung out in bars in the pedestrian parks. The city center was alive. But I remember, too, feelings of insecurity and the threat of crime. We visited, when we had enough money to pay for parking and a cover charge, the new hotel's bar, but, even in these spaces, businesses took care to create a regulated ambiance. On one occasion, my friends and I were denied our request for hip-hop music: they "didn't play that type of music." At other times, I witnessed businesses in the city center becoming, in effect, private spaces, controlling who could enter, excluding those whose dress or skin suggested poverty or lower status.

Everyday life for residents of public housing, the poor, and blacks thus moves between government-controlled neighborhoods and designated public city spaces. Many in public housing say their days are dominated by staying home and by activities around their own communities, such as taking young children to school. Many are at home most of the day, washing clothes, cooking, visiting friends inside the gates, organizing community activities, hanging out at the community center when it is unlocked, playing dominoes. Beyond the neighborhood, the city center provides shopping, churches, and work. A popular shopping spot is the nearby Centro del Sur Shopping Mall (east of Gándara), where many shop at the discount department store for household items; a few use the supermarket in La Rambla Shopping, but public housing residents mainly like to buy groceries in "cash-and carries" (discount supermarkets) beyond walking distance from their homes in the Caobos or Santa Teresita areas, even though few had cars. Many walked or rode bicycles, took public transportation or buses, or depended on rides from friends or family. Inside their government-controlled housing, there were no places to shop, such as a grocery store or pharmacy. Except for the elementary school, they had to go to the center for any service.

The public-private economic and business development that Ponce en Marcha set forth supported the private gardens for the rich while releasing the poor to the public streets. Other elements of the plan, like building golf courts, building a mega hotel, and improving the facilities of Coffin Island just off the coast of Club Náutico created more private gardens for the rich. As crime increased, prisons were built as part of the plan, and the wealthy of Ponce moved to spacious suburban dwellings along the northern fringes of the city or secluded themselves behind the fences of social clubs, in what the environmental sociologist Andy Szasz refers to as an "inverted quarantine": the elite abandoned the public spaces once used by all in Ponce.[63] Open public spaces, provided and monitored by the city, now are used mostly by the poor. The public spaces, in their vulnerability to insecurity, fail to serve as substitute gardens. The city's public spaces and gated private clubs denote the deep chasm between rich and poor, regarded as so natural that few even mention it. While the poor travel a distance to reach contested public spaces, the rich cultivate private botanical clubs and secret gardens.

The "Green Veneer"

As spaces (fauna, flora, or urban renewal planning projects) are crafted into botanical Edens for the rich or public spaces for the poor, Ponce created, and maintains, a city of segregated and class-designated spaces: one space is composed of home and club gardens, with protected mangoes and orchids; the other comprises concrete basketball courts and noisy public spaces. As municipal projects construct an orderly city through regulated public spaces, Ponce's elite escape "unwholesomeness and dirt."[64] Gardens have become a common way to beautify and improve spaces in the modern city, understanding that beauty symbolizes care and that flowers and nature can be a palliative for physical as well as social ills. In the field of criminology, "broken windows" theories posit that dilapidated buildings that need paint breed crime by symbolizing a lack of order and care, indicating that nobody is watching, overseeing, or protecting.[65] Similarly, gardens have become the focus of an urban greening movement that sees them as barriers to decay and abandonment, hence important components of urban revitalization. They have become central to programs throughout the world to create communities that are aesthetically pleasing, stronger, better, and healthier—more "humane," "more *green*, more *healthy and safe*, more *people friendly*, and more *equitable*," suggests Rutherford H. Platt.[66] Since the 1970s, urban gardens have been used as interventions to save poor communities; gardens are purported to be effective community builders, good sources of locally grown produce, and even vehicles of resistance among the poor.[67] But "greening" movements fail to recognize that nature is already in the city, because the city, for the poor, is already a garden, but not one that is green and carefully landscaped but rather a "cement garden" that symbolizes discipline and control.[68]

For the rich, the pots, flowers, and horse manure represent a fertile lifestyle of modern-day Puerto Rico. An Alhambra resident said that her sister in Extensión Alhambra was reclaiming a garden lifestyle via the gates: "En Extensión Alhambra de verdad que la criminalidad ha bajado. O sea, yo te lo digo por mi hermana que ella vivió ahí y no podía tener muebles en el balcón porque se los llevaban. Y desde que cerraron, está lucida porque tiene un poquito de vida más tranquila" (In Extensión Alhambra crime decreased. I tell you because my sister lived there and she couldn't have furniture on the porch, because they would steal it. And since they closed the gates, she is happy because she has a more peaceful life).[69] Extensión Alhambra, thus, has been able to reclaim the street as a common garden: "Al tener acceso controlado la gente está en la calle, hace barbecue afuera, hacen fiestas y como sólo tienen el tránsito del que vive allí, pues ellos pueden interaccionar unos con otros más" (Since they have controlled access, people are on the street. They barbecue outside, hold parties, and since they only have traffic of people who live there, they can socialize with each other more).[70]

The elite, supported by government policies, controls nature for their benefit. Carolyn Merchant writes that "Edenic spaces ostracized those 'others' of different classes and colors who did not fit into the story. The green veneer became a cover for the actual corruption of the earth and neglect of its poor; that green false consciousness threatened the hoped-for redemption of all people. . . . The new suburbs existed at the cost of poor minorities who lived with polluted wells, blackened slums, and toxic dumps."[71] Urban improvement projects in homes and public spaces resegregate people and impede the very integration social idealists like the New Deal and Luis Muñoz Marín, the governor of Puerto Rico in the 1950s, envisioned and sought to create.

In an era of what William Walters calls "domopolitics," which "embodies a tactic which juxtaposes the 'warm words' of community, trust, and citizenship, with the danger words of a chaotic outside—illegals, traffickers, terrorists; a game which configures things as 'Us vs. Them,'"[72] gardens, like public improvement projects, have become ideal codified ways to separate and control those who live in the city. Frances Hodgson Burnett wrote that "as long as one has a garden one has a future; and as long as one has a future one is alive."[73]

In *The Secret Garden*, her famous story, children brought an abandoned and neglected garden back to life and, with the garden, a boy who had expected to die. Although gardens are purported to be an extension of life, and urban renewal projects are deemed to make life in the city better, they can also limit and stagnate the life of a city. Mumford notes that "soon, in breaking away from the city, the part became a substitute for the whole. . . . Play became the serious business of life; and the golf course, the country club, the swimming pool, and the cocktail party became the frivolous counterfeits of a more varied and significant life. . . . In suburb and in metropolis, mass production, mass consumption, and mass recreation produce the same kind of standardized and denatured environment."[74] Thus, gardens and urban projects meant to beautify may create a regressive urban experience where disparate people are segregated behind perverted symbols of beauty and order.

Chapter 6

Neighbors More Remote than Strangers

> Social space is to the practical space of everyday life, with its distances which are kept or signalled, and neighbours who may be more remote than strangers, what geometrical space is to the "travelling space" (*espace hodologique*) of ordinary experience, with its gaps and discontinuities.
>
> —Pierre Bourdieu, *Distinction*

It is cleaning day in Doña Lucrecia's house. Doña Lucrecia, a middle-aged, white woman in one of the larger homes in Extensión Alhambra, guided me through a maze of furniture to a back terrace garden crowded seating clusters, tables, and a tiny pool; it was the setting, no doubt, of many small social gatherings. An olive-skinned woman with a duster, a mop, a broom, and a bucket was at work. She was, said Doña Lucrecia, "the one who helps around the house." Doña Lucrecia, in her conversation with me, worried about "sounding offensive or inhumane."[1]

Gates identify separate yet interdependent roles between the gated communities of rich and poor, and they also represent a secure source of income for poor women and a "decent" and ready labor pool for the upper class.[2] As an Extensión Alhambra resident explained, "Puedes tener una gente que te ayude en la casa y esas personas llegan a pie y se van solas, o sea que no tengo que salir a buscarlos a ningún sitio y a la hora que terminan se van solitos" (You can have people help you in the house who get here on foot and leave on their own, so that I don't have to go get them. When they are done they leave on their own).[3] New Deal ideals of side-by-side interclass placement—intended to foster social interaction—are realized in an ironic way. The well-off have their own assessed and trustworthy labor pool, conveniently located in adjacent space. Joaquín, of Alhambra, said, "Sí, es correcto que en la barriada aquí en Dr. Pila vive mucha gente decente porque el jardinero de aquí vive en Dr. Pila y hay mucha gente decente" (It is true that in the barrio in Dr. Pila there are many decent people. Our gardener lives in Dr. Pila and there are many decent people there).[4]

The trusted poor are allowed into the gated spaces of the well-to-do to serve the purposes of the rich:

> Realmente yo te diría que en esta comunidad por muchos años se conocía a las personas que trabajaban en las casas de los demás, o sea que no tan sólo conocían a los vecinos sino también a los ayudantes de los vecinos y todavía aquí nosotras compartimos, porque por ejemplo el señor que me hace el patio yo sé que ha venido a esta casa, va donde [Carmen] o sea que nos lo pasamos y de casa de [Carmen] entonces me llama para decir que a [Carmen] le están robando las chinas y si el perro de [Carmen] se quedó afuera. O sea, que yo entiendo que aquí hay comunidad donde hay interacción, no tan sólo de los residentes, sino también de las personas allegadas.

> (In this community, for many years, you would know the people who worked in other people's homes. We knew not only the neighbors but also the neighbors' helpers. We still share, because the man who works on my yard comes to this house and goes to Carmen's. We pass them around. He calls to tell me that Carmen's oranges are being stolen, and that Carmen's dog was left outside. As I understand it, there is a community here with a lot of contact of the residents and of people close to us.)[5]

These hired helpers, sometimes men but mostly women who clean and launder and iron and care for children, tend to the same interior and exterior gardens that youth from their own communities (punishing their own families) were said to threaten. The contradictions of hiring the poor are not lost on Dr. Pila residents. Vanessa, a feisty woman, told me, "Terminan necesitando de los residenciales. Cuando necesitan quien le limpie las casas los buscan en los residenciales públicos. Son unos vagos" (In the end, they need public housing. When they need someone to clean their homes they look for that person in public housing. They're lazy). At the same time, Jessy confided:

A nosotros ... nos dan a entender ... al ponernos la verja ... no es que quieren proteger la barriada, ni a los residentes. ... Lo que quieren es aislar a los residenciales de las personas pudientes. Eso no lo debe hacer porque son comunidades. Son comunidades en general. Ellos no tienen porqué irse por encima a nosotros. Somos todos personas de carne y hueso.

(They give us ... the message ... by putting up our gate ... that it is not that they want to protect our community, nor its residents ... What they want is to isolate public housing from wealthy people. They have no reason to think they're better than us. We're all people, of flesh and bone.)[6]

Employer-employee relationships go only as far as defined and hierarchical labor transactions. There is little or no mobility and little confusion. The gates of each solidify class distinctions. Or, as Foucault said of structures of discipline and punishment, "It is a segmented, immobile, frozen space. Each individual is fixed in his place. And, if he moves, he does so at the risk of his life, contagion or punishment."[7] An Alhambra resident reminded me: "Porque yo a Pila y Gándara voy cuando tengo personas que me hacen algún tipo de trabajo las llevo y las traigo" (I go to Pila and Gándara when I hire people to work for me and I take them home or bring them here). But the resident would only accompany the worker to the gate: "Hasta el gate pero no me atrevo a entrar porque como lo cerraron y ahora hay policía, pues no" (I don't brave walking in past the Dr. Pila gate because they closed it and now a police officer is there. So, no).

As Puerto Rico's social economy turned away from agriculture and toward manufacturing and industrialization during the 1950s and after the oil crisis of the 1970s, the island increasingly became dependent on service industries like tourism. As in many Latin American and Caribbean countries, the gap between poor and rich continues to increase.[8] In Dr. Pila and Gándara more than 70 percent of residents are poor, about 40 percent are unemployed, and the median household income is $37,229.[9] In Alhambra and Extensión Alhambra the unemployment rate in 1999 was at 14 percent and the median household income was $62,800.[10] About half of the families include a married couple; only 16 percent of the households are headed by single females. The statistics alone are insufficient to explain the stark ways in which class is identified and enforced. Melvin Tumin's 1961 study on class in Puerto Rico identified "discernible strata" in Puerto Rico beyond differences in education, income, and residence: "These classes are units upon whom different average fates descend. . . . They are unequally burdened. . . . They share unequally in the rewards of prestige and property."[11]

In the 1950s, class seemed to be more fluid and appeared to have moved into a period of realignment, away from the fixed divisions of the nineteenth century.[12] As Tumin found, New Deal policies had led to a general optimism among the "lower classes," a feeling that society "is open . . . that new opportunities are not something of the remote future, but almost immediately available."[13] By the late twentieth century, the gated communities had surrendered the ideal. Mobility and spontaneous contacts across class have been unsuccessful. Arnold van Gennep elaborates the point when discussing territorial passages: "When milestones or boundary signs . . . are ceremonially placed by a defined group on a delimited piece of earth, the group takes possession of it in such a way that a stranger that sets foot on it commits a sacrilege analogous to a profane person's entrance into a sacred forest or temple," or what van Gennep calls a magico-religious trespass.[14]

Keyla, of Dr. Pila, explained the differences between Dr. Pila and the upper-class neighboring communities:

Bueno . . . todo es por nombre. Porque La Alhambra . . . se deja llevar de gente que tiene dinero, tienen sus propias casas, y tiene de todo. Pero somos iguales que ellos. Porque no tenemos una casa, pero a veces somos más felices que ellos mismos. No tenemos dinero, pero tenemos un techo. Comemos bien, cuando ellos a veces lo que comen es fast food. Nosotros no, nosotros comemos bien. Y pues, la calidad de ser humano. La persona que viven en un residencial son bien humanitarios y saben ser amigos, y a veces la gente de alta sociedad son bien groseros y te miran por encima del hombro. Yo creo que en nada nos parecemos a ellos.

(Well, everything is based on where you are from. Because in La Alhambra, people focus on others with money, they have their own homes, they have everything. But we are equal to them. We don't have a house, but sometimes we are happier than they are. We don't have money, but we have a roof over our heads. We eat well, when sometimes they eat fast food. Not us, we eat well. And of course, the quality of human being, people in public housing are humanitarian, they know how to be a friend. And sometimes the people from high society are rude, they look down on you. I don't think we are alike at all.)[15]

In Dr. Pila and Gándara, some residents assumed a posture of defense, of resisting stereotypes others use for their community. A Gándara resident said, "Si uno vive aquí [lo] dice. Vivo en un residencial con orgullo. . . . yo digo vivo en residencial, y es así. El que no le guste mi amistad por vivir en urbanización no la necesito" (If I live here, I claim it. I live in public housing, proudly. . . . I say I live in public housing, and that is that. I don't need the friendship from anybody who, because of living in a private subdivision, doesn't like me).[16]

In Alhambra and Extensión Alhambra, residents spoke to me with pride of their stable relationships, a community in which lifestyles and incentives, capital and cultural, are shared:

Nos parecemos en que hemos tenido hijos que han estudiado en el mismo sitio. Tenemos negocios propios casi todos. . . . Están los muchachos en la misma escuela, hacían deportes juntos . . . y hemos continuado la amistad. Aparte de eso amistades de mi esposo cuando él estudiaba . . . hemos continuado la amistad . . . viajamos juntos y tenemos muchas actividades que hacemos juntos. Son . . . profesionales.

(We are alike in that our children went to the same school. Almost all of us have our own businesses . . . our kids went to school together, participated together in sports. . . . We have continued these friendships. On top of that, my husband's friends, who studied with him, . . . we have continued the friendship . . . we travel together and take part in a lot of activities together. They are . . . professionals.)[17]

Public housing communities were considered *totalmente diferente* (totally different). "El estilo de vida de allá es más que de gente pobre. . . . Hay mucha falta de conocimiento de lo que es moral, de estilo de vida. Ellos, de verdad que la diferencia es bien grande, completamente diferente. Ellos se sienten que tienen menos y que aquí son los que tienen más y entonces hay esa discordancia" (The lifestyle there is more than people of poverty. . . . There is little morality. The difference [between us] is big, completely different. They feel they have less and that we have more and so there is discord between us).[18]

Class and group distinctions, according to Pierre Bourdieu, are elaborated through habitus, a "structuring structure, which organizes practices and the perception of practices, but also a structured structure: the principle of division into logical classes which organizes the perception of the social world" and distinction.[19]

The familial and social contacts of both rich and poor communities are restricted to others like them, aligned by neighborhood boundaries. "Nos conocemos porque los residenciales siempre están con los residenciales, unidos. Cuando hacen actividades residencial con residencial, no residencial con urbanización" (We know each other because the public housing residents are always within other public housing projects, never in private subdivisions).[20] Public housing residents, in both Dr. Pila and Gándara, reported that most of their extended families and friends lived in other Ponce public housing sites such as Portugués, López Nussa, Lirios del Sur, and Rosales. They knew people in other low-income communities as well, among them Bélgica, San Antón, La Yuca, Cantera, and Cotto Laurel. Some had social contacts with residents of *urbanizaciones* of lower-class, lower and working middle-class, or middle-class communities, like Valle Alto, Santa Teresita, and Santa Marìa. Many who have friends in other public housing sites explained that their daily activities coincide. So, for example, their children go to the same school or take part in the same basketball league or in activities organized by public housing's private management company. The social circles of the poor follow their fault lines.[21]

The people of means offer the same explanation of their social circles and they share areas of common concern and activities in the same locations. "[Tenemos] las mismas aspiraciones, el mismo modo de vida. Nos gustan los mismos temas. Frecuentamos los mismos sitios, los mismos supermercados, las mismas tiendas" ([We have] the same aspirations, the same way of life. We like the same topics. We frequent the same places, the same supermarkets, the same stores).[22] "Sean personas del mismo estatus de uno. Uno ve las personas que más o menos actúan y piensan similares" (Persons of the same status, we see people who more or less act and think similarly).[23]

Tumin noted that, in Puerto Rico, "class membership and [a] common style of life are virtually synonymous"[24] and that cross-class relationships are promoted or inhibited by concepts of community membership, and identity of self and other. The social psychologist Gordon Allport's theory of contact suggests that when groups meet under conditions of equal status, interdependence, cooperation, or support from authority, positive integration is achievable, but when physical or symbolic boundaries, such as gates, are erected, groups and categories are experienced as distinct and separate, regardless of proximity in space, time, or character.[25] As Kevin Lynch and Gerald Suttles proposed, physical artifacts, in Puerto Rico the gates, define and outline social universes and directly shape social action.

The social worlds of the rich and poor are independent of each other, except as employer and employed, and home spaces are equally restricted. Before the gates of Extensión Alhambra went up, residents of Gándara would trick-or-treat in Extensión Alhambra (but not the other way around). No longer: "En Halloween daban como tres casas. Adentro del portón. Creo que era la segunda y otra. Las casas no quedan juntas. Siempre eran las mismas. No era una cosa que tuviéramos amistad pero ellos sabían que iban gente de aquí" (At Halloween about three homes inside the gate gave [treats]. Not that we had friendships, but they knew people from here went there).[26] Now, many who live in Dr. Pila and pass through the streets of La Alhambra on their way to the city center have never set foot inside a home in Alhambra and know no one who lives there. Gándara residents, too, pass through only on their way to schools or other locations. The gated Extensión Alhambra is even more remote, with no accessible streets from the outside through the gates except for residents and their guests. Most in Dr. Pila and Gándara have never had a reason to be admitted to Alhambra or Extensión Alhambra and, unless hired as domestics or landscapers, have never trespassed. The exclusion imposed on the poor by the gates of the rich and the fence and gates installed by the guards of the city defeat the very purposes of integration intended by the New Deal in locating public housing next to private housing in Puerto Rico's cities. The experiment failed; it led to gates that partition space and made class more rigid.

Managing Women, Rich and Poor

It is a woman's world, behind the gates, in the closed communities of both the rich and the poor. In Dr. Pila and Gándara, in Extensión Alhambra and Alhambra, women were the most visible, the ones whose authority was on display. They were the administrators, the Resident Council presidents, the neighbors. In both types of housing, they defined and managed their homes and communities' boundaries and purposes, though among the elite they demonstrated a deference to men. Doña Lucrecia in Extensión Alhambra kept telling me in our interview that her husband could have provided more "intellectual" answers. When I left, her husband was arriving but was too busy for conversation. It was obvious that my work was women's business. Although I spoke primarily to women in communities that were both rich and poor, the number of single-female-headed households is far higher among homes of the poor.[27] In Gándara and Dr. Pila, a majority of the residents are female: a number, so it is said, do not declare that they are married because it would mean loss of benefits. Between half and three-quarters of the households are headed by single females.[28] In Extensión Alhambra and Alhambra, 16 percent of household heads were single in 1999.[29] Yet the effect and impression are the same across class lines—men were not visible or present when I was interviewing. Overall, I saw more men in Dr. Pila and Gándara than in the affluent communities.

The gates manage women without regard to wealth or class; during the day they are, or appear to be, in both communities without spouses. Dolores Hayden considers the modern home to be a gendered spatial geography. The gates of Puerto Rico have re-created and reinforced a gendered geography; in the city, there is a spatial sorting of men by degree of privilege.[30] The elite gated communities along with sanctioned city spaces like the social clubs, like suburbs within a city, have become the site of a cloistered womanhood, meeting, as Lewis Mumford puts it, "the needs of child-bearing and child-rearing: with woman predominating in this community throughout the day . . . a sort of return to the archaic matriarchy,"[31] a refuge from the open spaces of the dangerous city. Privileged children, too, play behind home and club gates. Gates release elite men for "real" work in the world of power arrangements, business, and government and public policy.

Behind the private enclosures of Extensión Alhambra I encountered women at different levels—homemakers, community makers, workers—but at each level, except for some professional women, access to the open outer world was restricted, carefully choreographed, and limited to specific places. Doña Lucrecia in Extensión Alhambra had ensured that her home and family were well taken care of even if not by her own hand. The outside world was transmitted to her through images conveyed by her husband from work or by her children. Her home was her principal arena and universe—a protected island of flowers, furnishings, equipment, and domestic tasks. Her neighbor, Rebecca, a plant-loving neighborhood association president, extended her reach to the wider city, but only into the nearby streets, by connecting neighbors and choosing causes to support. The neighborhood itself seemed to be an adult playground, an extension of the home. Rebecca moved outside of the loop and the gate principally for social occasions. For most women, like Doña Lucrecia, the gates seemed to indicate and organize a circumscribed routine—a job, a hair appointment, a shopping excursion. Even in the open city itself, women's movements were circumscribed. In Alhambra, many women do work outside the home, running businesses with their husbands or in professional positions. Ramona, a teacher, had greater reach: she worked every day outside her gate and neighborhood; she encountered people from varied walks of life, taught students of diverse backgrounds, and had more knowledge of the city. Such women may also move beyond the home for social activities or to provide their children with broader social opportunities that are unavailable in their neighborhood. The city—at least the open, unrestricted parts of it—is not inviting but threatening and carefully managed.

Children, as an extension of women, are a constant and are central to the gated experience, particularly for women in public housing. In Dr. Pila, for example, 49 percent of residents were eighteen and younger; in Gándara, about 50 percent.[32] Some of my interviews in both occurred in the presence of young children, and, even when not present, children's schedules often dominated the interviews in the communities. Lorna, a resident council chair of a Dr. Pila subdivision, met me with her toddler-aged daughter in pigtails, dressed in pink from head to toe. Women looked at their watches— children had to be picked up and otherwise cared for. I would agree to cut the interview short, but some were torn between children and me—I had offered a cash incentive to public housing residents to compensate them for their time.

The tensions between making money and caring for children, between being a provider and a nurturer, affect unmarried poor women behind the gate. Although women are far more visible than men, the policies of gating, with the National Guard raids and the helicopters, impose a superficial aggressive masculinity that misrepresents the actual character of these woman-dominant neighborhoods as simultaneously (and simultaneously expected to be) in control and nurturing as well as out of control and male. Punitive interventions and programs tend to portray inept single-female heads of household and criminal young males.[33] Women as representing "a tangle of pathology" in the Moynihan report, the "culture of poverty" of Oscar Lewis, in the United States as in Puerto Rico, ignore the complexities of lived experience.[34] Alhambra residents echoed a view of how they felt the public housing family lifestyle was an inferior culture.

Entonces mira, casi todas las muchachas del caserío no se casan porque si se casan pierden, por ejemplo, los cupones. Les aumentan las viviendas porque dependiendo de los ingresos es que ellos pagan renta y casi todas las mujeres aparecen viviendo solas con niños. Ahora mismo todos los años o cada dos años el gobierno federal viene a visitar el residencial. Ahora todas están sacando la ropa y llevándola a casa de la familia para cuando vengan a inspeccionar el apartamento. [Para que] allí no haya nada de hombre porque ellas viven solas y pues para coger su bono y para pagar menos.

(So then, most women in public housing don't get married, because if they do, they lose their benefits. Rents rise because the amount they pay depends on their income so most women appear as if they live by themselves with their children. Right now, every year, or every other year, when the federal government comes to visit public housing, they take clothing out of their rooms to family members' homes until the inspection is over. [So that] the government finds no men's things in their homes and assumes they live alone. Then they can get their benefits and they pay less rent.)[35]

Yo te digo, porque una persona que yo conozco, que papi y mami lo ven de aquí, vive con su mujer y tiene hijos y él no aparece como el jefe de familia y de vez en cuando chequean.

(I tell you this because a person I know, that my father and mother can see from here, lives with his wife and children but he doesn't appear as head of household. Once in a while they get checked.)[36]

A neighbor followed up with "Mienten mucho, tú los entrevistas y no se atreven a decir la verdad, te dicen 'no, yo vivo sola' y no viven solas" (They lie a lot. You interview them and don't dare say the truth. They tell you "no, I live alone" but they don't live alone).[37] Poor families, thus, tend to be seen as devious and, therefore, in need of reform and in need of containment behind gates. Public housing residents elaborate the distinction too. In contrast to them, the privileged are pictured as not being family-oriented: "La persona que vive en residencial está más directo con la familia que ellos. Porque ellos van a un restaurant, pero no se llevan al hijo. . . . Nosotros cargamos con los muchacos para dondequiera" (The people who live in public housing are more involved with the family than they are. Because they go to a restaurant, but don't take their child. . . . We take our kids wherever we go).[38] Elite women live in gated communities that seek to protect their privilege, because they are prized beings that require, and deserve, protection from the chaotic city. But, says Mumford, because protection "did not apply to the women and children of the working classes,"[39] something more than gender was at stake.

Race, Whiteness, and the Contours of Preference

With the intersection of gender and class differences enforced, a racial stigma, too, is imputed and enforced, if subtly, and with a psychology of denial. From the nineteenth century onward, a race and class geography has been imprinted on urban San Juan, in the words of Teresita Martínez-Vergne: "a process of gentrification (read whitening) shortly after midcentury [occurred] as the government earmarked certain neighborhoods for state monumental architecture and forcefully moved the working-class populations."[40] Assessing who is who, who lives where, and who is permitted access and contact is mediated through race. Kenia explained, "Al ser de residencial público formamos parte de los residenciales públicos. Nos ven como ellos. Podemos estar en cualquier puerta de residencial público y nos van a abrir. Yo voy a Alhambra a tocar una puerta y no me van a abrir" (Because we live in public housing, they see us in them. If we are at any door in a public housing project, the door will be opened. But if I go to Alhambra to knock on the door no one will open).[41] Kenia's skin is brown. She is aware that poverty in Puerto Rico has been racialized and, thus, stigmatized. Phenotypes, such as dress, talk, and general comportment, are shaped into an intersectional profile of a racial poverty that identifies who is safe and who is dangerous, who is good or bad, and who is worthy.

Neighborhoods—private versus public, rich versus poor, gated versus nongated—help mark and navigate a socio-racial geography. But, in Puerto Rico, this is not a simple combination of skin color or other physical characteristics, because actual skin color often belies the claim or stigma of racial identity.[42] Historically seen as a society unafflicted by racial problems, newer scholarship has begun to address the ways in which race operates on the island.[43] This scholarship has mostly focused on pinioning the boundaries of racial categorization, as well as the discursive negation of blackness.[44]

Particularly for racial categorization, context has been deemed most important for racial ascription.[45]

Housing and neighborhoods frame race. If race is "slippery" or "fugitive" in language, as the anthropologist Isar Godreau notes, in physical structures it is frozen. Space, the built environment, I suggest, exposes the activated racist contours of its imaginations.[46] Those in the elite communities of Alhambra and Extensión Alhambra see themselves as, and are perceived to be, *blanquitos* (whites). Almost all residents in Extensión Alhambra and Alhambra claim to be white, whatever their color tone. In the 2000 U.S. Census, almost all (98 percent) in these two communities identified themselves as white.[47] In my own interviews there, residents labeled themselves, and their neighborhoods, as inhabited primarily by *Blanco* (white) or *Caucásico* (Caucasian) people. But racial identification and skin tone were not synonymous. Nelly, who identified herself as Blanca, is olive-toned with children darker than she. I came to understand that, in the context of Puerto Rico, her class position and her residence in a gated elite neighborhood had awarded the privilege of whiteness. Such negotiation occurs with neighbors, not outsiders alone.

The concept of whiteness in the United States is a product of a scholarly attempt to identify an unacknowledged—by science as well as those who hold the privilege—racial category and structures of racial privilege; whites are the Other, the opposite side of disadvantage (in the United States, typically represented by blacks).[48] Recognizing privilege, however, breeds insecurity, leading, in turn, to an evasion of race and, hence, to new forms of "racism" (aversive, color-blind, laissez-faire, symbolic).[49] In Puerto Rico, among the neighbors of Extensión Alhambra and Alhambra, whiteness is proudly claimed, seen as obvious and unchallengeable, and not something to be ashamed of, because of its links to systems of racial bondage, supremacy, and hierarchy.

In an exchange between two neighbors during one interview, Rosanna said she was Caucásica, and Gloria retorted, "*Aquí el que no tiene dinga tiene de mandinga*" (Here, everyone has some kind of African blood or other).[50] A claim to or denial of multiracial ancestries and, specifically, of African descent has validated discourses of racial equality in Puerto Rico for many years. The claim is contradictory. Everyone, because of assumed widespread miscegenation, has someone who came, originally, from Africa and is, therefore, "black" or has black "blood." Thus, no one can logically assume racial superiority over anyone else. But a biological and essentialist debate overlooks the long-standing ways in which Puerto Ricans construct race in the everyday—creating, sorting, and aligning symbols of status, with white almost always the superior—and, in turn, act upon them according to status: although many people in Puerto Rico claim to be white, to others outside of that locally informed structure of racial hierarchy, they may instead appear as brown or black.

For their part, Dr. Pila and Gándara residents construct the *riquitos* (rich) as blanquitos, relying not just on actual color but on who thinks they are better and look down on those who are poor. Yet they see behind color and status. One Gándara resident told me that Alhambra residents were always "hiding," "*los de cuellito blanco*" (the ones with white collars), and engaged in much of the illicit activities for which the poor are blamed.[51] Cubans, the scholar Jorge Duany suggests, "mingle freely with 'white' Puerto Ricans from the upper and middle sectors of society, the so-called *blanquitos*."[52] Duany describes how "blanquito" is used in everyday language:

> Blanquito suele ser un individuo de origen europeo, ingresos eleva- dos, ocupación diestra, educación universitaria y residencia exclusiva. Muchos de los llamados blanquitos son los herederos de los hacen- dados criollos del siglo XIX, ahora transformados en políticos, em- presarios, médicos, abogados y otros profesionales. Algunas personas logran "blanquearse" a través del dinero, la educación o el matrimo- nio y escalan una posición social superior a la de su familia de origen.
>
> El uso común del diminutivo "blanquito" sugiere el desprecio de los sectores subalternos hacia los dominantes. Frecuentemente se em- plea en tono de burla para poner en su sitio a quienes ostentan ínfulas de grandeza, hablan de manera rebuscada o niegan sus antepasados menos afortunados. A los blanquitos se les atribuyen ideas elitistas, como creerse mejores que otros grupos estigmatizados como "cafres," "cocolos," "cacos," "chusma," "tusa" o simplemente gente "de color." La sabiduría popular es implacable con los blanquitos. Así, pueden oírse comentarios críticos sobre escuelas, universidades, urbanizacio- nes, condominios, clubes, tiendas, restaurantes, deportes y músicas de blanquitos. Incluso, pueden denunciarse ciertas políticas públicas (como la privatización) como "embelecos de blanquitos."

(A "Whitey" tends to be an individual of European descent, of high income, skilled occupation, college educated and good residence. Many of the so-called "Whiteys" are heirs of 19th century creole land- owners, now politicians, business owners, doctors, lawyers, and other professionals. Some people can "whiten" themselves through money, education, or marriage, and move up to a higher social stratum than the one held by their family of origin.

The common use of the diminutive of white, "Whitey," suggests rejection of subordinate groups by the dominant sectors.[53] It is frequently used to parody or neutralize those who think themselves better, those who speak in inflated ways, or negate their less fortunate ancestors. Whiteys are attributed with elitist ideals, like thinking they're better than other stigmatized groups like "cafres," "cocolos," "cacos," "chusma," "tusa," or simply people "of color." There are a lot of popular ideas about Whiteys. You can hear critical comments about Whitey schools, universities, private subdivisions, condominiums, clubs, stores, restaurants, sports and music. In fact, even public policies (like privatization) are sometimes qualified as maneuverings of Whiteys.)[54]

A racial and class negotiation—what Norelia, a resident of Extensión Alhambra, describes as a "*confrontamiento . . . que más bien [es] diferencia social*" (a confrontation . . . that more than anything is based on social differences)[55]—takes place in Puerto Rico through the gated and open spaces of public and private communities. Renata, of Alhambra, elaborates on the confrontations:

Había mucha agresividad de la barriada hacia la Alhambra. Tiraban piedras. . . . "Mira, la Señora Rica esta tirándonos dulces. Vengan, vengan." . . . y te pagan con piedras. Miren, yo no soy una señora rica. Yo soy una persona que he trabajado y mi esposo trabaja mucho para tener lo que tengo y si ustedes en un futuro en vez de tirar piedras se ponen a estudiar pueden tener una casa y un trabajo.

(There was a lot of aggression in public housing toward La Alhambra. They would throw rocks. . . . "Look, the rich lady is throwing candy. Come, come." . . . and they pay you with rocks. Look, I'm not a rich woman. I'm a person who has worked and my husband works a lot so that we can have what we have. If you, in the future, instead of throwing rocks go to school, you can have a house and a job.)[56]

Criminals are most often seen as unemployable dark young males who live in public housing. Rafa, a bored, young dark man, explained: "¿Qué yo cambiaría en el residencial? El discrimen que tienen en la oficina. . . . Tu vas y le preguntas si tienen algo [de trabajo] y dicen que no tienen, y [después] se lo dan a la gente preferida . . . a los escogidos" (What would I change about public housing? The discrimination in the office. . . . You go and ask if they have [jobs available] and they say they don't. And then they give the job to the favorites . . . the chosen). Being turned down for jobs was common, seen as a nuanced and spontaneous calculation based on residence. Don Ramon, an employer at a job fair organized by the social workers in Dr. Pila, told me that he was there to provide job opportunities other employers denied to residents of public housing. Dinora, a resident, described one such incident: "Yo tenía una entrevista. . . . Pues cuando llegué el supervisor me dijo, '¿De dónde tú eres?' Cuando le dije que era de Dr. Pila entonces cambió la actitud, como que 'pues yo te llamo cualquier cosita.' De una actitud que estaba como que ese trabajo era seguro y después cambió a una actitud, al decir el sitio [donde vivo], de te llamaré después" (I had an interview. . . . Well, when I got there, the supervisor asked me, "Where are you from?" When I told him I was from Dr. Pila, his attitude changed to "I'll call you if anything comes up." He went from an attitude that the job was for-sure to an attitude, once I said where I lived, of I'll call you later).[57] Jobs and occupations are important social distinctions. The rich and poor considered jobs to demonstrate an important difference between their neighborhoods, a distinction that Tumin found correlated to skin color.[58] Analyses of Census data show a correspondence in Puerto Rico of perceived whiteness with more privileged socioeconomic positions.[59] This means not that the whites are the privileged but that the privileged are whites.

When I arrived to interview someone well-to-do, I made a note at the time about the experience as "interviewing while black." The affluent people who interrogated me before I began the interview about where I lived and where I had been were reading "race symbols" and were doubtlessly suspicious or confused about me because of my brown skin, and therefore, that there might be reason for concern.[60]

Duany suggests that the term "blanquito" confuses race and class. Being white doesn't necessarily access whiteness. He asks, "*Pero, ¿no es posible ser blanco sin ser blanquito o ser blanquito sin ser blanco?*" (But, isn't it possible to be white without being a "Whitey" or to be a "Whitey" without being white?). Whiteness in Puerto Rico, accessible to some, is more than just about hair texture or skin color; it is a sorting of racial privilege by class, of having access to opportunities reserved for the elite. Such whiteness is systematically less accessible to the poor.

Cuando yo vivía en el bloque 31, que queda para esa área [Alhambra] uno se cree que esa gente son de dinero. Pero hay gente humilde. Una vez hubo un desagüe porque llovió mucho y cayó de la barriada el agua a casa del Señor. El Señor dio la vuelta, habló con nosotros y nos dijo que la gente cree que él tiene dinero, pero a él le cuesta arreglar eso, y eran aguas negras. Él lo que es un señor de carros públicos. Con su sudor se compró su casa. Hay gente como nosotros ahí.

(When I lived in Block 31, right next to Alhambra, one might think all those people have money. But there are some humble people. There was once a flood. There had been a lot of rain and the sewage over-flowed to the man's house. The man turned around and talked to us and told us that people thought he had money, but that it was costly to fix what happened. He was a public car driver. He bought his house with his own sweat. There are people like us living there.)[61]

As there are "blanquitos," and white privilege, there are also "negritos," "gente de color," "prietos," "Dominicanos," and "yoleros" often seen as lawless and poor and contaminating the island. In Puerto Rico, there is evidence of these emplaced bodies being discriminated against in employment, as well as policed aggressively and violently by law enforcement.[62] The question Duany asked may be posed in reverse: Is it possible to be black without being a crim-inal, poor, Dominicano, or uneducated? To answer yes, in both cases, essen-tializes race and proposes that it is something more than a socially signified category. In a negative response, we acknowledge that imaginaries of race (in their intersection with class, gender, and neighborhood) are solidified, acted upon, and structured socially.

That these imaginaries grant and distribute privilege is easily overlooked in Puerto Rico, as the anthropologist João Costa Vargas notes, referring to Brazil, where there is a "hyperconsciousness/negation race dialectic," in which racial awareness coexists with a highly racialized system.[63] The archi-tectural historian Dianne Harris, speaking of the United States, confirms that preserving privilege (whiteness) is behind the negation of racial inequality and that the built environment is suitable to this negation:

Hiding in plain sight[,] which is a hallmark of white privilege, is equally true for a range of ideologies that are designed into the spaces that surround us. Landscapes, for example, are particularly well suited to the masking of such constructions because they appear to be completely natural, God-given, and neutral. But landscapes, and indeed architecture, are never thus. They are always powerful symbols and containers of cultural values, just as they simultaneously work to construct culture. Given this equivalence of invisibility between the ideologies of constructed space and constructions of race, built form and ideologies of whiteness become more than usually complicit in the manufacturing of societal norms. Racial privilege and exclusion become visually naturalized in verdant spaces that appear wholesome and even precious, the seeming ineffability of boundaries linked to that of an apparently organic spatial structure.[64]

Thus, whether subjects are articulated as black, white, women, men, straight, or lesbian, people act and structures are erected, as if they are (sometimes exclusively) black, white, women, men, straight, or lesbian, with all the significations, opportunities, and limits that these and other intersecting positionalities award and allow. Imaginaries are, indeed, actualized and encoded in social structures. Their encryption enhances their structuration, for their articulation (in ideology) is arguable yet, to use an Althusserian logic, undeniably "real."[65] Stuart Hall writes that

> both Althusser and Gramsci . . . insist that ideology . . . is not a simple form of false consciousness, to be explained as a set of myths or simple false constructions in the head. All societies require specific ideologies, which provide those systems of meaning, concepts, categories and representations which make sense of the world, and through which men come to "live" (albeit unconsciously, and through a series of "misrecognitions"), in an imaginary way, their relation to the real, material conditions of their existence (which are only representable to them, as modes of consciousness, in and through ideology). . . . Both insist, however, that ideologies are not simply "in the head," but are material relations . . . which shape social actions, function through concrete institutions and apparatuses, and are materialized through practices.[66]

To echo Barbara Fields, "ideology is a distillate of experience," structured in the everyday.[67] For Stuart Hall, as for Paul Gilroy, "race is the modality in which class is 'lived.'"[68] Thus, even if fluid and hard to pinion, race constructions (physical and symbolic) have real consequences for the city and its inhabitants, in Ponce as it has in the United States, and, although in different guises, undoubtedly in societies all over the world.

Home Exclusions

Most of the Alhambra houses contiguous to Dr. Pila have been abandoned: the intersecting spatial boundaries of race and class have been reinforced by a fortress of house ruins. As race, class, and gender are frozen and rearticulated, ideas and policies of distinction between adjacent neighborhoods both distance and segregate the communities of Ponce.

Pierre Mayol suggests that "belonging to a neighborhood, when it is corroborated by belonging to a specific social milieu, becomes a marker that reinforces the identification process of a specific group."[69] Gates demarcate and enhance distance; they segment identities as they "mark" the "unmarked."[70] They position and remind specific bodies of their rightful place, delineating the limits of their identity and the neighborhood that embodies those limits and discouraging dislocations of time and place. A white Alhambra woman described the misplaced poor who were parading at night down her ungated affluent street outside her gated house:

> Pasan tecatos y drogadictos por ahí todo el tiempo mirando a uno. . . . Y tú los ves pasar y tú te quedas en el balcón y ellos te miran. Pasa una cantidad que tú no te puedes imaginar, locos, borrachos y drogadictos. Yo estoy con mi compadre hablando en el balcón con la luz apagada y empiezan a pasar y decimos, "¿Pero qué es esto?" De doce a una de la mañana, se ve una de personajes que tú jamás los ves. Muchos de los deambulantes pasan por esta triste calle, todos los que piden chavos en las luces."

> (Crackheads and addicts go by every minute, all the time looking at us. . . . You see them pass by, and you stay in your porch, and they look at you. There are so many going by, you can't even imagine, demented, drunks, addicts. And I am with my *compadre* talking in the porch, with the light off and they start to go by and we ask "What is this?" From midnight to one in the morning, you see a series of characters that you never see. Many of the homeless pass on this sad street, all the ones that beg for money at the traffic lights.)[71]

The gates have inverted the New Deal promise of adjacent neighborhoods of rich and poor with a consequent integration of class (and race) in the neighborhood. The opposite has occurred. Gated homes and neighborhoods have codified otherwise shifting dimensions of race, class, and gender, suggesting them as static. Henri Lefebvre believes "every shape in space, every spatial plane, constitutes a mirror and produces a mirage effect; . . . an ever-renewed to-and-fro of reciprocal reflection, an interplay of shifting colours, lights and forms. A mere change of position, or a change in a place's surroundings, is enough to precipitate an object's passage into the light: what was covert becomes overt, what was cryptic becomes limpidly clear."[72]

The Gated Library

> If you saw the old library, situated as it was, in a big, old wooden
> building painted a shade of yellow that is beautiful to people like
> me, with its wide veranda, its big, always open windows, its rows
> and rows of shelves filled with books, its beautiful wooden tables
> and chairs for sitting and reading, if you could hear the sound of
> its quietness (for the quiet in this library was a sound in itself), the
> smell of the sea . . . the heat of the sun . . . the beauty of us sitting
> there like communicants at an altar, taking in, again and again, the
> fairy tale.
>
> —Jamaica Kincaid, *A Small Place*

In 2010, Ponce's municipal library—Biblioteca Municipal e Infantil Mariana
Suárez de Longo y Archivo Histórico de Ponce—was finally finished. I was
visiting family that January, and I was excited to find a place where I could
write, with free wi-fi and silence. My mother, my aunt, and my cousin had
been searching for alternatives for days: the McDonald's in Santa Isabel, the
Burger King in Avenida Las Americas, the public plaza in the center of town,
but none were places for contemplation. I could see gates everywhere. But the
library offered peace. The Gándara residents had complained, years ago, that
the abandoned courthouse building in the lot where the library now stands
was ugly and dangerous, a shooting clinic: "un pasto, [con] basura y el residencial está al ladito. La gente pasa por ahí y dicen 'qué feo es eso al lado del
pasto'" (a field, full of trash right next to the project. People go by there and
say "that project next to the field is horrible").[1]

By August 2007, the courthouse had been razed and the new library had been built but only gradually opened to the public.[2] It reminded me in appearance of colonial government houses: it was massive, immaculate, painted in pale peach with complementary brick and white trimmings. A staff person described it to me: *"preciosa, hermosa"* (precious, beautiful). Giant square pillars and manicured green grounds fronted a symmetrical architecture. At the center of two horizontal extensions, a peaked triangular ceiling provided a stately quality. A manicured green lawn, modest flowerbeds, and bushy palm and tropical trees framed the front, with a footpath, bordered by lawn lighting, curving to the door.

But then I saw fences around the front perimeter, a seemingly endless row of green iron poles linked by spaced ten-foot-high cement pillars protecting the lawn. There is a gate at the front, locked when the library is closed (and sometimes, even, when it is open). An about ten-foot cement wall (also peach) with complementary square pillars, separates the public housing of Gándara from the access road to the library's drop-off rotunda and parking lot. The road at the side of the grounds is interrupted by a sidewalk with green iron bars on one side and the trees and cement wall of Gándara on the other side. From outside to inside, navigation is intricate. From the back drop-off rotunda, the pedestrian entry is hidden by a tower. Inside, right and left walkways lead around the periphery of a square garden—a secret garden—that is three steps down, sunken in the middle of an open pillared terracotta-tiled hallway, adorned with planters. (A library staff person told me the garden had recently been used by the French Alliance for a cocktail reception.) Green shutter doors off the open hallway lead to three air-conditioned library halls, with framed glass windows. To the north, a majestic triple-arched entryway faces the street that leads to Ponce's city center. On each side of the entryway, brown and gold plaques credit the mayor, government officials, architects and builders, and they recognize Mariana Suárez de Longo, for whom the library is named, as the first female Superintendent of Schools in Puerto Rico. To the west of the garden is a hall intended for the municipal archives, not yet transferred from the city center; in early 2010 it was a tax orientation center. To the south is a small Exposition Hall, sometimes used for student art exhibits or for book presentations. The director said that any who request it may use it. Behind the hall is a colorful but small *rincón de lectura* (reading corner) for young children and a small hall for older children. To the east is a two-story hall, a "traditional library," with stacks of reference books, tables and chairs, and computer stations. It is there where I wrote, entering under an electronic security arch. A new security system with video cameras and monitors was to be installed, paid for by a large federal grant put aside for security, books, and data. Three or four guards on relay shifts provide round-the-clock watch; they used to walk around the grounds but now the guards are locked, by the new system, in a room of monitors. Security cameras are posted in corners.

No one can take books out of the library yet. In order for the library to become a lending library, a staffer explained, it needs *políticas que rijan esos servicios* (policies to guide those services). Visitors who read books or write or can undertake research must hand over an identification card when they enter—typically a driver's license—and sign a log, recording time of entrance and departure. One morning, after strolling around the garden taking photographs, I sat in the "traditional library" area. I had been asked for more information than usual, to give my ID and sign in on the log, as usual, but also to write my name, address, and phone number on a separate form, needed, so I was told, in case I left my ID behind or needed to use the public computers. I began to think the multiple eyes of persons and cameras had been watching me. The library's architecture suddenly seemed like a panopticon, every movement monitored, and, like, a panopticon discipline, it enforced via its many "tiny theatres."[3]

On the days I wrote in the library, a few others were there, a middle-aged woman and a middle-aged man writing on their laptops, and other adults, mostly men, came in to use the computer stations. Once, four college-aged youth sat and chatted a bit. A middle-aged man called out "*¡Silencio!*" A staff person had told me that she had been instructed to devise strategies to "educate" users on the proper use of a library:

> Cuando se percató de que había internet, era más uso social que académico. . . . Vienen a socializar y chatear y no estudiar . . . un centro social de adolescentes, desordenando, parejas por ahí, hay que sacarlos de las escaleras y esquinas. . . . Se dieron dinámicas fuertes . . . viendo pornografía en computadoras, fotos en el recycle bin, páginas de video pornográfico.

> (When people became aware that we had Internet, the use was more social than academic. . . . They would come to socialize and chat, rather than to study . . . a social place for adolescents, scrambling, couples around, we had to take them out of the stairwell and corners. . . . We had many confrontations . . . looking at pornography in the computers, pictures in the recycle bin, pornographic web pages.)

New security tactics, a filtering software for web pages, staff vigilance, and enforcement of regulations are helping the library meet its objective.

The library website lists rules of comportment, and the rules are also posted at the entrance on yellow, peach, and black illustrated sheets of construction paper. The text in English and in Spanish says, "Gathering and chit-chatting inside the library is forbidden. Please use a low tone of voice while using the facilities"; "Must present photo identification and/or water or electricity bill to open up a [computer] account and make book loans"; "Backpack, pocketbooks, and bags will be left in the Hall of Ponce and Puerto Rico. Laptop bags will be checked on entry and exit"; "People with shirts, blouses sleeveless, strapless, halter, necklines, mini skirts or shorts or other attire not appropriate for the facilities is not allowed on the premises"; and "If the user does not meet all of the above he/she may be withdrawn from the facilities, to keep the order and to safeguard the faithful implementation of standards."

I wondered how many Gándara and Dr. Pila public housing residents, or Alhambra and Extensión Alhambra private community residents for that matter, were using the splendid new library. I wondered if it was really a common civic space, a site of integration. The director was capable and eloquent, brown-skinned, not a member of the elite and with an idealistic philosophy: "Se recibe desde los más educados, de alto recurso, hasta los más humildes, sencillos, personas de poca escolaridad" (We receive everyone, from the more educated and high-income people to the more humble, simple, less educated people). She spoke proudly of the library's outreach to public schools and to public housing communities—librarians bring information about the library and conduct storytimes. Staffers visit their public schools and erect bike racks at the library for those without cars. People from these communities, she explained, "vienen con hermanitos" (come with young siblings) or "vienen en bicicletas" (come on bikes). Distinctions between poor and rich emerge in unexpected ways; according to the director, one difficulty in opening the library to all is "cuestión de vestimenta" (a clothing issue). "Por no limitar a personas de bajo recursos" (In order not to limit people of low-income), the library set up a clothing bank with jackets and sweaters, because "personas de bajo recurso vienen esportcita, enseñando las boobies" (people of low income come very underdressed, showing their boobs). "No cerramos puertas, sino que las educamos a vestirse más tapaditas" (We don't close doors, but educate patrons to dress more conservatively).

Doors are not always unlocked during open hours (8:00 AM to 8:00 PM on weekdays, and 9:00 AM to 5:00 PM on weekends, with a more limited itinerary during the summer), and the fences, gates, the big cement wall between the library and Gándara, the security mechanism, and the regulations limit access physically and psychologically. The fences, I noticed, made it hard to navigate the grounds. Regulations demanded having an ID card and a purpose, a clear function to perform. There were no areas to sit in on the grounds: the lawn was inaccessible as a loitering-proof, anticommunity design.[4] Once, trying to exit the grounds myself through the path to the front gate, I found barriers upon barriers and had to turn around. The library is cleverly designed to be approached by car, from the back, but many in Gándara and Dr. Pila have no cars. The front façade and pedestrian entries are not easily accessed by pedestrians; instead, the entrances are often closed and no outside signage directs a visitor to approach the library by a different route. This public space, in effect, identifies and sorts out rich from poor, with physical boundaries and symbolic ones.

The library, a public service, an allegorical opening to the world of books and to the mind, has been walled off, in a sense, to be used in limited and predetermined ways and negotiated in intricate ways. It symbolizes the good society Ponce and Puerto Rico have become, a society divided by class and race, defeating the purpose and richness of diverse urban life a city is intended to provide.

The Gated City

Gates continue to be erected in Puerto Rico. They are unavoidable. And although some controlled access infrastructures in public housing have fallen into disrepair, the fences of Mano Dura, as those of the elite, remain and recall important social divisions.[5] In 2011, as crime once again emerged as a national emergency, fortresses are being expanded and amplified. To move about in Puerto Rico, a society whose people live in secluded worlds, and visit the library is to confront a landscape of gates that affects the aesthetics and feel of the city and its power arrangements.

The city has been considered to be a place where heterogeneous individuals come naturally into contact, in neighborhoods, parks, workplaces, transportation systems, shops, libraries, and streets.[6] Lewis Mumford wrote that the city "begins as a meeting place to which people periodically return . . . this ability to attract non-residents to it for intercourse . . . remains one of the essential criteria of the city, a witness to its inherent dynamism, as opposed to the more fixed and indrawn form of the village, hostile to the outsider."[7] But in Ponce, Puerto Rico, as many cities in the world, outsiders are no longer welcome and interactions are carefully choreographed, limited to those who are known well.

Early urban sociologists, like Louis Wirth and Robert Park, proposed that secondary nonfamilial relationships would predominate over primary family relationships in a city, with competition and control replacing kinship. In the gated city, a posturban society has set up formal physical structures of social control that increasingly segment space and life, reducing so-called presumed secondary contacts and preserving presumed primary ones. Neighbors no longer encounter the street and seldom each other; homes and private spaces have become the locus of social life, and the private unit of the family has, again, become the central unit of society, eroding the spontaneous contact the urban lifestyle promised.

In this posturban society, exclusionary trends of competitive individualism and the quest for sameness in the name of community has taken over the city.[8] David Sibley writes that home, locality, and nation all shape social space and influence geopolitical relationships.[9] Exclusion, in turn, is elaborated across these spaces, as moral boundaries are spatialized and imprinted in the urban form. The city of inclusion has been taken over by, to use Giorgio Agamben's terms, the "camp" of exclusion where "city and house became indistinguishable."[10] Puerto Rico's community gates represent urban exclusion—by class, race, and gender.[11] Residents of private and the public neighborhoods increasingly inhabit different social universes and, without relations with each other, suspicion and fear, not urban creativity and contact, predominate.

Puerto Rico's twentieth-century policy push for housing was intended to provide a home for individuals and families, but also for communities in interrelationships. Housing, and particularly public housing, was meant to equalize, to fulfill basic human rights of shelter and protection from the elements, not to segregate and denote social status.[12] The original social experiment of the New Deal was meant to build public housing and place public and private homes side by side; however, this plan has failed to advance social integration. The gated home and community have formalized not integration but segregation and separation.

Gated homes have made concrete divisions that discourage contact across social boundaries. In this posturban world, the walls of social distinction are no longer "invisible."[13] Yet the exclusions are rarely, if ever, named, even as they are emphatically structured in practice and form. By encoding exclusion, the city's built environment actively structures social imaginaries. Physically visible but symbolically encoded boundaries become more formal; race and class inequality are disguised by legitimate concerns of "security," "community," and "rights." In the modern posturban city, where distance and exclusivity are at a premium, built structures—homes, gates, libraries—are complicit in establishing private interests as central and public interests as peripheral.

Integration, this posturban city suggests, requires extraordinary efforts; environments and neighborhoods at the heart of the idea of "community" bring people together as they reaffix social divisions. Gordon Allport and others have suggested that contact can disrupt the stereotypes that fuel prejudice and racism.[14] In the United States, efforts to integrate public housing residents in mixed-income developments still result in internal balkanizations mirroring sociopolitical cleavages and inequities of the broader society.[15] To be brown and live in these communities is to be read as poor; to be white in these communities is to be read as paying market value.[16]

What is true is that cities, in the way they are built and the policies that drive them, pave the way for inequality. As Sharon Zukin reminds us, "Occupation, segregation and exclusion on every level are conceptualized in streets and neighborhoods, types of buildings, individual buildings and even parts of buildings. They are institutionalized in zoning laws, architecture and conventions of use. Visual artifacts of material culture and political economy thus reinforce—or comment on—social structure. By making social rules legible, they re-present the city."[17] Neoliberal legislation sanctioning privatization and gated communities, and validating an unequal, capitalist market organization of housing, land-use planning, and urbanization, violates the common democratic social contract.[18] Much of the creation, construction, and maintenance of the urban form is under the purview and control of government bodies: planning boards, urban development programs, development efforts, housing programs, and zoning laws. As the sociologists John Logan and Harvey Molotch contend, government matters.[19] The built environment, housing in particular, does not have to reflect and perpetuate the inequities exhibited in other social relationships; it has the potential to be a democratizing agent.[20]

The optimism that enveloped the New Deal, the construction of public housing, and the promise of industrial development in Puerto Rico were starting to evaporate in the late 1960s. The fear and disenchantment today have been cemented into gates, fences, and walls.[21] A resident of Dr. Pila

Figure 17. A security device in the library. Photo by author.

Figure 18. The closed gates of the Ponce library. Photo by author.

↓ No se permiten personas con blusas de manguillos, strapless, holter, escotes, faldas o pantalones cortos o cualquier otra vestimenta no apropiada para las facilidades.

↓ People with shirts, blouses sleeveless, strapless, halter, necklines, mini skirts or shorts or other attire not appropriate for the facilities is not allowed on the premises.

Figure 19. The dress code for the library. Photo by author.

suggested to me that the municipality should arrange social activities that would bring the private and public housing communities together. In an era where people "bowl alone,"[22] communities of interest are getting narrower, leisure is exclusive, and the civic pact bows down to neoliberal processes of privatization and the prioritization of a market logic, the resident's idea seems naïve and simplistic. But this resident understands the very central role of government, of policy, of social programs, to effect a communal bond on the one hand or to drive inequality on the other. In Ponce, as throughout Puerto Rico, the original high hopes for trouble-free cities on the island and for integration have not come to pass. Or, perhaps, not yet.

Methodology

People like me cannot really think in abstractions, people like me cannot be objective, we make everything so personal. You will forget your part in the whole setup.

—Jamaica Kincaid, *A Small Place*

When I began *Locked In, Locked Out* I was already an involved observer. Objectivity is highly valued in science's gathering and production of knowledge, but, by the traditional definition, I was never, have never been, objective. By my own understanding of objectivity, the unobstructed, honest, clear understanding of research, I was and am subjective. This book and the research on which it is based are very much about me; it is shaped by me as all books are by their authors, but it is also reflective of me, therefore, by the traditional definition, subjective, understood to be clouding the vision, obscuring the truth. It is my belief that the relevance of this study to me has added dimension, not reduced it.

In graduate school at Michigan, I never contemplated what dissertation project I would pursue. I was not disinterested; rather, it was so obvious that I didn't need to contemplate. There was no "aha" moment, just a self-understanding that I would study race and space. By the time I returned to Puerto Rico, with my research hat on, I wanted to investigate the policies I had heard a lot about and secretly (well, maybe not so secretly) despised—Mano Dura, the raiding and gating of public housing for the poor. I disliked the policies because I considered them racist; they marked public housing communities as dangerous because they were populated by poor people, some of whom had committed crimes. I hadn't lived there but I had friends—black, of limited economic means—who had and they were not dangerous; public policy said otherwise.

I tried, first thing, to get in touch with officials of the Department of Housing and Urban Development (HUD) in Puerto Rico. One of my friends from graduate school who worked at the HUD graciously introduced me to them. In two interviews, I learned a lot about Mano Dura as seen through the HUD's eyes. Then I proceeded to collect the crime data that had been cited as justifying the police raids and the gates that followed; I (and later with a friend I recruited) copied that data from book logs in the statistics office of the central Puerto Rican police headquarters in Río Piedras. At my computer, in an office where others were decorating a Christmas tree, I sifted through dusty books of handwritten spreadsheets. As I began to talk to people, and to try to locate and access more data, innumerable excuses were offered for delay—lunch, having to "do something," talking on the phone or chatting with coworkers. I spent a lot of time waiting. At the Puerto Rico Public Housing Authority (PRPHA), I shuttled between floors and visited multiple desks before gaining a brief appointment with Carlos Vivoni, the director of the PRPHA. He provided a list of public housing projects that Mano Dura had "rescued." Again, I did much waiting. Between trips from 2000 to 2004, I met with other representatives from the HUD and PRPHA, the Puerto Rico Planning Board, and public housing management staff, and I conducted semistructured open-ended interviews to try to understand the policies and their intended consequences. I met with administrators of the specific public housing projects I had chosen for the study and with homeowners' association representatives to learn the history of the residential developments, the changes of program or design, and the rationale. The following list shows the guiding questions that were employed in my interviews with HUD and PRPHA officials, public housing site managers, and homeowner association representatives.

A. Homeowner association representatives
When was this residential development built?
Do you have pictures or plans of the development throughout the
    years?
How many units are in the development?
Do you have statistics on average family housing size, average in-
    come, and other characteristics?
How would you characterize the community in terms of people who
    live here?
When was the controlled access built?

Why was it gated?

How was the process of gating done? Who participated? How was
the decision made?

Who decided how and where the gate would be built?

Who was the architect/builder of the controlled access?

How is the infrastructure of the gate financially maintained?

B. HUD officials and PRPHA officials

Why was Mano Dura conceived?

What was the political backdrop?

What did the policies entail?

What were the interventions?

What were the expected outcomes?

C. Public housing managers

When was this residential development built?

Do you have pictures or plans of the development throughout the
years?

How many units are in the development?

Do you have statistics on average family housing size, average income, and other characteristics?

How would you characterize the community in terms of people who
live here?

When was the controlled access built?

Has the gating been effective?

Do you see a difference in management between before and after
gating?

Has the gating been infrastructurally maintained?

Have you had problems in providing maintenance to the gating?
(Are there people using alternative entryways?)

I consulted newspapers and legal documents to establish a detailed chro-
nology of events, and I reviewed the web archive of a popular Puerto Rican
newspaper, *El Nuevo Día*, and documents at the University of Puerto Rico
Libraries, the Municipal Archives in Ponce, the Luis Muñoz Marín Foundation, and the Puerto Rico Planning Board. Then I began my research at the
housing sites.

Research Design

My research design for the fieldwork was a two-way comparison of four residential sites in Ponce, along two axes: (1) public or private housing, and (2) gated or not gated. I decided to study (1) "CG," gated public housing; (2) "CN," not gated public housing; (3) "UG," gated private residential areas; and (4) "UN," not gated private residential areas.

The sites included not only public housing sites for which the city policy was intended, but also adjacent residential neighborhoods. I selected among public housing and adjacent residential sites: Residencial Doctor Manuel de la Pila (CG), Residencial José N. Gándara (CN), Urbanización Alhambra (UN), and Urbanización Extensión Alhambra (UG). Dr. Pila, a public housing project, had been built right next to La Alhambra, one of the most affluent urban neighborhoods in Ponce. Under the Mano Dura policies, Dr. Pila had been "rescued," and gated, during the early 1990s because it had been a place of extreme criminal activity. The affluent neighborhood La Alhambra had not been permitted to gate itself, though it tried hard. However, a middle/upper-middle-class residential development (*urbanización*), Extensión Alhambra, next to Alhambra, had been successful in gating itself. Across the street from Extensión Alhambra was another public housing site, Gándara, which was not gated because of its reputation as a "safe" public housing site.

Table 4. Research Site by Type

		Axis 2	
		Gated "G"	Not Gated "N"
	Public Housing (Caserío) "C"	Dr. Pila [CG]	Gándara [CN]
Axis 1	Private Housing (Urbanización) "U"	Ext. Alhambra [UG]	Alhambra [UN]

Gating public housing sites was a central component of the Mano Dura policies, from the 1990s onward. Private residential neighborhoods in Puerto Rico were not affected by Mano Dura. But more and more private residential developments, originally built as open neighborhoods, retrofitted themselves with gates. The dynamics of the gating for private and public housing sites differ—one was a state-sponsored policy; the other was the neighborhood's choice. Studying the impact of gating on public housing and on private housing provided an important comparison, especially because the gating of private neighborhoods occurred contemporaneously with Mano Dura interventions in public housing. If Mano Dura was meant to reduce crime by gating, then one may consider that the effect on private communities in the process of gating or already gated would differ from the impact to communities that were not gated.

Sample

My field research included focus groups, individual interviews, and participant observations. I conducted twenty focus groups across the four residential sites. (See Table 5 for a description of the sample in each community.)

Table 5. Description of Sample

	Dr. Pila	Gándara	Alhambra	Ext. Alhambra	Total
Number of focus groups	7	4	4	5	20
Number of household respondents	32	18	8	7	65
Number of females	28	16	8	6	58
Mean age	37	45	47	59	
Mean number of years in community	21	20	22	22	
Mean household size	3.6	<3	>3	2.3	
Mean yearly income	$3,700	n/a	$80,000	$54,000	

Interviews at different sites required different approaches. Specifically, issues of private versus public, violence and crime, levels of community monitoring, management agencies and their practices, forms of gating, size of the community, and points of entry affected the sample selections.

Dedicated fieldwork in Ponce was conducted between the fall of 2003 and early 2004. Because Ponce is my hometown, I was able to move around more readily than if I had been a stranger. I approached the two public housing communities via a list of private management agencies, to which the PRPHA had subcontracted management for the sites. I called the management company for each public housing site to find an appropriate means of entry. I was fortunate in being able to study two public housing sites being managed by the same company—Westbrook Management.[1] In the private housing communities, I relied primarily on individuals who knew residents there, primarily using snowball sampling; then, residents referred me to others they knew.

It turned out that I knew the management director of Westbrook from my days as an athlete. I set up a meeting, and he referred me, in turn, to the director of resident services, who helped me organize meetings with the Resident Councils, the management directors, and the social workers for both Dr. Pila and Gándara. When I met with representatives from each site to present my research project, everyone, and especially the members of the Resident Council, suggested how I might publicize my project and what methods would be possible and effective. Of particular concern for me and my research, in Dr. Pila, were a recent murder and nightly shootouts—as one resident described it the area was *"El Viejo Oeste"* (the Wild West)—and related safety issues. It became clear that words such as *investigación* (investigation or research), could not be used in any flyers, consent forms, documents, or oral descriptions of my research. Instead I described my work as *"un estudio"* (a study) or *"haciendo un perfil de la comunidad"* (building a profile of the community): both of these phrases would help keep me safe and avoid potentially dangerous misunderstandings of my presence and my role.[2]

In Dr. Pila, I conducted seven focus-group interviews, with a total of thirty-two respondents (of these, only four were males). The average age was thirty-seven: the youngest person was nineteen; the oldest, sixty-seven. The average time a resident had lived in the community was about twenty-one years; the most recent had arrived two years before the interview; one interviewee had lived there all of her forty-five years. The average household size was 3.6 persons: the smallest household had one, and the largest had seven family members. Many families relied on welfare benefits, including food stamps and the Programa de Asistencia Nutricional (PAN, or Food Stamps) program, and some residents received Social Security. Incomes averaged about $3,700 a year.

It became obvious that my research would require sanctioning by the Resident Councils and would be controlled and managed primarily by them. The council representatives and the management company were my research allies and promoters, although sometimes they were uncollaborative with each other. After dissuading me from knocking on doors, and a few revisions of my recruitment flyer, the management staff agreed to pass out my flyer to those whom they thought would be cooperative and "safe" to interview.[3] Each person would receive a modest stipend in order to compensate for his or her time. The management staff would do its part by spreading the word and telling those to whom they provided service about the study. The flyer, approved by the Resident Council representatives, would be posted in the community center building, which was shared by the management offices.[4] Both council representatives and management staff referred persons to me. A job fair, at Dr. Pila, which I attended, was a successful recruitment site. Also, residents who participated in the focus groups referred others to me. This recruitment effort necessarily biased the sample of respondents who participated in the focus groups for Dr. Pila. Overall, it is accurate to say that my view of the community came from those most engaged in the community and not from those who were seen as pariahs, or persons new to the community, or those sufficiently detached from the community network as to avoid the community center's postings and activities.

In Gándara, recruitment was more systematic. Because the Gándara community is small and because the community was not experiencing tension, I could send out flyers to each household. Flyers were distributed, along with other informational materials, in weekly management mailings. The flyers informed all households that I would be present at the community center to sign up individuals for focus groups. At the suggestion of the management staff and a resident, the modest financial incentive I proposed was not mentioned in the flyer.

Reunión para Orientación
Estudio de la Comunidad

Residentes de Gándara:

Los invitamos a una reunión informativa para orientarte sobre un estudio que se está haciendo de la comunidad

por Zaire Dinzey, una estudiante de doctorado de la Universidad de Michigan, para su tesis doctoral.

La reunión será el
Día: este VIERNES, 24 de octubre
Hora: 2:00 PM
Lugar: Centro Comunal Gándara

Si no puede ir a la reunión informativa, por favor comuníquese con Zaire Dinzey directamente al [deleted phone number] para hacer una cita para participar en el estudio.

Gracias por su cooperación.
Zaire Dinzey

**(Orientation Meeting
Community Study**

Gándara Residents:

We invite you to an information meeting that will orient residents on an ongoing study of the community, being done by Zaire Dinzey, a doctoral student of the University of Michigan, for her dissertation.

The meeting will be on:
**Date: this Friday, October 24
Time: 2:00 PM
Place: Gándara Community Center**

If you can't attend the information meeting, please get in touch with Zaire Dinzey directly at [deleted phone number] to set up a time to participate in the study.

Thanks for your cooperation.
Zaire Dinzey)

Residents got in touch with me, and I signed some up. They recruited other residents. I conducted four focus groups in Gándara, from eighteen households. As with those from Dr. Pila, Gándara participants undoubtedly represented those who were most engaged in the community. Again, most were female; only two males participated. Ages ranged from twenty-six to sixty-nine, with an average of forty-five. Most had lived in the community for long periods of time: the longest reported living there for the last fifty-four years, probably close to the time the project had opened. A few families had lived in the community a year or less. The average time spent in the community was twenty years. Residents reported that few vacancies occurred; when an apartment was vacated, a new family soon moved in. The small size of the apartments available often led to bigger families living in smaller apartments. The average household size was just under three household members; some households had only one member and the largest had five. Many households relied on welfare, either from the PAN program; a number had monthly Social Security benefits.[5]

Puerto Rican middle-class and upper-class communities are particularly hard to access for research purposes, and in the private communities, gaining entry was more challenging. Physically and socially, such communities have become less and less accessible. Few persons ever knock at someone's door. Physical contact has become less spontaneous and is likely to lead to questions, especially in communities that have been unable to get permission to gate themselves. Architecture, too, plays a significant part in preventing a spontaneous response; guards at gates demand that you know somebody in the neighborhood in order to obtain entry or that you have an already approved purpose for visiting. Also, the fear of crime prevents residents from answering doors to unrecognized visitors. I, therefore, avoided a door-to-door strategy for recruiting participants in the study; instead, I relied on acquaintances and on their referrals and other residents for focus-group interviews and, at times, for individual interviews as well.

In Alhambra, I conducted four interviews with eight households. All who took part were female, except in one case where a man and a woman participated (however, the woman provided the household information). Those who took part tended to be middle-aged, with an average age of forty-seven. There was greater variation in the length of time in households than in the other communities. Some had lived there many years and several were recent arrivals; the average length of stay was close to twenty-two years. The household size was between two and six, and the average was just over three persons. The average household income for Alhambra was just under $80,000.

In Extensión Alhambra, I conducted five interviews with a total of seven households. One man participated in the interviews, and the rest were women; the average age was close to fifty-nine. Most had lived there for long periods of time, averaging twenty-two years across the seven households. The shortest time of residency reported was five years; the longest, forty years. The average household size was 2.3 persons per household. The yearly income average was $54,000: the highest was more than $95,000; the lowest, $25,000.

Data Collection

Overall, I conducted twenty focus groups, with each ranging from forty-five minutes to two hours. Some other interviews were conducted with individuals who, for various reasons, could not participate in a group interview. The semistructured open-ended interviews, with between one and six participants, focused on residents' impressions of the housing policy, impressions and satisfaction with the physical qualities of their neighborhoods, frequency and quality of contact within and outside the public housing community, residents' impressions of safety and crime, and residents' involvement with community organizations. The English translations of the usual discussion questions follow here.

Focus Group Protocol

Part 1. The neighborhood

1. Please point out the limits of your neighborhood.
   - Streets
   - Landmarks
2. What is your neighborhood called?
3. If you were to describe this neighborhood to people who had never been here, how would you describe it?
   - Who lives in your neighborhood? Race? Ethnicity? Income? Rent vs. own? Household sizes? Families vs. singles?
   - What does your neighborhood look like physically?
4. Do most people that live in this neighborhood stay for a long time or do they move out frequently? Why do you think people stay or move out? What other neighborhoods do people prefer to move out to?
5. What are the major differences or similarities between your neighborhood and other neighborhoods?
6. What are the differences between your neighborhood and the next-door neighborhood [the other neighborhoods being studied] and yours? What are the similarities between them?
7. If you could, would you change anything about the place you live in?
8. If you could, would you change anything about your neighborhood/community? What and why? Ideally, how would you have this neighborhood look (physical changes)?
9. If you could, would you change anything about your next-door neighborhood/community? What and why? Ideally, how would you have that neighborhood look (physical changes)?
10. Do you think your place of residence is attractive?
11. Do you think other neighborhoods around you are attractive?

Part 2. Social interaction

1. What places do you and members of your family frequent?
2. Where are these places located?

3. What routes do you take to get to those places?
4. What type of transportation do you take to get there?
5. Since the [gating/controlled access], did any of these change?
6. Whom do you interact with in your house and in your work, and which families or friends do you visit?
7. In your immediate area, whom do you interact with (which households)? How often? What is the nature of the interaction? How many people do you know? Where do the people you know live?
8. Outside your immediate area, whom do you interact with (which households)? How often? What is the nature of the interaction? How many people do you know? Where do the people you know live?
9. Before 1992, did you ever visit the neighborhoods next door? Why or why not?
10. After 1993, have you visited the neighborhoods next door? Why or why not?

Part 3. Mano Dura and crime

1. Do you consider any parts of your neighborhood/community unsafe? Why, and what areas are those?
2. Do you consider any parts of the next-door neighborhoods/communities unsafe? Why, and what areas are those?
3. Do you think there have been changes in crime levels in the last ten to fifteen years? If so, what do you think caused these changes?
4. How do you feel about controlled access in your neighborhood or in the neighborhoods around you? Do you think it is positive or negative? Why or why not?
5. What did you think of the Mano Dura policies established in the early 1990s?
6. Compared to the late 1980s and early 1990s, do you think your neighborhood is safer? Why?
7. Compared to the late 1980s and early 1990s, do you think the neighborhoods around you are safer?
8. What do you think of the privatization of public housing projects?
9. What do you think of the police role in your and other neighborhoods?
10. What do you think of the recent renovations?
11. What do you think of the community centers/recreational facilities?
12. In your view, what have been the major changes brought about by Mano Dura?

Surveys for Individuals

1. Name?
2. Gender?
3. Age?
4. Race?
5. City and country of birth?
6. How long have you lived in the community?
7. What is the location of your residence in the community?
8. When walking, what street do you use to enter and exit the community?
9. Do you mostly walk or use a car to enter and exit your community?
10. What is your household's size?
11. More or less, what is your household's income?
12. If there is anything that you were unable to express during the interview, or if you have additional comments about this study, please use this space for any additional comments.

The interviews provide rich qualitative information on the quality of residential life, on perceptions of the impact of Mano Dura interventions on their own lives, and on the spatial character of life, in general. Interviews within groups allowed people to build knowledge collectively, representing the goal of my study to see the community as the unit of analysis as socially affected by policies and the changing built environment. All focus-group interviews were tape-recorded with the consent of the participants and were later transcribed.

Everyone in focus groups was provided with a consent form informing them of the purpose of the study and specifying that participation was voluntary and confidential. For the recording of the interview, I asked each resident to come up with a pseudonym. Every resident had a place card with his or her pseudonym, in order for all to use these names in conversation. At first I conducted focus groups by myself, but I later hired a research assistant from Dr. Pila to aid in the setup logistics of a group interview—distributing consent forms, collecting them, keeping a log of the first word stated by each person so that I would be able to follow who spoke every line of the recording. A friend had agreed to serve as a research assistant, but I was unable to hire him because he was a light-skinned man from outside the community; I thought that he might be seen as a police officer, thus contributing to fears from residents that I was part of law enforcement. Serena (a pseudonym), my research assistant from Dr. Pila, accompanied me to focus groups in Dr. Pila and Gándara. Her presence on occasion created uncomfortable situations, especially in Gándara, for some recognized her as a resident of Dr. Pila, and they feared violations of confidentiality. I had, however, trained Serena and thoroughly explained the confidentiality issue to her and others. Serena, a single mother, was a return migrant from the United States, and she was eager to go back. She was responsible and ready and contributed greatly to the data collection effort in this project.

Participant observations made possible a sense of the response of individuals to their spatial milieu. Such observations were necessarily unsystematic and defined by circumstance. In some communities, I was able to walk around (both chaperoned or unchaperoned) to take pictures and observe but most observations occurred in my day-to-day research, such as when I conducted the focus groups and recruited participants. I also drove through the sites for quick observations and, at times, when I deemed it safe, I took notes while parked in my car on the grounds. I reconstructed other notes shortly after a period of observation. My aim was to see how people managed their environment, with whom they related and how. Observation periods served to supplement but also to challenge the narratives that emerge from focus groups and my other methodologies.

Data Coding

In coding the data, I used a grounded theory method, in which I began without a theory and postponed ad hoc impressions; the data itself guided me toward the development of theory. Thus, no codes were predetermined. I used in vivo line-by-line coding, in which all transcripts and notes were to be reviewed along with salient points, issues, words, or phrases restated in the margins. The line restatements were grouped into general coding categories, and I began identifying links as well as emergent and recurring themes in the data and among the thematic codes.

The coding process involved beginning to identify possible causal explanations for themes apparent in the data. It also offered a prime opportunity for me to think about my codes and the intentions of my research, as well as to begin to understand how my research was in dialogue with others' prior research. This constellation of activities paved the way for theorizing and for presenting the results of the study.

Of Ethnography and Limitations of Research

This project was necessarily limited, as much by me and my own interests as by context. I first envisioned it as a mixed-method project, including historical, quantitative, and qualitative techniques. While the quantitative aspect lent a great deal to my knowledge of the policy and its impact and to the story that I tell here, it is the interviews and participant observations from qualitative techniques that are most visible here. But it is important to understand that this story emerges from a mixed-method enterprise rather than from an ethnographic project per se. The difference is that the study's breadth and a comparative epistemological frame were of concern, rather than depth and context, which is true of a pure ethnographic enterprise. This necessarily shapes the story I am able to tell: some details are missing, I didn't have sustained personal contact with many informants, and the time period for the study is narrow. Instead, this project relied on what I refer to as "ethnographic incisions," made in order to compare with historical and quantitative results I was simultaneously collecting. And, although they may appear buried in these pages, the quantitative and historical research centrally shape this story.

Qualitative and quantitative methodologies have been posed as an epistemological pole in social science research. At one end, quantitative methods, following the Scientific Revolution of the 1600s, invoke a positivistic approach to social phenomena (an approach employed by Adam Smith, Darwin, Newton, Descartes, Galileo, and Copernicus) that seeks to parallel the natural science disciplines. This approach is represented by fixed measurements, hypothesis testing, and statistical analyses that privilege what are argued to be objective observational social phenomena. Qualitative methods, on the other hand, are typically represented as flexible, fluid inquiries that allow knowledge to be built from the ground up. With a qualitative methodology, the "actor" and his or her view of the world are as integral to the phenomena as the phenomena—although it is true that you are not always made privy to the actor's exact identity.

Distinctions between quantitative and qualitative methodologies are often based on the positivistic versus inductive epistemological nature of the two methods of inquiry, but they also involve other concerns such as the questions that are best answered by each. For example, some have argued that quantitative methodology is best for answering "what?" and qualitative methodologies allow us to understand "how" social phenomena take place.[6] This understanding of the two methodologies as being mutually exclusive yet complementary has inspired a mixed-method approach that has come to be called *triangulation*. Defined by Norman Denzin, triangulation involves the combination of methodologies, observers, and theoretical perspectives in the study of the same phenomenon.[7] There are different types of triangulation, including "within-method," which includes using different techniques within the same method, or "between-method," which involves applying different methods for one research problem. Whereas "within-method" triangulation involves a concern with consistency and reliability, "between-method" triangulation tests the external validity of research results.[8] In addition, as stated by Todd Jick, triangulation "can also capture a more complete, *holistic*, and contextual portrayal of the units(s) under study,"[9] and this suggests that triangulation achieves desirable results because (1) it leads us to uncover convergence and divergence in our results that give validity to corroborate our findings, or it leads us to unexpected and unplanned findings; and (2) it allows us to be confident in our results; (3) it can lead to creative new ways of capturing a problem; (4) it can help in theory building by highlighting inconsistencies; and (5) it can pave the way for theoretical triangulation that results in a synthesis of theories. Jick suggests that one limitation of triangulation is that it results in inquiries that are hard to replicate.

Like triangulation, this project relies on a multi-method approach employing quantitative, qualitative, and historical methodologies. A portion of my work applies triangulation techniques in the traditional sense, because I compare the results using qualitative versus quantitative approaches; but mainly I attempt to identify proper methodologies to certain lines of inquiry. My concern is less with corroboration of a finding than with gaining a complex understanding of outcomes and how the texture of everyday social life is constituted. I follow Judith Freidenberg's insistence on having research examine "the discrepancies between informants' constructions of social experience and interpretative views of those experiences by others."[10] But a mixed-method approach highlights, or demands that the researcher accepts, that knowledge is always partial and incomplete. The discontinuities and gaps here presented, thus, are likely to be more evident than in projects that follow one path of inquiry.

Practical limitations, for one, are exposed. Once finished with historical and quantitative analyses, I aimed to do comparative case-study research in Ponce and San Juan. In both cities, I planned to walk through four communities, knock on doors, talk to people, and invite them to group interviews. But my plans quickly changed when I began the research in Dr. Pila. What the historical and quantitative aspects of the research failed to forecast were the very real and practical difficulties of being "on the ground." The fear of crime and violence was a massive hurdle, present from day one. On the first afternoon I sat with Dr. Pila's Resident Council, a boulder was thrown through the window of a car parked right by the one I rode in, and residents talked about a "drug war" that forced them indoors before nightfall. When I completed my work in Ponce, emotionally exhausted and feeling lucky for having survived (and with no clear sense of the accuracy of the feeling), I began contacting people to begin my work in San Juan projects, but I found the same deterrence—"there is a drug war." I decided I couldn't do it again. Readjusting plans came to be a permanent part of this project, begging questions of what constitutes thorough research and how practical matters, and the researcher's own identity, are weighted against the pursuit of knowledge and the ontological view of what that pursuit is.

This balancing act necessarily makes this research appear schematic and uneven at times, biased and personal at others. What I've done is to try to take advantage of the multiplicity of different types of data that this research endeavor yielded. If the methodology for this research project had been represented as visual art, it might be a Picasso painting from his Cubist stage. Or it might look like those abstract paintings in which a clear picture starts to emerge, only upon taking a detained, hazy look. The lines are there, but it is only in looking at the lines in their relationship to other lines that the form gains relevancy. This research endeavor, thus, is intentionally, admittedly blemished; it represents an effort to provide comprehensive understandings of a phenomenon by taking samples and dissecting them and, once dissected, gaining a profile without losing awareness of the pieces that constitute the whole. The multiple methodologies I used occur at different scales, from different viewpoints, and with different tools; similar to what Eviatar Zerubavel calls "theoretical sampling."[11] This research study and its methods and results are not just, as Merton suggested, "egocentric" but are revealing of what the, or my, reality was and is.

Notes

Prologue

1. A note on why I use the word *negrita* (a diminutive term for black) is in order. *Negrita*, many have noted, is derogatory and reflects racist efforts to infantilize people of African descent. In contrast, growing up, within the confines of my house, with my family, we used the term to declare an allegiance, to evoke a sense of pride, and to claim power in response to past or present injustices. I remember how we would sit in front of the television cheering for any negrito/a competitor, prioritizing a vague, yet clear, racial typology informed primarily by phenotype over national affiliations. To say that the term worked in that way within our family does not cancel out its racist historical etymology, but it simply reflects how, in the everyday, we had taken control over its meaning.

2. For a wider discussion of the insider/outsider debate, see Maxine Baca Zinn, "Field Research in Minority Communities: Ethical, Methodological, and Political Observations by an Insider," *Social Problems* 27, no. 2 (1979).

3. For what observations are encouraged or hampered by the insider or outsider status, see Robert K. Merton, "Insiders and Outsiders: A Chapter in the Sociology of Knowledge," *American Journal of Sociology* 78, no. 1 (1972). Also see Alford Young, Jr., "Experiences in Ethnographic Interviewing about Race: The Inside and Outside of It," in *Researching Race and Racism*, ed. Martin Bulmer and John Solomos (New York: Routledge, 2004).

4. See Earl Lewis, "To Turn as on a Pivot: Writing African Americans into a History of Overlapping Diasporas," *American Historical Review* 100, no. 3 (June 1995): 765–87.

5. Patricia Hill Collins, "Learning from the Outsider Within: The Sociological Significance of Black Feminist Thought," *Social Problems* 33, no. 6 (1986).

6. On "color-blind racism" and whiteness, see Eduardo Bonilla-Silva, *Racism without Racists: Color-Blind Racism and the Persistence of Racial Inequality* (Lanham, Md.: Rowman and Littlefield, 2006); Charles Gallagher, "Color Blind Privilege: The Social and Political Functions of Erasing the Color Line in Post-Race America" in *Rethinking the Color Line*, ed. Charles A. Gallagher, 3rd ed. (New York: McGraw-Hill, 2009); and Joe Feagin, *White Racism* (New York: Routledge, 2001).

7. See George Lipsitz, *The Possessive Investment in Whiteness: How White People Profit from Identity Politics* (Philadelphia: Temple University Press, 2006).

8. David R. Roediger, *The Wages of Whiteness: Race and the Making of the American Working Class* (New York: Verso, 1991).

9. Isabelo Zenón Cruz, *Narciso descubre su trasero: El negro en la cultura puertorriqueña*, vol. 1 (Puerto Rico: Editorial Furidi, 1974). My translation, referring to the poem "Rutas Perdidas" by Jesus Hernández Ortiz.

10. The relationships between home, self-identity, and community identity have been widely discussed by scholars. See, for example, Lee Rainwater, "Fear and the House as Haven in the Lower Class," *Journal of the American Institute of Planners* 32, no. 1 (1966): 23–31; Gerald Suttles, *The Social Construction of Communities* (Chicago: University of Chicago Press, 1973); Geoffrey Hayward, "Home as an Environmental and Psychological Concept," *Landscape* 20 (1975): 2–9; J. Douglas Porteous, "Home: The Territorial Core," *Geographical Review* 66, no. 4 (October 1976): 383–90; Yi-Fu Tuan, *Space and Place: The Perspective of Experience* (Minneapolis: University of Minnesota Press, 1977); Maria V. Giuliani, "Towards an Analysis of Mental Representations of Attachment to the Home," *Journal of Architectural and Planning Research* 8, no. 2 (1991): 133–46; Doreen B. Massey, "The Conceptualization of Place," in *Place in the World? Places, Cultures and Globalization*, ed. Doreen B. Massey and Pat Jess (Oxford: Oxford University Press, 1995), 87–132; Peter Somerville, "The Social Construction of Home," *Journal of Architectural Planning and Research* 14, no. 3 (1997): 226–45; Peter Saunders and Peter Williams, "The Constitution of the Home: Towards a Research Agenda," *Housing Studies* 3, no. 2 (1998): 81–93; Yi-Fu Tuan, "Community, Society, and the Individual," *Geographical Review* 92, no. 3 (July 2002): 307–18; Lynne C. Manzo, "Beyond House and Haven: Toward a Revisioning of Emotional Relationships with Places," *Journal of Environmental Psychology* 23, no. 1 (March 2003): 47–61; Hazel Easthope, "A Place Called Home," *Housing, Theory and Society* 21, no. 3 (2004): 128–38; Shelley Mallett, "Understanding Home: A Critical Review of the Literature," *Sociological Review* 52, no. 1 (February 2004): 62–89; Claire Cooper Marcus, *House as a Mirror of Self* (Lake Worth, FL: Nicolas-Hays, 2006);

11. See, for example, Dianne Harris, "Little White Houses: Critical Race Theory and the Interpretation of Ordinary Dwellings in the United States, 1945–60," Proceedings from the Warren Center for American Studies Conference on Reinterpreting the History of the Built Environment in North America, August 3, 2005, http://warrencenter.fas.harvard.edu/builtenv/Paper%20PDFs/Harris.pdf (accessed October 20, 2011).

12. For Brazil, see Theresa P. R. Caldeira, *City of Walls: Crime, Segregation, and Citizenship in Sao Paulo* (Berkeley: University of California Press, 2000); Sandra da Costa, Gustavo Forlin, Mateus Godoi Maria, Rafael Lucio da Silva, and Monique Bruna Silva Carmo, "Urban Sprawl and New Forms of Urbanization in Brazil: The Characteristics of Gated Communities in the Valley of the Paraíba River, São Paulo State," presented at the 2011 International RC21 Conference, http://www.rc21.org/conferences/amsterdam2011/edocs/Session%207/7-1-Da-Costa.pdf (accessed May 29, 2012). For South Africa,

see Andy Clarno, "A Tale of Two Walled Cities: Neoliberalization and Enclosure in Johannesburg and Jerusalem," *Political Power and Social Theory* 19 (2008): 159–205; Martin J. Murray, *Taming the Disorderly City: The Spatial Landscape of Johannesburg after Apartheid* (Ithaca, N.Y.: Cornell University Press, 2008); Jacob R. Boersema, "Guilt behind the Gate: White South Africans and the Experience of Gated Living in Post-Apartheid South Africa," presented at the 2011 International RC21 Conference, http://www.rc21.org/conferences/amsterdam2011/edocs2/Session%207/7-1-Boersema.pdf (accessed May 9, 2012); and Manfred Spocter, "Non-metropolitan Residential Gated Developments in the Western Cape Province, South Africa," presented at the 2011 International RC21 Conference, http://www.rc21.org/conferences/amsterdam2011/M_Spocter%20paper.pdf (accessed May 29, 2012).

13. Stuart Hall, *Myths of Caribbean Identity* (Coventry: Walter Rodney Memorial Lecture, Centre for Caribbean Studies, University of Warwick, 1991).

14. Jamaica Kincaid, *A Small Place* (New York: Farrar, Straus and Giroux, 2000).

15. José Luis González, *El país de cuatro pisos y otros ensayos* (Río Piedras: Ediciones Huracán, 1984). Juan Flores finds a similar claim predating José Luis González "by eighty years." See Juan Flores, "Labor of Love, Love of Labor: Work and Culture of the Puerto Rican Diaspora," in *Labor,* ed. Antonio Martorell and Susana Torruella Leval (New York: Hunter College, 2011), 10–16.

Chapter 1

1. For a historical perspective of gating, see Setha Low's *Behind the Gates: Life, Security, and the Pursuit of Happiness in Fortress America* (New York: Routledge, 2003), chapter 1, and also Edward J. Blakely and Mary Gayle Snyder, *Fortress America: Gated Communities in the United States* (Washington, D.C.: Brookings Institution Press, 1999).

2. For research on gated communities worldwide, see Sameer Bagaeen and Ola Uduku, eds., *Gated Communities: Social Sustainability in Contemporary and Historical Gated Developments* (Washington, D.C.: Earthscan, 2010); Blakely and Snyder, *Fortress America*; Theresa P. R. Caldeira, *City of Walls: Crime, Segregation, and Citizenship in Sao Paulo* (Berkeley: University of California Press, 2000); Mike Davis, *City of Quartz* (London: Verso, 1990); Low, *Behind the Gates*; Ivelisse Rivera-Bonilla, "Divided City: The Proliferation of Gated Communities in San Juan" (PhD diss., University of California, Santa Cruz 2003); Kevin Romig, "The Upper Sonoran Lifestyle: Gated Communities in Scottsdale, Arizona," *City and Community* 4, no. 1 (2005): 67–86; Rowland Atkinson and Sarah Blandy, *Gated Communities: International Perspectives* (New York: Routledge, 2006); Georjeanna Wilson-Doenges, "An Exploration of Sense of Community and Fear of Crime in Gated Communities," *Environment and Behavior* 32, no. 5 (2000): 597–611. The majority of these studies focus on the rise of this physical form as an intervention of "fear," constructed by privileged residential clusters in the quest for security or a rationalized sense of security from crime, from the fear of crime, from declining property values, or in the name of privilege and prestige.

3. See João Costa Vargas, "When a Favela Dared to Become a Gated Condominium:

The Politics of Race and Urban Space in Rio de Janeiro," *Latin American Perspectives* 33, no. 4 (July 2006): 49–81; Andrew James Clarno, "The Empire's New Walls: Sovereignty, Neo-liberalism, and the Production of Space in Post-Apartheid South Africa and Post-Oslo Palestine/Israel" (PhD diss., University of Michigan, 2009); and Mike Davis, *Planet of Slums* (New York: Verso, 2006).

4. Lewis Mumford, *The City in History* (New York: Harcourt, 1961), 65.

5. Ibid., 65–66.

6. Ibid., 66, 358.

7. Ibid., 330.

8. "Royal Ordinances for the Laying Out of New Cities, Towns or Villages," Archivo Nacional, Madrid, Ms. 3017 Bulas y Cedulas para el Gobierno de las Indias, July 3, 1573, trans. Zelia Nuttall, *Hispanic American Review* 5 (November 1921): 249–54, in *The Urban Ambience: A Study of San Juan, Puerto Rico*, ed. T. Caplow, S. Stryker, and S. Wallace (Totowa, N.J.: Bedminster Press, 1964).

9. Arturo Morales Carrión, *Puerto Rico: A Political and Cultural History* (New York: W. W. Norton, 1983), 12.

10. Ibid., 14.

11. Ibid., 23.

12. "Royal Ordinances for the Laying Out of New Cities, Towns or Villages," 28.

13. Ibid.

14. Mumford, *City in History*, 66.

15. "Royal Ordinances for the Laying Out of New Cities, Towns or Villages," 29.

16. The phrase "motley laboring class" is used by Kelvin A. Santiago-Valles, " 'Forcing Them to Work and Punishing Whoever Resisted': Servile Labor and Penal Servitude under Colonialism in Nineteenth-Century Puerto Rico," in *The Birth of the Penitentiary in Latin America*, ed. Ricardo D. Salvatore and Carlos Aguirre (Austin: University of Texas Press, 1993), 134.

17. Ibid., 139.

18. Michel Foucault, *Discipline and Punish: The Birth of the Prison* (New York: Vintage, 1995), 200.

19. Ibid.

20. Santiago-Valles, " 'Forcing Them to Work," 140.

21. Ibid., 141–43.

22. Ibid., 145.

23. Ibid., 147.

24. Teresita Martínez-Vergne, *Shaping the Discourse on Space: Charity and Its Wards in Nineteenth-Century San Juan, Puerto Rico* (Austin: University of Texas Press, 1999), 19–20.

25. Ibid., 22.

26. Ibid., 25.

27. Ibid., 24.

28. Ibid., 25.

29. John Michael Vlach notes that as cities became more crowded in the antebellum South, many slave owners allowed their slaves to live outside the home. Many slaves ended up living at the fringes of the city and not the core. See Vlach, "'Without Recourse to Owners': The Architecture of Urban Slavery in the Antebellum South," *Perspectives in Vernacular Architecture: Shaping Communities* 6 (1997): 150–160.

30. Marisa Fuentes, "Buried Landscapes: Black Women, Sex, Confinement and Death in Colonial Bridgetown, Barbados and Charleston, South Carolina" (PhD diss., University of California, Berkeley, 2007).

31. Foucault, *Discipline and Punish*, 108.

32. Edgardo Rodríguez Juliá, *Cortijo's Wake/El Entierro de Cortijo*, trans. Juan Flores (Durham: Duke University Press, 2004), 20.

33. Ibid.

34. For a summary of the crime rates in Puerto Rico between the 1940s and 1990s, see Humberto García Muñiz and Jorge Rodríguez Beruff, eds., *Fronteras en conflicto: Guerra contra las drogas militarización y democracia en El Caribe, Puerto Rico y Vieques* (San Juan: Red Caribeña de Geopolítica, Seguridad Regional y Relaciones Internacionales, 1999), 53–57. Between 1950 and 1970 Type I offenses rose by 222 percent and personal violence crimes rose by 484 percent. By 1994, Interpol reported that the murder rate per 100,000 inhabitants in Puerto Rico (26.89) was three times higher than in the United States (9), and higher than in Nicaragua (25.57) and in Venezuela (22.14). Between 1987 and 1994, murders almost doubled in Puerto Rico, numbering 509 in 1987, 865 in 1992, and 995 in 1994. Rodríguez Beruff (in *Fronteras en conflicto*) reports that a study by Dora Névarez (from 1996) reported that 1992 resulted in the highest levels of Type 1 offenses in the history of Puerto Rico, with 3,600 incidents per 100,000 inhabitants, seven times and thirteen times the crime incidence of 1950 and 1940, respectively. The director of the Drug Enforcement Administration (DEA) reported in 1997 that the number of homicides in Puerto Rico was 992 in 1984, 864 in 1995, and 868 in 1996, compared to New York City, where the homicide rate fell 50 percent to about 1,000 between 1984 and 1996. The DEA director also reported that Puerto Rico led the nation in carjacking incidents, with more than 8,000 armed carjackings between 1993 and 1997.

35. Ibid.

36. Ibid., 56. My translation.

37. Caldeira, *City of Walls*.

38. Interview, February 5, 2004.

39. Martin Linsky and Harvey Simon, "Mano Dura: Mobilizing the National Guard to Battle Crime in Puerto Rico," Kennedy School of Government Case Program, Case No. C109-97-1390.0 (1997), http://www.ksgcase.harvard.edu/. (Accessed July 20, 2010)

40. Ibid.

41. LexJuris Puerto Rico, Ley de Control de Acceso de 1987, Ley Num. 21 del 20 de mayo de 1987, según enmendada en el 1988, ley 156; 1992, ley 22; 1997, ley 77; 1998, ley 336. The law reads: "Los municipios podrán conceder permisos para el control del tráfico de vehículos de motor y del uso público de las vías públicas en paseos peatonales,

calles, urbanizaciones y comunidades residenciales, públicas o privadas, con un solo acceso de entrada y salida o que tengan más de un acceso de entrada o salida, pero que ninguna de sus vías públicas se use para la entrada o salida a otra calle, urbanización o comunidad que no haya solicitado control de acceso. Cuando las calles, urbanizaiones o comunidades sean parte de más de un municipio, la jurisdicción recaerá en aquel municipio en que se ubiquen la mayor parte de las fincas" (The municipalities will be able to provide permission for controlling traffic of motor vehicles and the public use of public streets in pedestrian walkways, streets, urbanizaciones, and residential communities, public or private, with only one or more entry and exit access points, as long as none of the public ways are used for the entry or exit to another street, *urbanización*, or community that has not solicited controlled access. When the streets, the *urbanizaciones*, or communities are part of more than one municipality, the jurisdiction will fall in the municipality that holds the larger portion of the lot).

42. Ibid. My translation. The law has been amended a number of times. This comes from the 1998 amendment, ley 336.

43. Blakely and Snyder, *Fortress America*, and Oscar Newman, *Community of Interest* (Garden City, N.Y.: Anchor Press/Doubleday, 1980).

44. Blakely and Snyder, *Fortress America*, 30.

45. Low, *Behind the Gates*, and Caldeira, *City of Walls*.

46. Caldeira, *City of Walls*, 20.

47. See Jane Jacobs, *The Death and Life of Great American Cities* (New York: Vintage, 1961); C. R. Jeffery, *Crime Prevention through Environmental Design* (Beverly Hills: Sage Publications, 1971); Oscar Newman, *Defensible Space: Crime Prevention through Urban Design* (New York: Macmillan, 1972); and B. Poyner, *Design against Crime: Beyond Defensible Space* (London: Buttersworths, 1983). This literature has highlighted the role that communities and specifically neighboring communities play in preventing crime. The scholarship has developed the concept of "collective efficacy," in which the ability of a community to use its social and cultural capital to monitor itself and children's behavior within it will determine the amount of antisocial behavior present in a given community. See Robert Sampson and W. B. Groves, "Community Structure and Crime: Testing Social-Disorganization Theory," *American Journal of Sociology* 94, no. 4 (1989): 774–802; Robert Sampson and William Julius Wilson, "Toward a Theory of Race, Crime, and Urban Inequality," in *Crime and Inequality*, ed. John Hagan and Ruth Peterson (Stanford, Calif.: Stanford University Press, 1995), chapter 2; Robert Sampson, F. Earls, and Jeffrey Morenoff, "Beyond Social Capital: Spatial Dynamics of Collective Efficacy for Children," *American Sociological Review* 64 (1999): 633–60.

48. See C. Shaw and H. McKay, *Juvenile Delinquency and Urban Areas* (Chicago: University of Chicago Press, 1942); L. E. Cohen and M. Felson, "Social Change and Crime Rate Trends: A Routine Activity Approach," *American Sociological Review* 44 (1979): 588–608; M. Sanchez-Jankowski, *Islands in the Street: Gangs and American Urban Society* (Berkeley: University of California Press, 1991); Philippe I. Bourgeois, *In Search of Respect: Selling Crack in El Barrio* (New York: Cambridge University Press, 1996).

49. Bill Hillier, "Can Streets Be Made Safe?" *Urban Design International* 9, no. 1 (2004): 31–45; Newman, *Defensible Space*; Jacobs, *Death and Life of Great American Cities*.

50. Jeffery, *Crime Prevention through Environmental Design*.

51. F. J. Fowler and T. W. Mangione, "A Three-Pronged Effort to Reduce Crime and Fear of Crime: The Hartford Experiment," in *Community Crime Prevention: Does It Work?* ed. D. P. Rosenbaum (Beverly Hills: Sage, 1986), 87–108; Blakely and Snyder, *Fortress America*.

52. R. B. Taylor, *Human Territorial Functioning: An Empirical, Evolutionary Perspective on Individual and Small Group Territorial Cognitions, Behaviors and Consequences* (Cambridge: Cambridge University Press, 1988); R. Atlas and W. G. LeBlanc, "The Impact on Crime of Street Closures and Barricades: A Florida Case Study," *Security Journal* 5 (1994): 140–45.

53. Davis, *Planet of Slums*.

54. Eviatar Zerubavel, *The Fine Line: Making Distinctions in Everyday Life* (New York: Free Press, 1991), 7.

55. Michel de Certeau, *The Writing of History*, trans. Tom Conley (New York: Columbia University Press, 1988), xv.

56. Zerubavel, *Fine Line*.

57. J. B. Jackson, *Discovering the Vernacular Landscape* (New Haven, Conn.: Yale University Press, 1984), 13.

58. Edward M. Peters, "Prison before the Prison: The Ancient and Medieval Worlds," in *The Oxford History of the Prison: The Practice of Punishment in Western Society*, ed. Norval Morris and David J. Rothman (Oxford: Oxford University Press, 1995), 3.

59. Foucault, *Discipline and Punish*, 113.

60. Ibid., 116.

61. See Edward C. Tolman, "Cognitive Maps in Rats and Men," in *Image and Environment: Cognitive Mapping and Spatial Behavior*, ed. Roger M. Downs and David Stea (New Brunswick, N.J.: Aldine Transaction, 2005), 27–50; and Kevin Lynch, *The Image of the City* (Cambridge, Mass.: MIT Press, 1960).

62. Lynch, *Image of the City*, 6.

63. Ibid., 7, 16.

64. Ibid., 47, 62.

65. Ibid., 48, 81.

66. Ibid., 47.

67. Ibid.

68. Erving Goffman, *Stigma: Notes on the Management of Spoiled Identity* (New York: Simon & Schuster, 1963), 2.

69. Ibid., 43.

70. Ibid.

71. Gerald Suttles, *The Social Construction of Communities* (Chicago: University of Chicago Press, 1972), 22.

72. Building on Goffman's concepts, Glenn Loury, in *The Anatomy of Racial Inequality* (Cambridge, Mass.: Harvard University Press, 2002), suggests that African Americans are stigmatized and attributed a "spoiled" identity based on race that deviates from their life history, which entails doubting the person's worthiness and "consigning him or her to a social netherworld." Also adapting Goffman's theory, Elijah Anderson, in *Streetwise: Race, Class, and Change in an Urban Community* (Chicago: University of Chicago Press, 1992), uses the notion of becoming streetwise, meaning being adept at subtly decoding the markers presented to one in the streets, which may include race and class as key indicators to learn how to navigate the streets. Richard Grannis's study, "The Importance of Trivial Streets: Residential Segregation" (*American Journal of Sociology* 103, no. 6 [1998]: 1530–64), also displays how race is read via the environment when he found that there is a correlation between the street patterns of neighborhoods and communities' racial identities.

73. Herbert Blumer, "Race Prejudice as a Sense of Group Position," *Pacific Sociological Review* 1 (1958): 3–7.

74. Pierre Bourdieu, *Distinction: A Social Critique of the Judgment of Taste*, trans. Richard Nice (Cambridge, Mass.: Harvard University Press, 1984), 172.

75. Ibid., 479.

76. See Thomas F. Gieryn, "What Buildings Do," *Theory and Society* 31 (2002): 35–74; and Thomas F. Gieryn, "A Space for Place in Sociology," *Annual Review of Sociology* 26 (2000): 26. In addition to seeing buildings as social structures in process ("What Buildings Do," 65), the sociologist Thomas Gieryn claims that "place saturates social life" and advocates for a "sociology [that is] sensitive to place" ("A Space for Place in Sociology," 467). Gieryn suggests that all social phenomena are "emplaced," making the material form of the environment, its location, and its meaning important for social life. Gieryn favors the use of the term *place* to refer to the concept he is conveying. He argues that "place is not space—which is more properly conceived as abstract geometries (distance, direction, size, shape, volume) detached from material form and cultural interpretation" (ibid., 467). While I agree with Gieryn's ideas that a place has form, is material, has a location, and is satiated with meaning, I embrace a more general concept of place that is interchangeable with "space" in order to embrace the position that abstract geometries—distance, direction, size, shape—are not and are never meaningless. This vision of space/place is in line with Kevin Lynch's work on the imageability of cities and the links between form and meaning. Sharon Zukin speaks of the legibility of the environment. See her essay "Space and Symbols in an Age of Decline," in *The City Cultures Reader*, ed. Malcolm Miles, Tim Hall, and Iain Borden (New York: Routledge, 2000), 81–91; and in Zukin, *The Cultures of Cities* (Cambridge, Mass.: Blackwell).

77. Jonathan Charley, "Industrialization and the City: Work, Speed-up, Urbanization," in *The City Cultures Reader*, ed. Malcolm Miles, Tim Hall, and Iain Borden (New York: Routledge, 2000), 67–68.

78. Zukin, "Space and Symbols in an Age of Decline."

79. See David Sibley, *Geographies of Exclusion, Society and Difference in the West* (New York, Routledge, 1995), and Davis, *City of Quartz*.

80. Although gated communities have been of widespread interest for researchers over the last ten years, most of the scholarship deals with privileged gated communities. Blakely and Snyder's *Fortress America* details the growing presence of gated communities in the United States. Caldeira's *City of Walls* explores the rise of securitization in Brazil and the political and economic conditions that led to them. Low's *Behind the Gate* describes life behind the gates for members of privileged communities. An edited volume by Rowland Atkinson and Sarah Blandy, *Gated Communities*, explores the international trend to gated communities for the rich.

81. The introduction of the gate in a poor community in Brazil is addressed by Costa Vargas, "When a Favela Dared to Become a Gated Condominium." Mike Davis, in *Planet of Slums*, briefly engages the trend toward gated communities and how this affects the lives of the poor. The trend to gate the poor is on the rise worldwide, as a recent *New York Times* article on "migrant walled villages" in China has found. See Helen Gao, "Migrant 'Villages' within a City Ignite Debate," *New York Times*, October 3, 2010.

82. See Sibley, *Geographies of Exclusion*. Also Anderson, in *Streetwise* (1992) describes how social relations are spatialized in neighborhoods in Philadelphia and the physical cues that mark the neighborhoods and make them defendable. In "The Importance of Trivial Streets," Grannis analyzes the relationship of street patterns to community identities and finds that street patterns are significant in delineating community identities. Mario Small similarly highlights how spatial patterns function as barriers to interactions among public housing residents and the members of more privileged adjacent communities. See Small, *Villa Victoria: The Transformation of Social Capital in a Boston Barrio* (Chicago: University of Chicago Press, 2004). Authors like Dolores Hayden ("The Power of Place," *Journal of Urban History* 20, no. 4 [1994]: 466–85) have criticized the tendency of historical preservation boards to not preserve buildings that "represent the social and economic struggles of the majority of ordinary citizens" (466–67), which results in a spatially unequal milieu of social interaction. Master city plans and urban development programs, seeking to control chaos, complement industrialization, or implement civic democracy in the urban space, have similarly reproduced the order of spatial inequality and exclusion (Sibley, *Geographies of Exclusion*; Davis, *City of Quartz*). A feminist geography literature that elucidates the processes of gender exclusion and subordination that have been encoded and produced in the built environment has bloomed as a result. The literature on the effects of spatial production on the poor, and especially the poor and poor communities of color, is rare. Sociological theorists of the underclass, such as Robert J. Sampson and William Julius Wilson have inserted a cursory conceptualization of space into their analyses on race, poverty, crime, and segregation. See their essay "Toward a Theory of Race, Crime, and Urban Inequality."

These accounts are often used in place of explicitly spatial accounts of the production of the city and of the city's social interaction with poor communities of color. Like the earlier Chicago School ethnographies, studies about racial housing segregation often hint at but leave unexplored the process whereby the state, the market, and people confront and are confronted by productions of space.

83. Zaire Dinzey-Flores, "Cache vs. Cas[h]eríos: Puerto Rican Neighborhoods under Siege," in *The Caribbean City*, ed. Rivke Jaffe (Kingston: Ian Randle, 2008).

84. A sense of safety, rather than an actual decline in crime, has been discovered to be the greatest benefit of gating. See Fowler and Mangione, "A Three-Pronged Effort"; Taylor, *Human Territorial Functioning*; Atlas and LeBlanc, "The Impact on Crime of Street Closures and Barricades"; Blakely and Snyder, *Fortress America*.

85. The term "legibility" is used by Kevin Lynch to refer to how easy it is to read the environment. See Lynch, *Image of the City*.

86. For a discussion about cosmopolitanism in the city, see Louis Wirth, "Urbanism as a Way of Life," *American Journal of Sociology* 44, no. 1 (1938): 1. Also see Georg Simmel, *The Sociology of Georg Simmel* (New York: Free Press, 1964). For a discussion of the challenges for cities to meet these ideals of cosmopolitanism, see Fatimah Williams Castro, "Afro-Colombians and the Cosmopolitan City: New Negotiations of Race and Space in Bogotá, Colombia," *Latin American Perspectives* (forthcoming).

Chapter 2

1. Ivelisse Rivera-Bonilla, "Divided City: The Proliferation of Gated Communities in San Juan" (PhD diss., University of California, Santa Cruz 2003).

2. Vivoni quoted in Martin Linsky and Harvey Simon, "Mano Dura: Mobilizing the National Guard to Battle Crime in Puerto Rico," Kennedy School of Government Case Program, case no. C109-97-1390.0 (1997), http://www.ksgcase.harvard.edu/, 2 (accessed July 20, 2010)

3. As stated by "Evaluación Operacional," put out by the AVP/PRPHA in Atlas. The privatization effort had been spearheaded by the Popular Democratic Party (PPD) administration of Rafael Hernández Colón, who occupied the governorship during 1988–92. The PPD administration had laid the foundation for Mano Dura through the Comisión para Combatir el Crimen (Commission to Combat Crime) initiatives in the last quarter of its administration, which included the occupation of a few public housing sites by the Fuerzas Unidas de Rápida Acción (United Forces for Rapid Action). See Humberto García Muñiz and Jorge Rodríguez Beruff, eds., *Fronteras en Conflicto: Guerra Contra las Drogas Militarización y Democracia en El Caribe, Puerto Rico y Vieques* (San Juan: Red Caribena de Geopolítica, Seguridad Regional y Relaciones Internacionales, 1999), 60.

4. It is questionable when the first raid occurred under the PNP administration. There is evidence that the plan, with involvement of the National Guard, was being rehearsed in January 1993, albeit not under the name of Mano Dura.

5. Linsky and Simon, "Mano Dura."

6. The figure of eighty-two projects comes from a document titled "List of Occupied Projects," provided to me in 2002 by the Puerto Rico Public Housing Authority Administrator, Carlos G. Laboy-Díaz. There is conflicting evidence on the timing and

total number of public housing sites occupied under the Mano Dura policies. During my February 2, 2002, interview with Laboy-Díaz, he himself reported that eighty-three projects had been occupied. The Kennedy School case study of 1997, however, reports that seventy-four interventions occurred between June 1993 and January 1996 (Linsky and Simon, "Mano Dura"), while Rodríguez Beruff, in *Fronteras en conflicto*, states that by 1997, eighty public housing sites had been intervened across the island. Furthermore, Rodríguez Beruff presents a table provided by the National Guard of Puerto Rico (in 2000) which reports the total number of operations in which the National Guard participated in public housing totaled close to ninety. It is likely that the National Guard figures double-count some public housing sites in which the National Guard participated more than once between the years of 1993 and 1998, or that the National Guard participated in some interventions that were not part of the bundle of Mano Dura policies. Because of its primary source, I am taking the list provided by the Puerto Rico Housing Authority as the most accurate representation of the total number of public housing sites intervened.

7. Interview with Carlos G. Laboy-Díaz, February 26, 2002.

8. This association between housing design and crime is supported by law enforcement records as well as a vast tradition of criminological work. See, for example, Oscar Newman, *Defensible Space: Crime Prevention through Urban Design* (New York: Macmillan, 1972), 22–24; and Henry G. Cisneros, *Defensible Space: Deterring Crime and Building Community, Second in a Series of Essays* (Washington, D.C.: U.S. Department of Housing and Urban Development, February 1995). The literature on gated communities has also noted this tendency to associate smaller size with safety. Kevin Romig, for example, noted that the perception is that "the smaller your territory is, the easier it is to defend and control." See Romig, "The Upper Sonoran Lifestyle: Gated Communities in Scottsdale, Arizona," *City and Community* 4, no. 1 (2005): 67–86.

9. On October 6, 1992, the Hope VI program was "developed as a result of recommendations by the National Commission on Severely Distressed Public Housing, which was charged with proposing a National Action Plan to eradicate severely distressed public housing." The commission's final report "recommended revitalization in three general areas: physical improvements, management improvements, and social and community services to address resident needs." The U.S. Department of Housing and Urban Development (HUD) reports that "the specific elements of public housing transformation that have proven key to HOPE VI include: Changing the physical shape of public housing[;] Establishing positive incentives for resident self-sufficiency and comprehensive services that empower residents[;] Lessening concentrations of poverty by placing public housing in nonpoverty neighborhoods and promoting mixed-income communities[; and] Forging partnerships with other agencies, local governments, nonprofit organizations, and private businesses to leverage support and resources." http://portal.hud.gov/hudportal/HUD?src=/program_offices/public_indian_housing/programs/ph/hope6/about (August 12, 2011). The Puerto Rico Housing Authority received a $50 million HOPE VI "Revitalization Grant" in 1994 and a $400,000 "Planning

Grant" in 1995. http://portal.hud.gov/hudportal/documents/huddoc?id=DOC_10014. pdf and http://portal.hud.gov/hudportal/documents/huddoc?id=DOC_10013.pdf (accessed August 12, 2011). Evaluating Hope VI programs has proven to be challenging, given the diverse set of interventions and programs implemented under its funding umbrella. Research findings show that there have been successes and failures; residents, in particular, have often not benefited from the programs. For a full review of the research evaluating Hope VI programs, see Susan J. Popkin et al., "A Decade of Hope VI: Research Findings and Policy Challenges," Urban Institute, Brookings Institution (May 2004).

10. See Figure 2 on p. 63 in Zaire Dinzey-Flores, "Criminalizing Communities of Poor, Dark Women in the Caribbean: The Fight against Crime through Puerto Rico's Public Housing," *Crime Prevention and Community Safety* 13, no. 1 (2011): 53–73

11. In "Personas Muertas en los Residenciales de Puerto Rico por Area, Distrito y Total por Residencial" (1994, 1995, 1996, 1997, 1998, 1999, 2000, 2001), compiled by the Puerto Rico Police Department. It is important to note that the crime data provided by the Puerto Rico Police Department are not necessarily reliable. A 2011 Department of Justice report cited widespread corruption in the Puerto Rico Police Department. Included in the problems of the department were inconsistent and inaccurate data collection and record keeping. The data on the size of projects can be found at http://www .gobierno.pr/AVP/ListadoResidenciales/Ponce/Ponce/ (accessed August 12, 2011). Data keeping, however, is a widespread problem in Puerto Rico, and even the Puerto Rico Housing Authority has been a "troubled agency" for much of the late twentieth and early twenty-first centuries, plagued by fiscal and managerial problems and improprieties.

12. This date (November 8, 1993) comes from a report in the newspaper *El Nuevo Día*. "Se Mudan al Sur los Operativos Conjuntos en los Caseríos" (November 9, 1993), Archivo Digital *El Nuevo Día*, www.adendi.com. However, other reports make it unclear what the exact date is. Ivelisse Rivera-Bonilla, in "Divided City: The Proliferation of Gated Communities in San Juan," replicates a table published in *El Nuevo Día* on January 18, 2000, p. 30, that lists an occupation date of September 10, 1993.

13. "Se Mudan al Sur los Operativos Conjuntos en los Caseríos," November 9, 1993.

14. Linsky and Simon, "Mano Dura."

15. A 1993 newspaper report reflects this alliance: "El Congreso de Calidad de Vida está contemplado en la ley que permitió la privatización del mantenimiento y la administración de los residenciales y que entró en vigor el cuatrienio pasado. . . . Los privatizadores son uno de los puntales en la estrategia de intervención en los residenciales" (The Quality of Life Congress is contemplated in the law that permitted privatization of public housing management and that began during the past administration. . . . The private management companies are central to the public housing intervention strategy). "A raíz del problema en el residencial/servicios sociales/ educación/cuerpo de" (June 14, 1993), Archivo Digital *El Nuevo Día*, www.adendi.com.

16. Zaire Z. Dinzey-Flores, "Temporary Housing, Permanent Communities," *Journal of Urban History* 33 (2007): 467–92.

17. Today, saying *"caserío"* is equivalent to calling a public housing site a "ghetto," whereas "residencial" is a more accepted term. While conducting research in 2003–4, I noted that the accepted term varied across locales and across people. All government personnel, and especially those working in the Housing Authority, referred to the sites exclusively as residenciales and at times corrected others who used the term *caserío*. Also, residents of these sites referred to them as *residenciales* or *caseríos* depending on the situation and context. Outsiders, however, tended to call the projects *caseríos* unless they were consciously making efforts to represent themselves as being sympathetic. Also see Zaire Z. Dinzey-Flores, "Cache vs. Cas[h]eríos: Puerto Rican Neighborhoods under Siege," in *The Caribbean City*, ed. Rivke Jaffe (Kingston: Ian Randle, 2008), 209–26.

18. In García Muñiz and Rodríguez Beruff, *Fronteras en Conflicto*, 54–55.

19. Newman, *Defensible Space*, 22–24.

20. Ibid.

21. Cisneros, *Defensible Space*.

22. Rafael Hernández, "Ahora Seremos Felices," Decca, 1939.

23. The "hopeful rhetoric" description is used in Frances Fox Piven and Richard A. Cloward, *Regulating the Poor: The Functions of Public Welfare*, updated ed. (New York: Random House, 1993), 87.

24. Fox Piven and Cloward, *Regulating the Poor*, 85. Also see Sidney M. Milkis and Jerome M. Mileur, "Introduction: The New Deal, Then and Now," in *The New Deal and the Triumph of Liberalism*, ed. Sidney M. Milkis and Jerome M. Mileur (Amherst: University of Massachusetts Press, 2002), 1–22.

25. For an explanation of how Roosevelt saw the New Deal as a way to save "capitalism and the business classes—despite themselves," see Fox Piven and Cloward, *Regulating the Poor*, 85. For a general introduction of public housing policy and design and its logics in Puerto Rico, see Dinzey-Flores, "Temporary Housing, Permanent Communities."

26. Fox Piven and Cloward, *Regulating the Poor*, 89.

27. In the United States, the New Deal home mortgage finance policies effected a similar result, as they opened up opportunities for suburban homeownership. But suburban mobility was limited by race and class, creating an urban/suburban racial and class segregation, which resulted in segregated, blighted inner-city ghettos. To understand how policies promoted racially segregated cities, see Douglas S. Massey and Nancy Denton, *American Apartheid: Segregation and the Making of the Underclass* (Cambridge: Harvard University Press, 1993), 51–59.

28. See Dinzey-Flores, "Cache vs. Cas[h]eríos."

29. The "Hogar Seguro de Puerto Rico," Law #53, was established on July 11, 1923.

30. Telésforo Carrero, *Housing in Puerto Rico* (Santurce: Junta de Planificación de Puerto Rico, 1950).

31. The PRERA was established in 1934 as part of the New Deal. On May 28, 1935, the PRERA was substituted by the PRRA under a more expansive jurisdiction and a more directed focus on developing the socioeconomic infrastructure. See Luz Marie

Rodríguez, "Suppressing the Slum! Architecture and Social Change in San Juan's Public Housing," in *San Juan Siempre Nuevo: Arquitectura y Modernización en el Siglo XX*, ed. Enrique Vivoni Falagio (Río Piedras: Archivo de Arquitectura y Construcción Universidad de Puerto Rico AACUPR, 2000), 86.

32. Carrero, *Housing in Puerto Rico*.

33. See Puerto Rico Housing Authority, *Housing Progress in Puerto Rico, 1938–1948* (San Juan: Puerto Rico Housing Authority, 1948), 4. See also Carrero, *Housing in Puerto Rico*, 21.

34. Puerto Rico Housing Authority, *Housing Progress in Puerto Rico*, 4.

35. Carrero, *Housing in Puerto Rico*, 19, 35–36. Explaining the failure, the Planning Board Report said, "In 1935 the Federal Emergency and Relief Administration built Barriada Hoare in Santurce 250 detached frame dwellings, averaging in cost about $456.95. These houses were granted free to low income families from existing slums. An investigation made in 1938 (three years later) among 170 of the occupants showed that only 102 (60%) of the original beneficiaries were occupying the houses. Another investigation conducted in 1946 (eleven years after construction) showed that only 54 (31.8%) of the original beneficiaries were occupying them. Some of them had sold their homes for less than its original cost (for as low as $100) and these same houses had been resold once or twice for $700, $800, and $900, in spite of the 11 years depreciation. There were cases of persons owning more than one house, and others in which the original beneficiary was renting the house to another person. The bare truth is that this housing project has degenerated into a slum."

36. Rodríguez, "Suppressing the Slum!" 98–99. The design consisted of 2,300 units of detached concrete dwelling units to accommodate 16,000 people. The project was constructed in stages and, by 1950, 635 detached units had been built. Rodríguez claims that "the plan of the 'Eleanor Roosevelt' settlement was the most obvious difference from the RA [Resettlement Administration] projects. Curves were not used in the PRRA developments. In the Greenbelt Towns, especially in Greenbelt and Greenhills, the curve was the element which organized the town scheme" (127). Although the curve was part of Greenbelt and not of the PRRA developments, the axial form was true to housing plans from the City Beautiful Movement, through the more modernist grid, straight-line patterns of garden cities (e.g., Radburn), greenbelt towns, and later public housing developments.

37. Rodríguez, "Suppressing the Slum!" 127. Greenbelt towns were conceived of by Rexford Tugwell under the Resettlement Administration (RA), a federal agency in charge of providing government-planned housing for low-income urban and rural families. Also see Marygrace Tyrell, "Colonizing the New Deal: Federal Housing in San Juan, Puerto Rico," in *The Caribbean City*, ed. Rivke Jaffe (Kingston: Ian Randle, 2008), 69–93.

38. Carrero, *Housing in Puerto Rico*, 20; Rodríguez, "Suppressing the Slum!" 134. The third housing project, Morell Campos, on the western outskirts of Ponce, had 150 detached concrete single-family units, intended for relocating slum dwellers. There were schools and a community center.

39. Rodríguez, "Suppressing the Slum!" 91. The lot for the project was located "to the north of the Seboruco road, near the municipal cemetery." There were thirteen one-bedroom units, ninety-two two-bedroom units, and twenty-six three-bedroom units, and some others were studios without bedrooms.

40. Ibid., 92.

41. Ibid., 92–93.

42. Ibid., 95. The buildings were arranged "peripherally and symmetrically within the lot" around a central courtyard, with the stairs, landings, and corridors linking the buildings on the first floor, as entrances to buildings, or on the upper floors, in balconies shared by two apartments. Rodríguez complains that the shared balcony ignored "the importance of the balcony within the social and architectural reality of the Puerto Rican family," but the shared balconies were probably designed in accordance with U.S. PWA requirements. In the Carl Mackley Houses in Philadelphia, apartments shared porches because fire laws required each apartment to have two exits. See Eric J. Sandeen, "The Design of Public Housing in the New Deal: Oskar Stonorov and the Carl Mackley Houses," *American Quarterly* 37, no. 5 (Winter 1985): 652. If architectural cultural preferences influenced the design, federal programs also guided it. Inside the courtyard was a two-story building, intended as a nursery and preschool but also used as a community center with administrative offices, a reading room, and a small clinic; in between the enclosed square of buildings were to be green public spaces with paved walkways "only . . . accessible on foot" (Rodríguez, "Suppressing the Slum!" 95). Built in the Moderne variant of art deco, this style was an Americanized version of a style that "incorporates the machine" (95–96). Also see Carrero, *Housing in Puerto Rico*, 19–20.

43. Charles Fourier (1772–1837) was a French philosopher and sociologist who advocated a system of interaction in which individuals lived in *falansterios*, which were organized human collectives with the objective of promoting the well-being of each member through free labor. For a detailed account of the debate that led to the name "El Falansterio" and the introduction of the name by the press, see Rodríguez, "Suppressing the Slum!" 74–117.

44. Dolores Hayden, *Redesigning the American Dream: The Future of Housing, Work, and Family Life*, rev. and expanded ed. (New York: W. W. Norton, 2002), 157–61.

45. Law #64 of the May 14, 1945, gave the Planning Board the power to declare a slum as any run-down urban sector and to label it "M," meaning "para mejorarse" or "to be improved." See Departamento de la Vivienda, *Vivienda: Metas, objetivos y programas* (San Juan: Estado Libre Asociado de Puerto Rico, 1990).

46. Rafael Picó, "The Role of Planning in Puerto Rico," *Annals of the American Academy of Political and Social Science* 285 (1953): 72. The plan was executed through zoning laws that marked these areas as "M" districts, meaning "Mejoramiento." In 1953, the Planning Board estimated that by 1956 more than 18,000 families would be moved out of San Juan slum areas. Additionally, 3,298 low-cost dwelling units had been built between 1940 and 1953, and 11,000 more were expected by 1957. And in the summer

of 1952, Puerto Rico had under construction 8,799 public housing units costing around $44 million.

47. Carrero, *Housing in Puerto Rico.*

48. Departamento de la Vivienda, *Vivienda.*

49. This super-block design comes from Ebenezer Howard and was then adopted by Le Corbusier. Juan Ponce de León marked the introduction, en masse, of a Le Corbusier-reminiscent multidwelling architectural style for public housing developments on the island. The projects were essentially identical when they were constructed. The French architect Le Corbusier focused intently on the home and its relationship to work and industry. Le Corbusier had a functional ideological vision of the city where all (and only) formal urban uses, of which the most central were housing and industry, had to be logically accommodated to exist in amicable relationships. Most central to his plan was the institutionalization of the home's function so that it was in harmony with industry. Interestingly enough, his solution to overcrowding, slums, disease, and chaos brought about by urban migrations was to increase density through the construction of super-blocks of geometrically arranged high-rise buildings; this idea was interestingly reminiscent of Howard's garden cities: "We must decongest the centers of our cities by increasing their density." See Peter Hall, *The Cities of Tomorrow: An Intellectual History of Urban Planning and Design in the Twentieth Century*, updated ed. (London: Blackwell, 1988). Le Corbusier's household units would all be uniform and contain the same furniture—they would be stripped-down "cells" that fulfilled basic human sentimental and physiological needs. All functions of the buildings would be institutionalized to fit the work day and the industrial interests. Le Corbusier's vision of institutional housing would become the prime design pattern of housing for the poor in the United States. See Sudhir Venkatesh, *American Project* (Cambridge, Mass.: Harvard University Press, 2000). Le Corbusier's high-rise super-block design was welcomed in the 1930s and 1940s with the U.S. New Deal programs for housing. In Puerto Rico, public housing developments typically consist of a group of two- to four-story buildings freely organized in a large super-block. Therefore, the modernist movement toward high-rise public housing design that took over the United States was not predominant in Puerto Rico. The structural orientation of buildings in a super-block, with formally defined open spaces, was adopted, but the high-rise component was not. Although a few high-rise public housing buildings were built, medium- and low-rise buildings remained the preferred architectural form of public housing in Puerto Rico. While in places like New York or Chicago the super-block was imposed over a preexisting grid of small blocks, in Puerto Rico the super-block involved the creation of a new spatial organization. The super-block in New York or Chicago literally meant the sum of many small blocks, while in Puerto Rico the super-block was built in either slum communities without rationalistic top-down planning order or on empty lots. Thus, although in New York, Chicago, and Puerto Rico the public housing super-block came to look the same, the process of turning the city housing into that spatial arrangement differs. Thus, Puerto Rico was molded into Chicago and New York even though the tropical canvas was radically different than the

cities dictating the model. By the time Tugwell left office, many public housing projects like Ponce de León had been built on the island.

50. For a description of the resistance to move to public housing, see Kurt W. Back, *Slums, Projects, and People: Social Psychological Problems of Relocation in Puerto Rico* (Durham: Duke University Press, 1962); and Helen I. Safa, *The Urban Poor of Puerto Rico: A Study in Development and Inequality* (New York: Rinehart and Winston, 1974).

51. Oscar Lewis, *La Vida: A Puerto Rican Family in the Culture of Poverty* (New York: Random House, 1965); and Safa, *The Urban Poor*.

52. Safa, *The Urban Poor*, 18–19.

53. Ibid., 19.

54. Ibid., 18–19.

55. Ibid., 82.

56. Lewis, *La Vida*, 661–62.

57. Carlos Alvarado, *Public Housing in Puerto Rico: Housing for a Lower Segment, a Special Case* (New York: John Wiley, 1974).

58. Gordon K. Lewis, "Puerto Rico: A Case Study in an Under Developed Area," *Journal of Politics* 17 (1955): 614–50. Lewis suggested that in order to further the sought-after economic development, Muñoz went along with programs that provided most federal investments.

59. Sepúlveda Rivera, "Viejos Cañaverales, Casa Nuevas: Muñoz versus el Síndrome Long," in *Luis Muñoz Marín, Perfiles de su Gobernación, 1948–1964*, ed. Fernando Picó (Río Piedras: Fundación Luis Muñoz Marín, 2003), 166–207.

60. See Dinzey-Flores, "Cache vs. Cas[h]eríos."

61. Puerto Ricans favored homeownership. Kurt W. Back, in *Slums, Projects, and People*, states that Puerto Ricans weren't willing to pay rent for a house that they did not own. In *The Urban Poor*, Helen Safa suggests that slum residents lost social control of the neighborhood when moving into public housing. This loss of control was especially difficult for men, who disliked public housing because the control is taken away from them—they no longer own their own home, they depend on project management for repair and maintenance, and they must report every change in occupation or salary to management. Safa cites one resident, who complained that "*aquí todo es público y uno no puede mandar en nada*" (here everything is public and one has no authority in anything). She also states that residents feel that there is more respect among neighbors in shantytowns than in public housing, where disputes are referred to housing management (81) and that kin and neighborhood bonds and trust developed in the slums were broken.

62. Luis Muñoz Marín followed the lead of the prominent New Deal official and last American-appointed governor to the island, Rexford G. Tugwell, who beginning in 1941 oversaw the urban planning enterprise to develop housing and propel an aggressive public housing program. Tugwell, along with Muñoz Marín's Popular Democratic Party, was responsible for the promotion of Puerto Rico as a "social laboratory," a model for modern development. See Michael Lapp, "The Rise and Fall of Puerto Rico as a Social Laboratory, 1945–1965," *Social Science History* 19, no. 2 (Summer 1995): 169–99.

63. Anonymous, "La Filosofía del Gobierno de Puerto Rico y los Programas de la CRUV" (unknown date), Datos Sobre Vivienda, Fundación Luis Muñoz Marín Archives, sección 5, serie 16 #10, caja 4. Original in Spanish; author's translation.

64. Alvarado, *Public Housing in Puerto Rico.*

65. There is a lot more that can be said regarding Muñoz's stance on the privileged vis-à-vis the public housing residents. Muñoz's writings reveal a paternalistic attitude toward the less privileged that is common to his era and is present in the federal housing policies of the time. Federal and local housing policies and design elements during that time sought to reeducate the public housing residents into modern, civil, and urban living. In addition, the letter continually elides the people of the *caserío* by failing to refer to the neighborhood by its name. While in the letter Muñoz persistently refers to the private residential development by its name, Dos Pinos, the *caserío* remains generic and unspecific. The people don't have a neighborhood that can be named: they simply live in a *caserío.*

66. Dinzey-Flores, "Temporary Housing, Permanent Communities."

67. See Dinzey-Flores, "Temporary Housing, Permanent Communities." *Caseríos* are defined as *"conjunto de casas en el campo"* (a group of houses on rural farmland), while residencial is an adjective referring to anything that needs personal housing (see Ramón García-Pelayo y Gross, *Diccionario Larousse del Español Moderno* [New York: Penguin, 1976]). It is not hard to see from the origins of these words how one would be preferred to others. Typically and since the era of privileged development in the 1950s, in Puerto Rico anything that is from the farmland is considered backward compared to the urban areas.

68. Memorandum de Luis Muñoz Marín á T. Carrero (Julio 14, 1954), Datos Sobre Vivienda, Fundación Luis Muñoz Marín Archives, sección 5, serie 16 #10, caja 4. Original in Spanish; author's translation.

69. Ibid.

70. See Dinzey-Flores, "Cache vs. Cas[h]eríos."

71. See ibid.

72. Departamento de la Vivienda, *Vivienda.*

73. Carlos A. Aurora Pérez, 15/16/II/1996, booklet, Secretaría de Arte y Cultura, in Archivo Municipal de Ponce, File: Machuelo (Barrio de Ponce), 012-M-247.

74. Although it was the first "suburban" *urbanización*, Alhambra was actually the second *urbanización* constructed. A few years earlier, around 1915, Urbanización Mariani had been built on the southeastern fringes of the city. According to a recollection of Ponce's Territorial Plan, its construction represents the move of the city's wealthy to the periphery. See *Memoria del Plan: Plan Territorial de Ponce* (Oficina de Plan y Territorio, Municipio de Ponce, October 1992).

75. Ibid.

76. By the 1970s, twenty new suburban private residential developments had been planned, were in construction, or had been constructed within the outskirts of the central city zone of Ponce. See Rosario C. Natal, *Ponce en su Historia Moderna*

1945–2002 (Ponce: Secretaría de Cultura y Turismo del Municipio Autónomo de Ponce, 2003), 126.

77. Dr. Pila has 906 units. It was built after Juan Ponce de León (300 units), Santiago Iglesias (280 units), Gándara (270 units), and Hogares Portugués (152 units).

78. Sepúlveda Rivera, "Viejos Cañaverales, Casa Nuevas," 200–207; Dinzey-Flores, "Cache vs. Cas[h]eríos.

79. Sepúlveda Rivera, "Viejos Cañaverales, Casa Nuevas," 200–201.

80. Anonymous, "La filosofía del gobierno."

81. Sepúlveda Rivera, "Viejos Cañaverales, Casa Nuevas," 201.

82. Iris Marion Young, *Justice and the Politics of Difference* (Princeton: Princeton University Press, 1990), 247.

83. Here I'm using Dovidio and Gaertner's "aversive" term to denote the encoded and nondirect nature of how inequality is maintained through housing structures in Puerto Rico. Dovido and Gaertner define late twentieth-century aversive racism as the discordance between a sincerely egalitarian value system that maintains that it is wrong to discriminate and rejects racial stereotypes, and unacknowledged negative feelings that are a result of being unable to escape cultural and cognitive forces. The aversive racist discriminates when normative structures within a given situation are weak, ambiguous, or conflicting. In the case of Puerto Rico, I suggest that aversive attitudes are encoded in discriminating structures. See John F. Dovidio and Samuel L. Gaertner, "Aversive Racism," *Advances in Experimental Social Psychology* 36 (2004): 1–52.

84. Anonymous, "La Filosofía del Gobierno."

85. Dinzey-Flores, "Temporary Housing, Permanent Communities."

86. Edgardo Rodríguez Juliá, *Cortijo's Wake/El Entierro de Cortijo,* trans. Juan Flores (Durham: Duke University Press, 2004).

Chapter 3

1. Michel Foucault, *Discipline and Punish: The Birth of the Prison*, 2nd ed., trans. Alan Sheridan (New York: Vintage, 1995), 215.

2. The "raw iron" description was used in an interview on February 6, 2004, with a resident of Extensión Alhambra.

3. Dr. Pila has an elementary school within the perimeter gate, located by the north entrance, used by children who live there. The school that is accessible through the eastern pedestrian gate is a middle school.

4. Unless there is reasonable suspicion of drugs or guns or such, I suppose any such searches are a violation of the Fourth Amendment's prohibition of unreasonable searches and seizures. But it is unlikely that the residents of Dr. Pila or other public housing communities would have thought that the ACLU might bring forth a suit on their behalf.

5. Interview, November 7, 2003.

6. "Ugly" was used to describe gated Dr. Pila in an interview, October 27, 2003.

7. Interview, October 27, 2003.

8. Interview, February 5, 2004.

9. Interview, February 6, 2004.

10. Field notes, February 4, 2004.

11. Interview, February 5, 2004.

12. Interview, February 6, 2004.

13. Interview, February 4, 2004.

14. Ibid.

15. Interview, October 21, 2003.

16. Interview, October 27, 2003.

17. Foucault states: "Hence, the major effect of the Panopticon: to induce in the inmate a state of conscious and permanent visibility that assures the automatic functioning of power. . . . To achieve this, it is at once too much and too little that the prisoner should be constantly observed by an inspector: too little, for what matters is that he knows himself to be observed; too much, because he has no need in fact of being so. In view of this, Bentham laid down the principle that power should be visible and unverifiable. Visible: the inmate will constantly have before his eyes the tall outline of the central tower from which he is spied upon. Unverifiable: the inmate must never know whether he is being looked at any moment; but he must be sure that he may always be so. . . . The Panopticon is a machine for dissociating the see/being seen dyad . . . one is totally seen, without ever seeing" (Foucault, *Discipline and Punish*, 201–2).

18. Interview, November 20, 2001.

19. For a discussion of the three phases of Mano Dura—"Rescue," Restore," and "Reempower," see Chapter 2.

20. Interview, October 31, 2003.

21. Interview, October 27, 2003.

22. Ibid.

23. Interview, October 22, 2003.

24. Foucault, *Discipline and Punish*, 249.

25. The references to *presos* (inmates) were frequent among Dr. Pila residents (interview, October 31, 2003), but Gándara residents also talked about Dr. Pila residents as being like presos or that they themselves would feel as if they were presos if a gate were ever erected in their community (interviews, October 27 and 31, 2003). Michel Foucault would call the residents "delinquents." He distinguished "convicts," defined by the acts that led them to be imprisoned, from "delinquents," defined by their existence in the "penitentiary operation." Residents in gated public housing were not convicted of specific acts but are living in a quasi-penitentiary operation, which effectively makes them "delinquents" (Foucault, *Discipline and Punish*, 252–53).

26. Interview, October 24, 2003. La Cucharas is a well-known prison complex system on the outskirts of Ponce.

27. Interview, October 22, 2003.

28. For a discussion of the processes of rules and regulations in public housing communities, see Chapter 4.

29. Interview, October 22, 2003.

30. Interview, February 5, 2004.

31. Ibid.

32. Giorgio Agamben identifies the wolf-man as "a monstrous hybrid of human and animal, divided between the forest and the city . . . in its origin the figure of the man who has been banned from the city." See Agamben, *Homo Sacer: Sovereign Power and Bare Life*, trans. Daniel Heller-Roazen (Stanford, Calif.: Stanford University Press, 1998), 63.

33. Interview, October 22, 2003.

34. Interview, October 27, 2003.

35. This concept of *gente de bien* (people of good) was prevalent throughout interviews with residents within the affluent communities.

36. Field notes, February 4, 2004.

37. Interview, February 5, 2004. That race is "read," and "real," in crossings across neighborhoods in Puerto Rico was captured by Edgardo Rodríguez Juliá in his description of entering the largest public housing site in Puerto Rico in order to attend the funeral of the popular musician Rafael Cortijo in 1982. See Edgardo Rodríguez Juliá, *Cortijo's Wake: El Entierro de Cortijo*, trans. Juan Flores (Durham: Duke University Press, 2004), 88.

38. Interview, October 29, 2003.

39. In her unpublished dissertation, Ivelisse Rivera-Bonilla does note that there are public housing gated communities in Puerto Rico, but she concentrates more on private gated communities. See Ivelisse Rivera-Bonilla, "Divided City: The Proliferation of Gated Communities in San Juan" (PhD diss., University of California, Santa Cruz, 2003).

40. Foucault, *Discipline and Punish*, 249, borrows from C. Lucas, *De la réforme des prisons* (1836), 69.

41. See, for example, Theresa Caldeira, *City of Walls* (Berkeley: University of California Press, 2000); Mike Davis, *City of Quartz* (London: Verso, 1990); Mike Davis, *Ecology of Fear: Los Angeles and the Imagination of Disaster* (New York: Metropolitan, 1998); Setha Low, *Behind the Gates* (London: Routledge, 2005); and Iris Marion Young, *Justice and the Politics of Difference* (Princeton: Princeton University Press, 1990).

42. Young, *Justice and the Politics of Difference*, 247.

Chapter 4

1. Jeffrey M. Berry, Kent E. Portney, and Ken Thomson, *The Rebirth of Urban Democracy* (New York: Brookings Institution Press, 1993), 6.

2. Pierre Bourdieu suggests that the elite's ability to offer a "political judgement" is a reflection of their very own class position and that it feeds a sense of "competence." See Bourdieu, *Distinction: A Social Critique of the Judgement of Taste*, trans. Richard Nice (Cambridge, Mass.: Harvard University Press, 1984), 399.

3. Ibid.

4. It is important to note that in retrofitting the previously open Extensión Alhambra with gates, some homes were left outside the gate. I was never referred to any community members who live in these homes, for interviews, likely a sign of their lack of integration within the now-gated sector of the community.

5. Interview, February 6, 2004.

6. Ibid.

7. Ibid.

8. See Jorge Duany, Luisa Hernández Angueira, and César A. Rey, *El Barrio Gandul: Economía Subterránea y Migración Indocumentada en Puerto Rico* (San Juan: Universidad del Sagrado Corazón, 1995); and Jorge Duany, "Caribbean Migration to Puerto Rico: A Comparison of Cubans and Dominicans," *International Migration Review* 26, no. 1 (Spring 1992): 46–66.

9. Interview, February 5, 2004.

10. Ibid.

11. Interview, February 4, 2004.

12. Class status also becomes very important in consolidating a sense of community for Extensión Alhambra residents. See Chapter 5 for a discussion of class connections and the sense of community cultivated beyond the neighborhood.

13. Interview, February 4, 2004.

14. "A Raíz del Problema en el Residencial/Servicios Sociales/Educacion/Cuerpode," in *A Raíz del Problema en el Residencial*, Archivo Digital *El Nuevo Día* (June 14, 1993), www.adendi.com. The act was part of a wider federal trend to integrate the private sector in urban development and to build and manage public works, including public housing projects. Consistent with the U.S. federal approach to public housing policies, the 1992 legislation to privatize Puerto Rican public housing projects was meant to be a strictly fiscal and managerial intervention to foster public-private partnerships with the purpose of significantly improving the living conditions and the effective organizational operations of and the fiscal allocation of funds to public housing projects. As stated in a report titled "Evaluación Operacional," put out by the AVP (n.d.), the policy was driven by "la necesidad de elaborar y poner en ejecución nuevos métodos y sistemas dirigidos a mejorar la calidad de vida, fomentar la actividad comunitaria, y el desarrollo personal y familiar de sus residentes, hace indispensable la intervención de ambos sectores, constituyendo una labor de equipo en el desarrollo de nuevas metas en favor de los puertorriqueños" (the necessity to elaborate and execute new methods and systems directed toward improving the quality of life, fostering community activity, and encouraging the personal and familial development of residents, makes the intervention of both sectors indispensable, constituting a team effort in the development of new goals in favor of Puerto Ricans). Retrospectively, this move toward the involvement of the private sector in the 1990s created opportunities for corruption and nepotism. Subsequently, in the first decade of the twenty-first century, many Puerto Rican officials and private-sector citizens were charged and convicted with corruption and federal larceny charges.

15. "One Strike and You're Out" screening and eviction guidelines for public housing

authorities, U.S. Department of Housing and Urban Development, Office of Public and Indian Housing, notice PIH 96-16 (HA), April 12, 1996.

16. "Política Pública para la Implantación de 'One Strike You Are Out Policy,'" Departamento de la Vivienda, Administración de Vivienda Pública, April 24, 1997.

17. Wackenhut was one of three companies originally awarded with a contract to manage public housing in Puerto Rico. Wackenhut is a well-known prison-management company: "Wackenhut Corrections Corporation. The Group's principal activity is to offer correctional and related institutional services to federal, state, local and overseas government agencies. Correctional services include the management of a broad spectrum of facilities, including male and female adult facilities, juvenile facilities, community corrections, work programs, prison industries, substance abuse treatment facilities and mental health, geriatric and other special needs institutions. Other management contracts include psychiatric health care, electronic home monitoring, prisoner transportation, correctional health services and facility maintenance. The Group has an in-house capability for the design of new facilities and offers a full privatization package to government agencies, including financing of new projects. The Group has 59 correctional, detention and healthcare facilities. The Group operates in the United States, Europe, Australia, New Zealand and South Africa." http://www.business.com/directory/government_and_trade/by_country/united_states/correctional_facilities/wackenhut_corrections_corporation/profile (accessed May 28, 2010).

18. Park Management managed twelve public housing sites in Ponce and three in Humacao, in the southeast. Westbrook Management Company inherited the twelve sites from Park Management, which oversaw 68 percent (or 2,673 units) of a total of twenty-five projects (or 3,951 housing units) that it manages accross nine municipalities in the Southwest region: Ponce, Peñuelas, Guayanilla, Adjuntas, Yauco, Maricao, Sabana Grande, Guánica, and Lajas. Two of the projects that Westbrook manages have at least one extension. Dr. Pila, in Ponce, has two extensions, which, for the purposes of the management company, makes it count as three housing projects. Santa Catalina, in Yauco, has one extension, which makes it count as two projects for the company. If we do not count the extensions of the projects as individual developments, the total number of projects Westbrook manages is twenty-two projects in the Southwestern region, including ten in Ponce. When speaking with the managers I noticed the different dispositions toward the community. One of the administrators in Dr. Pila, the one who manages one section of Dr. Pila, is a lifelong resident of another public housing project. I found this administrator to be very knowledgeable of the community and to be more understanding: the one who warned me about leaving "*cuando estaba caliente la cosa*" (when things were going down), the only one who dared to take me to an apartment, and the only one willing to take pictures for me. Another manager was also very forthcoming, while the third manager—the one in charge of the largest *uno ocho* (one eight) section of Dr. Pila—was unavailable for an interview. Residents confirmed having a different relationship with her. For example, one described it in this way: "Esa administradora no sirve. Siempre que viene a hablar con ella no está disponible. Sirve para cobrar rentas.

Sólo sirve para el desalojo. Si no pagas renta te da un desahucio" (The manager is no good. Whenever I go to talk to her, she is not available. She's good to collect rent. She's only good for eviction. If you don't pay rent, she gives you an eviction). In Dr. Pila, the three administrators and staff were originally housed in the same building, adjacent to the indoor community room. Eventually, one administrator was moved to the building previously occupied by the Puerto Rico police as a precinct. The administrator and staff in Gándara are housed in a separate building, close to the community room and back to back with the Resident Council office.

19. Interview, October 31, 2003.

20. While I conducted research, the most organized section and the one that drove most initiatives was the council of the original Dr. Pila uno ocho. The other two sections tended to be less active, although I did meet with the Resident Council representatives for those areas.

21. Interview, October 28, 2003.

22. Interview, October 24, 2003.

23. See James Scott, *Weapons of the Weak: Everyday Forms of Peasant Resistance* (New Haven, Conn.: Yale University Press, 1985); Rebecca Scott, "Former Slaves: Response to Emancipation in Cuba," in *Caribbean Freedom*, ed. Hilary Beckles and Verene Shepherd (Princeton: M. Wiener, 1996), 21–27; and Kusha Haraksingh, "Control and Resistance among Overseas Indian Workers: A Study of Labor on the Sugar Plantations of Trinidad, 1875–1917," in *Caribbean Freedom*, ed. Hilary Beckles and Verene Shepherd (Princeton: M. Wiener, 1996), 207–14.

24. Interview, October 31, 2003.

25. Interview, October 28, 2003.

26. Interview, October 22, 2003.

27. Interview, October 9, 2003. Lucy is a pseudonym.

28. Daniel Rivera Vargas, "Protesta a Son de Música," *El Nuevo Día*, December 3, 2005. This article is also discussed in Zaire Dinzey-Flores, "De la Disco al Caserío: Urban Spatial Aesthetics and Policy to the Beat of Reggaetón," *Centro: Journal of the Center for Puerto Rican Studies* 20, no. 1 (2008): 35–69.

29. Interview, February 6, 2004.

30. See Joan Petersilia, *When Prisoners Come Home: Parole and Prisoner Reentry* (New York: Oxford University Press, 2003).

31. Interview, February 5, 2004.

32. Ibid.

33. Mark Figueroa, Anthony Harriott, and Nicola Satchell, "The Political Economy of Jamaica's Inner-City Violence: A Special Case?" in *Caribbean City*, ed. Rivke Jaffe (Kingston: Ian Randle, 2008).

34. Although the first proponent of the "culture of poverty" term was Oscar Lewis (Oscar Lewis, *La Vida: A Puerto Rican Family in the Culture of Poverty* [New York: Random House, 1965]), the concept has been used and refashioned by numerous scholars. Notable examples are Daniel Patrick Moynihan, *The Moynihan Report:*

The Negro Family: The Case for National Action (Washington, D.C.: Office of Policy Planning and Research, U.S. Department of Labor, 1965); and William Julius Wilson, *The Truly Disadvantaged: The Inner City, the Underclass and Public Policy* (Chicago: University of Chicago Press, 1987). A recent volume, coedited by Mario Small, David Harding, and Michèle Lamont, has sought to recapture and specify the role of not "culture" but the process of "meaning making" that informs the experience of poverty. See Small, Harding, and Lamont, "Reconsidering Poverty and Culture," *Annals of the American Academy of Political and Social Science* 629 (May 2010). The volume has resulted in a public debate about the utility of the concept "culture of poverty." For the debate, see Patricia Cohen, "'Culture of Poverty' Makes a Comeback," *New York Times*, October 17, 2010, http://www.nytimes.com/2010/10/18/us/18poverty.html?_r=1&scp=1&sq=Patricia%20Cohen%20Culture%20Poverty&st=cse (accessed May 29, 2012); and Stephen Steinberg's response in Steinberg, "Poor Reason: Culture Still Doesn't Explain Poverty," *Boston Review*, January 13, 2011, http://www.bostonreview.net/BR36.1/steinberg.php (accessed May 29, 2012).

35. Moynihan, *The Moynihan Report*; Daniel Patrick Moynihan and Nathan Glazer, *Beyond the Melting Pot: The Negroes, Puerto Ricans, Jews, Italians, and Irish of New York City* (Cambridge, Mass.: MIT Press, 1970); Lewis, *La Vida*.

36. Interview, October 9, 2003. Francisco is a pseudonym.

37. Gerald Suttles, *The Social Order of the Slum: Ethnicity and Territory in the Inner City* (Chicago: University of Chicago Press, 1968), 3.

38. Interview, October 24, 2003.

39. Bourdieu, *Distinction*, 411.

40. Ibid., 399.

41. Interview, February 4, 2004.

42. Field notes, February 5, 2004.

43. These pleas presented a challenge for me. In response, I would tell residents that I was not the government, was not doing something on behalf of the government, and that I was not reporting to them. While I worried about being thought of as a government representative, I also worried about the expectations that residents had formed about participating in the interview.

44. Carlos Vargas, "The Impact of Migration on Political Participation: Environment Change and Political Incorporation of Puerto Rican Return Migrants," presented at the conference Transnational Citizenship Across the Americas, Rutgers University, March 26, 2010. A different version of the paper was presented at the thirty-fifth annual conference of the Caribbean Studies Association, held in St. Peters, Barbados, May 24–28, 2010.

45. Berry, Portney, and Thomson, *The Rebirth of Urban Democracy*, 3.

46. In electoral politics, Puerto Ricans behave more like Latin Americans than like North Americans. See Vargas, "The Impact of Migration."

47. David Harvey offers a neo-Marxist analysis of space, emphasizing the importance of capital to the production and experience of urban development. See David

Harvey, *Justice, Nature and the Geography of Difference* (Cambridge, Mass.: Blackwell, 1996).

48. Interview, February 4, 2004.

49. It is common for a central question in the real estate market to be if units are owner-occupied versus renter-occupied. Many co-ops put restrictions on renting or subletting units. Even the Federal Census asks about owner-occupied units, an important measure of neighborhood social and economic health. For more on how home-ownership is valued over renting, see Ruth Madigan, Moira Munro, and Susan Smith, "Gender and the Meaning of the Home," *International Journal of Urban and Regional Research* 14, no. 4 (December 1990): 625–47; Robert B. Riley, "Attachment to the Ordinary Landscape," in *Place Attachment*, ed. Irwin Altman and Setha M. Low (New York: Plenum, 1992), 13–35; Deryck Holdsworth, "Revaluing the House," in *Place/Culture/Representation*, ed. James Duncan and David Ley (New York: Routledge, 1993), 95–109; William M. Rohe and Michael A. Stegman, "The Effects of Homeownership on the Self-Esteem, Perceived Control and Life Satisfaction of Low-Income People," *Journal of the American Planning Association* 60, no. 2 (1994): 173–84; William M. Rohe and Leslie S. Stewart, "Homeownership and Neighborhood Stability," *Housing Policy Debate* 7, no. 1 (1996): 37–81; Ann Dupuis and David C. Thorns, "Home, Home Ownership and the Search for Ontological Security," *Sociological Review* 46, no. 1 (February 1998): 24–47; Denise DiPasquale and Edward L. Glaeser, "Incentives and Social Capital: Are Home-owners Better Citizens?" *Journal of Urban Economics* 45, no. 2 (March 1999): 354–84; William M. Rohe, Shannon Van Zandt, and George McCarthy, "Social Benefits and Costs of Homeownership," in *Low-Income Homeownership: Examining the Unexamined Goal*, ed. Nicolas Paul Retsinas and Eric S. Belsky (Washington, D.C.: Brookings Institution, 2002), 381–406; Lynne C. Manzo, "Beyond House and Haven: Toward a Revisioning of Emotional Relationship with Places," *Journal of Environmental Psychology* 23, no. 1 (March 2003): 47–61; Lynne C. Manzo, "For Better or Worse: Exploring Multiple Dimensions of Place Meaning," *Journal of Environmental Psychology* 25, no. 1 (March 2005): 67–86; Kevin R. Cox, "Housing Tenure and Neighborhood Activism," *Urban Affairs Review* 43 (September 2007): 107–22; and Alyssa Katz, *Our Lot: How Real Estate Came to Own Us* (New York: Bloomsbury, 2009).

50. See Frances Fox Piven and Richard A. Cloward, *Regulating the Poor: The Functions of Public Welfare*, updated ed. (New York: Random House, 1993). Residents of both Dr. Pila and Gándara were highly dependent on welfare. Close to two-thirds of residents across the three sections of Dr. Pila relied on public assistance—the Programa de Asistencia Nutricional (PAN; Program of Nutritional Assistance, or Food Stamps)—and a majority of them paid negative rent or under $25 a month for rent. The generalized perception of management company staff, however, was that 90 percent of residents in public housing relied on public assistance (interview, October 9, 2003).

Chapter 5

1. Rexford Guy Tugwell, *The Stricken Land: The Story of Puerto Rico* (New York: Greenwood, 1946), 75.

2. J. B. Jackson, *The Necessity for Ruins, and Other Topics* (Amherst: University of Massachusetts Press, 1980), 20.

3. Interview, February 5, 2004.

4. Ibid.

5. Ibid.

6. Interview, February 4, 2004.

7. Interview, October 27, 2003.

8. Interview, October 30, 2003.

9. Jackson, *The Necessity for Ruins*, 21.

10. Ibid., 23.

11. Ibid., 21. Christopher Grampp also notes that the garden was consonant with John Locke's "ethic of individualism—a desire to define themselves singly or as families rather than by community ties," achievable through ownership of private property. See Christopher Grampp, *From Yard to Garden: The Domestication of America's Home Grounds* (Chicago: Center for American Places at Columbia College, 2008), 17.

12. Lewis Mumford, *The City in History* (New York: Harcourt, 1961), 490, 492.

13. Interview, February 5, 2004.

14. Mumford, *The City in History*, 490. Ironically, the "garden" featured prominently in New Deal projects, following Ebenezer Howard's turn-of-the-century (nineteenth to twentieth) garden-city ideas promoting the marriage of town and country. See Ebenezer Howard, *Garden Cities of To-morrow* (London: Swan Sonnenschein, 1902). Howard's ideas were first made physically real by a British duo, Raymond Unwin and Barry Parker, in the New Earswick, Lechworth, Ealing, and Hampstead garden villages/cities/suburbs. Parker-Unwin ideas were replicated and extended in early and mid-twentieth-century Europe and United States. In the United States, garden cities were shepherded by Clarence Stein, Henry Wright, and Clarence Perry, resulting in projects like Forest Hills Gardens and Sunnyside Gardens in Queens, New York, and the Radburn planned communities, consisting of Radburn in New Jersey, Chatham Village in Pittsburgh, and Baldwin Hills Village in Los Angeles. Rexford Tugwell, through the Resettlement Administration, led the building of three greenbelt towns, mimicking and adopting some of the same principles: they were in Greenbelt, Maryland; Greenhills, Ohio; and Greendale, Wisconsin. Originally designed with socialist ideals of creating mixed-income communities, these communities primarily catered to the middle and upper classes and were racially and ethnically homogeneous. See Peter Hall, *Cities of Tomorrow: An Intellectual History of Urban Planning and Design in the Twentieth Century*, updated ed. (Malden: Blackwell, 1996), 87–132.

15. As quoted in Grampp, *From Yard to Garden*, 46.

16. Mumford, *The City in History*, 382.

17. Interview, February 5, 2004.

18. Grampp, *From Yard to Garden*, 176.

19. Interview, October 31, 2003.

20. "Ponce Informa: Boletín de Alcaldía," año 1, no. 5 (1991), in Archivo Municipal de Ponce. File: Barrio Sexto/Sector Cantera.

21. Ibid.

22. Interview, February 5, 2004.

23. Carolyn Merchant, *Reinventing Eden: The Fate of Nature in Western Culture* (New York: Routledge, 2003), 2. Also see Carolyn Merchant, ed., *Radical Ecology: The Search for a Livable World* (New York: Routledge, 1992).

24. The modern-day suburb came to be the ideal setting for the garden. Originating in England and globally exported by the United States, Peter Hall, in his history of urban planning, *Cities of Tomorrow*, calls Ebenezer Howard and his idea of the "suburb" as the "most important single character in [the] tale" (87), providing the possibility of escape to a "green ghetto dedicated to the elite" (Mumford, *The City in History*, 493). The suburban, as formulated in Ebenezer Howard's *Garden Cities of To-morrow* (1898) prioritized "beauty of nature," "fields and parks of easy access," and "bright homes and gardens," key phrases of Howard's town-county magnet. Even with great variety and innumerable differences, the "garden" has been a consistent promise of the suburb; if not in form, at least in name. In Spain, for example, a linear garden city (*la Ciudad Lineal*) promised "a cada familia, una casa, en cada casa, una huerta y un jardín" ("to each family a house; in each house, a orchard and a garden") (Hall, *Cities of Tomorrow*, 113). The garden-suburb configuration rippled through Puerto Rico as terms referring to nature and gardens became commonplace names for *urbanizaciones*. In Ponce, for example, many *urbanizaciones* follow Alhambra's and Extensión Alhambra's symbolic references by also using "gardens" in their names: Jardines del Caribe (Caribbean Gardens), Jardines de Ponce (Ponce Gardens), Quintas de Monserrate (after Francis Cook's palace and gardens in Portugal). Even the city of Caguas, located just outside the San Juan metro area, baptized itself *La Ciudad Jardín* (The Garden City), making reference to the New Deal–era suburban communities that sprouted throughout the United States.

25. This was also a trend on other Caribbean islands, during the pre-revolution era into early to mid-twentieth-century Cuba. See Maikel Fariñas Borrego, *Sociabilidad y Cultura del Ocio: Las Élites Habaneras y Sus Clubes de Recreo (1902–1930)* (La Habana: Fundación Fernando Oriz, 2009).

26. Mumford, *The City in History*, 487.

27. Ibid., 495.

28. Archivo Municipal de Ponce, File: Machuelo (Barrio de Ponce), 012-M-247.

29. Ibid.

30. Notas de Machuelo—Memoria, Archivo Municipal de Ponce, File: Machuelo (Barrio de Ponce), 012-M-247.

31. See http://www.galenusrevista.com/El-Dr-Manuel-de-la-Pila-Iglesias (accessed

February 25, 2010); http://wikimapia.org/8891152/Club-Deportivo-de-Ponce (accessed February 9, 2010).

32. Club Deportivo de Ponce, "Memoria anual reglamentaria presentada en la Junta General Ordinaria de 25 de Junio de 1916," 1915–16, Archivo Municipal de Ponce, File: "Club Deportivo de Ponce."

33. This bridge was built by inmates, showcasing the role that the punished and the undesirable play in creating the very environment and sense of privilege and exclusion for the elite. "Estampas de Machuelo: Rastros del Barrio y de la Familia," Archivo Municipal de Ponce, File: #012-M-247.

34. Club Deportivo de Ponce, "Memoria anual reglamentaria." The gendered segregation of the work of "building" is evident here, with women relegated to the aesthetic portion, involving flowers and gardens.

35. "Noticiero El Deportivo," January 1981, año 1, no. 1, Archivo Municipal de Ponce, File: "Club Deportivo de Ponce." Bomba y plena, a community/dance form practiced by African slaves, was transposed to this upscale setting, as claims of Puerto Rican authenticity—or "primordial Puerto Rican cultural practice," as Juan Flores would call it—were embedded in the community. See Juan Flores, *From Bomba to Hip Hop: Puerto Rican Culture and Latino Identity* (New York: Columbia University Press, 2000).

36. "Constitución y Reglamento: Ponce Yacht & Fishing Club, Inc.," 1979, p. 1, Archivo Municipal de Ponce, File: "Club Náutico de Ponce" #003-C-96.

37. Ibid.

38. "Commodore's Welcome," www.ponceyachtandfishingclub.com/index.php (accessed February 9, 2010); Carol Bareuther, "Yacht Club of the Month: Ponce Yacht and Fishing Club," *All at Sea: The Caribbean's Waterfront Magazine* (September 2006), www.allatsea.net/article/September_2006/Yacht_Club (accessed February 9, 2010).

39. "Commodore's Welcome."

40. Bareuther, "Yacht Club of the Month."

41. "Commodore's Welcome."

42. "Constitución y Reglamento," 29.

43. Ibid.

44. In Club Náutico, for example, there are many different types and ranks of membership, with strict guidelines for each. See "Constitución y Reglamento," capitulo V, beginning on p. 9

45. Capitulo VI, articulo 12 (a), in "Constitución y Reglamento," 12.

46. Capitulo VI, articulo 12 (c), in "Constitución y Reglamento,".

47. "Commodore's Welcome."

48. Interview, February 5, 2004.

49. Ibid.

50. Interview, February 4, 2004.

51. Bourdieu defines the aesthetic disposition as "a generalized capacity to neutralize ordinary urgencies and to bracket off practical ends, a durable inclination and aptitude for practice without a practical function, [that] can only be constituted within an

experience of the world freed from urgency and through the practice of activities which are an end in themselves, such as scholastic exercises or the contemplation of works of art. In other words, it presupposed the distance from the world . . . which is the basis of the bourgeois experience of the world" (*Distinction*, 54).

52. Ibid., 55.

53. Interview, February 6, 2004.

54. Bourdieu, *Distinction*, 54.

55. Mumford, *The City in History*, 488.

56. Interview, February 4, 2004.

57. Interview, November 7, 2003.

58. "Zona Histórica de Ponce: Una Evaluación," box 1, años 1951–85, Archivo Municipal de Ponce, File: "1961: Informe Evaluación Zona Histórica Ponce."

59. Ibid.

60. "Proyecto de Rehabilitación de Vivienda: Ponce en Marcha," 7 de Agosto de 1990 (Revisado 25 de Octubre de 1990), box 2, años 1986–1995, Archivo Municipal de Ponce, File: "Ayuntamiento Secc: Gobierno, Ss: Desarrollo Econ y Comunal, Se: Expediente, SS: Rehabiliticaión de Ponce Centro (Ponce en Marcha)."

61. Ibid.

62. "Zona Histórica de Ponce."

63. Andy Szasz, *Shopping Our Way to Safety: How We Changed from Protecting the Environment to Protecting Ourselves* (Minneapolis: University of Minnesota Press, 2007).

64. Mumford, *The City in History*, 488.

65. George L. Kelling and Catherine M. Coles, *Fixing Broken Windows: Restoring Order and Reducing Crime in Our Communities* (New York: Touchstone, 1996).

66. See Rutherford H. Platt, ed., *The Humane Metropolis: People and Nature in the 21st Century City* (Cambridge, Mass.: Lincoln Institute of Land Policy, 2006).

67. According to De Sousa, research has shown that greening "improves the well-being of city residents in a variety of ways, by reducing crime, reducing stress levels, strengthening neighborhood social ties, coping with 'life's demands,' and the like." See Christopher De Sousa, "Green Futures for Industrial Brownfields," in Platt, *The Humane Metropolis*, 156. For a discussion of local community garden movements and struggles, including Green Guerillas (a nonprofit organization in New York City), guerrilla gardening, and seed bombing in the late twentieth and early twenty-first centuries, see Sharon Zukin, *Naked City: The Death and Life of Authentic Urban Places* (New York: Oxford University Press, 2010), chapter 6; Sidney G. Tarrow, *The New Transnational Activism* (Cambridge: Cambridge University Press, 2005), chapter 4; Jamil Shariff, *50 Green Projects for the Evil Genius* (New York: McGraw-Hill, 2009), chapter 4, Project 14; and Margot Adler, "Environmentalists Adopt New Weapon: Seed Balls," April 15, 2009, http://www.npr.org/templates/story/story.php?storyId=103129515 (accessed February 25, 2010).

68. Anne Whiston Spirn, *The Granite Garden: Urban Nature and Human Design* (New York: Basic Books, 1984). This is one of the themes underlying the novel by Ian McEwan, *The Cement Garden* (New York: Anchor, 1994).

69. Interview, February 5, 2004.

70. Interview, February 4, 2004.

71. Merchant, *Reinventing Eden*, 3.

72. William Walters, "Secure Borders, Safe Haven, Domopolitics," *Citizenship Studies* 8, no. 3 (September 2004): 237–60.

73. Frances Hodgson Burnett, *In the Garden* (Boston: Medici Society, 1925)

74. Mumford, *The City in History*, 495.

Chapter 6

1. Field notes, February 5, 2004.

2. Evelyn Nakano Glenn notes the interdependent and constitutive process whereby class and racial identity are reinforced through the reproductive labor of domestics. See Evelyn Nakano Glenn, "From Servitude to Service Work: Historical Continuities in the Racial Division of Paid Reproductive Labor," *Signs* 18, no. 1 (Autumn 1992): 1–43.

3. Interview, February 5, 2004.

4. Ibid.

5. Ibid.

6. Interview, October 22, 2003.

7. Michel Foucault, *Discipline and Punish: The Birth of the Prison* (New York: Vintage, 1995), 195.

8. Latin America and the Caribbean make up the most unequal region in the world regarding financial equality between the rich and the poor. See United Nations Human Settlements Programme, UN-HABITAT, *State of the World's Cities 2008/2009 Harmonious Cities* (London: Earthscan, 2008). For Puerto Rico, see Orlando Sotomayor, *Poverty and Income Inequality in Puerto Rico, 1970–1990* (Río Piedras: Centro de Investigaciones Interdisciplinarias Universidad de Puerto Rico, 1998).

9. The median household income for the Dr. Pila and Gándara tracts is the mean for each tract: $25,558 for Dr. Pila and $48,900 for Gándara. The 2000 U.S. Census figures showed that 48.2 percent of the total Puerto Rican population had an income under the poverty level in 1999, 8 percent of the population were unemployed, and 20 percent of the population relied on public assistance. In 1999, 52 percent of Ponceños lived below the poverty line, with 24 percent depending on public assistance, and 10 percent of the labor-force population were unemployed. While between 70 and 80 percent of the population in the public housing tracts was below the poverty level, only 24 percent of the population in the private housing tract was below the poverty level. A greater percentage in the public housing tracts are unemployed (between 38.2 and 46.4 percent) than in the private housing tract, where only 14 percent of the population are unemployed. In the Dr. Pila tract, just under half of the households are headed by single females, while 37.7 percent of families in the Gándara tract are headed by single females.

10. 2000 U.S. Census.

11. Melvin M. Tumin and Arnold S. Feldman, *Social Class and Social Change in Puerto Rico*, 2nd ed. (Indianapolis: Bobbs-Merrill, 1971), 141.

12. See Teresita Mártinez-Vergne, *Shaping the Discourse on Space: Charity and Its Wards in Nineteenth-Century San Juan, Puerto Rico* (Austin: University of Texas Press, 1999), 5.

13. Tumin and Feldman, *Social Class and Social Change*, 164.

14. Arnold van Gennep, *The Rites of Passage* (London: Routledge, 2004), 16.

15. Interview, October 23, 2003.

16. Interview, October 27, 2003.

17. Interview, February 4, 2004.

18. Interview, February 5, 2004.

19. Pierre Bourdieu, *Distinction: A Social Critique of the Judgement of Taste*, trans. Richard Nice (Cambridge, Mass.: Harvard University Press, 1984), 170.

20. Interview, October 29, 2003.

21. This metaphor comes from Tomás Almaguer, *Racial Fault Lines: The Historical Origins of White Supremacy in California* (Berkeley: University of California Press, 1994).

22. Interview, February 6, 2004.

23. Ibid.

24. Tumin and Feldman, *Social Class and Social Change*, 188.

25. Also see *van Gennep, The Rites of Passage*; Eviatar Zerubavel, *The Fine Line: Making Distinctions in Everyday Life* (Chicago: University of Chicago Press, 1991); and Wayne Brekhus, *Peacocks, Chameleons, Centaurs: Gay Suburbia and the Grammar of Social Identity* (Chicago: University of Chicago Press, 2003) for a discussion on how distinctions are elaborated.

26. Interview, October 27, 2003.

27. Scholars have noted that women and children are the predominant residents in public housing and poor communities and that women participate and play an important role in community affairs. See, for example, Daphne Spain, "What Happened to Gender Relations on the Way from Chicago to Los Angeles?" *City and Community* 1, no. 2 (2002): 155–69; Milagros Ricourt and Ruby Danta, *Hispanas de Queens: Latino Panethnicity in a New York City Neighborhood* (Ithaca, N.Y.: Cornell University Press, 2003); and Rhonda Y. Williams, *The Politics of Public Housing: Black Women's Struggles against Urban Inequality* (New York: Oxford University Press, 2004).

28. Demographic profile of Dr. Pila, Westbrook Management Company; 2000 U.S. Census.

29. 2000 U.S. Census.

30. See Dolores Hayden, *Redesigning the American Dream: The Future of Housing, Work, and Family Life*, rev. ed. (New York: W. W. Norton, 2002).

31. Lewis Mumford, *The City in History* (New York: Harcourt, 1961), 492.

32. Community profile from Westbrook Management.

33. Zaire Dinzey-Flores, "Criminalizing Communities of Poor, Dark Women in the Caribbean: The Fight against Crime through Puerto Rico's Public Housing," *Crime Prevention and Community Safety* 13, no. 1 (2011): 53–73.

34. Robin Kelley remarks on how these experts have launched "vicious" insults at poor black women—"mamas"—in the ghetto. See Robin D. G. Kelley, *Yo' Mama's Disfunktional! Fighting the Culture Wars in Urban America* (Boston: Beacon, 1997). Also see Williams, *The Politics of Public Housing.*

35. Interview, February 5, 2004.

36. Ibid.

37. Ibid.

38. Interview, October 22, 2003.

39. Mumford, *The City in History*, 492.

40. See Mártinez-Vergne, *Shaping the Discourse*, 9.

41. Interview, October 22, 2003.

42. Harry Hoetink referred to a dominant somatic norm image of "white," which is slightly darker than the one used among Northwestern Europeans and is valued over darker shades. See Harry Hoetink, *Slavery and Race Relations in the Americas: Comparative Notes on Their Nature and Nexus* (New York: Harper & Row, 1973). Puerto Rican scholar Antonio S. Pedreira continually emphasized that the civilizing whitening of blacks was possible through racial mixture (Antonio S. Pedreira, *Insularismo* [1934; Rio Piedras, Puerto Rico: Editorial Edil, 1992]). An achievable impure whiteness showcases effort by Latin American people to portray themselves and their nations in the light of the European "civilizations." expanding the range of a desired whiteness. Edward Telles has argued that skin color, rather than racial identity, is a better measure for assessing discrimination in societies like Brazil, where a racial continuous structure is said to exist. See Edward R. Telles, *Race in Another America: The Significance of Skin Color in Brazil* (Princeton: Princeton University Press, 2004). I agree with Telles and would suggest that "place," too, for its reference to class and "culture," is crucial for understanding how race operates in these societies. Loïc Wacquant underscores the interdependent role of race, class, and place in his discussion of the ghetto: "The ghetto is not simply a spatial entity, or a mere aggregation for poor families stuck at the bottom of the class structure: it is a uniquely racial formation that spawns a society-wide web of material and symbolic associations between color, place and a host of negatively valued social properties" (Wacquant, "Urban Outcasts: Stigma and Division in the Black American Ghetto and the French Urban Periphery," *International Journal of Urban and Regional Research* 17, no. 3 [September 1993]: 366–83, 373). Also see Loïc Wacquant, "What Is a Ghetto? Constructing a Sociological Concept," in *International Encyclopedia of the Social and Behavioral Sciences*, ed. Neil J. Smelser, Paul B. Baltes, and P. B. London (New York: Pergamon, 2001); and Glenn Loury, *The Anatomy of Racial Inequality* (Cambridge, Mass.: Harvard University Press, 2002).

43. Early researchers characterized Puerto Rico as a racial democracy. See José Celso Barbosa, *Problema de Razas* (San Juan: Imprenta Venezuela, 1937); Luis M. Díaz Soler, *La Esclavitud Negra en Puerto Rico* (San Juan: Instituto de Cultura Puertorriqueña, 1957); María Teresa Babín, *Panorama de la Cultura Puertorriqueña* (New York: Las Americas, 1958); and S. Arana Soto, *Puerto Rico: Sociedad sin Razas y Trabajos Afines* (San Juan: Asociación Médica de Puerto Rico, 1976).

Today, scholarship on race in Puerto Rico and among Puerto Ricans has increased significantly, complicating the earlier view, and more researchers are studying how race is ascribed and experienced on the island and among its diaspora, as well as addressing the social consequences of racial inequality. See, for example, Angelo Falcón, "Puerto Ricans and the Politics of Racial Identity," in *Racial and Ethnic Identity: Psychological Development and Creative Expression*, ed. Herbert Harris et al. (New York: Routledge, 1995), 193–207; Roberto Rodriguez-Morazzani, "Beyond the Rainbow: Mapping the Discourse on Puerto Ricans and 'Race,'" in *The Latino Studies Reader: Culture, Economy, and Society*, ed. Antonia Darder and Rodolfo D. Torres (Oxford: Blackwell, 1998), 143–62; Jorge Duany, "Making Indians Out of Blacks: The Revitalization of Taíno Identity in Contemporary Puerto Rico," in *Taíno Revival: Critical Perspectives on Puerto Rican Identity and Cultural Politics*, ed. Gabriel Haslip-Viera (New York: Centro de Estudios Puertorriqueños, 1999), 31–55; Marya Muñoz Vázquez and Idsa E. Alegría Ortega, *Discrimen por razón de raza en los sistemas de seguridad y justicia en Puerto Rico* (San Juan: Comisión de Derechos Civiles, 1999); Isar P. Godreau, "La semántica fugitiva: 'Raza,' color y vida cotidiana en Puerto Rico," *Revista de Ciencias Sociales* 9 (2000): 52–71; Clara E. Rodriguez, *Changing Race: Latinos, the Census and the History of Ethnicity* (New York: New York University Press, 2000); M. A. Rivera Ortiz, *Justicia negra: Casos y cosas* (Hato Rey, Puerto Rico: Ediciones Situm, 2001); Marta Cruz-Janzen, "Latinegras: Desired Women—Undesirable Mothers, Daughters, Sisters and Wives," *Frontiers* 22, no. 3 (2001): 168–83; Jorge Duany, *The Puerto Rican Nation on the Move: Identities on the Island and in the United States* (Chapel Hill: University of North Carolina Press, 2002), especially chapters 10 and 11; Nancy S. Landale and R. S. Oropesa, "White, Black, or Puerto Rican? Racial Self-Identification among Mainland and Island Puerto Ricans," *Social Forces 81, no. 1* (2002): 231–54; William Darity, Jr., Darrick Hamilton, and Jason Dietrich, "Passing on Blackness: Latinos, Race, and Earnings in the USA," *Applied Economics Letters* 9, no. 13 (2002): 847–53; Clarence C. Gravlee, "Ethnic Classification in Southeastern Puerto Rico: The Cultural Model of 'Color,'" *Social Forces* 83, no. 3 (2005): 949–70; Clarence C. Gravlee, William W. Dressler, and H. Russell Bernard, "Skin Color, Social Classification, and Blood Pressure in Southeastern Puerto Rico," *American Journal of Public Health* 95, no. 12 (2005): 2191–97; Nancy S. Landale and R. S. Oropesa, "What Does Skin Color Have to Do with Infant Health? An Analysis of Low Birth Weight among Mainland and Island Puerto Ricans," *Social Science and Medicine* 61, no. 2 (2005): 379–91; Yeidy Rivero, *Tuning Out Blackness: Race and Nation in the History of Puerto Rican Television* (Durham: Duke University Press, 2005); Carlos Vargas-Ramos, "Black, Trigueño, White: Shifting Racial Identification among Puerto Ricans," *Du Bois Review* 2 (2005): 267–85; Luisa N. Borrell, Carlos J. Crespo, and Mario R. Garcia-Palmieri, "Skin Color and Mortality Risk among Men: The Puerto Rico Heart Health Program," *Annals of Epidemiology* 17, no. 5 (2007): 335–41; and Isar P. Godreau, "Slippery Semantics: Race Talks and Everyday Uses of Racial Terminology in Puerto Rico," *Centro Journal* 20, no. 2 (2008): 5–33.

44. See, for example, Godreau, "La semántica fugitiva," and Godreau, "Slippery

Semantics." Labeling racial language as "fugitive" or "slippery," Godreau shows the contextual basis of racial signification and labeling in the island. Also see Gravlee, "Ethnic Classification." Place is starting to be recognized, if implicitly, as an important factor in the attribution and negotiation of race. Godreau, for example, showed how blackness was relegated to the past in an urban revitalization project in Ponce. See Isar P. Godreau, "Changing Space, Making Race: Distance, Nostalgia, and the Folklorization of Blackness in Puerto Rico," *Identities: Global Studies in Culture and Power* 9, no. 3 (2002): 281–304.

45. See Godreau, "Slippery Semantics," and Gravlee, "Ethnic Classification."

46. José Fusté affirms this claim in his article "Colonial Laboratories, Irreparable Subjects: The Experiment of '(B)ordering' San Juan's Public Housing Residents," *Social Identities* 16, no. 1 (2010): 41–59.

47. In 2000, Puerto Ricans were asked by the U.S. Census Bureau to identify themselves racially for the first time in fifty years. In the Census, 80.5 percent of Puerto Ricans in the island identified as "White," 8 percent identified as "Black or African American," 6.8 percent identified as "some other race," and 4.2 percent identified as "two or more races." In the city of Ponce, the racial identifications were similar to the national pattern: 83.8 percent classified themselves as white, 9.5 percent identified as black or African American, and 5.1 percent identified as some other race. In Alhambra and Extensión Alhambra, 92.2 percent (using Census tracts), or 98 percent (using Census block groups, which is more accurate to the neighborhood boundaries), identified as white. The inclusion of the race question in the Puerto Rican Census was an issue of great political and social debate. Central to the debate was the utilization in the Puerto Rican Census of the exact same racial question utilized in the U.S. Census. Efforts were made by Puerto Rican populations on the island and by Latinos in the United States to remove the necessity for respondents who identified themselves as Latinos to have to choose a racial category. But other studies have shown a preference for whiteness among Latinos generally and Puerto Ricans specifically. See, for example, William A. Darity, Jr., Jason Dietrich, and Darrick Hamilton, "Bleach in the Rainbow: Latin Ethnicity and Preference for Whiteness," *Transforming Anthropology* 13, no. 2 (October 2005): 103–9. Also see Isar Godreau, "Blanqueamiento and the Celebration of Blackness as an Exception in Puerto Rico," in *Globalization and Race: Transformations in the Cultural Production of Blackness*, ed. Kamari Maxine Clarke and Deborah A. Thomas (Durham: Duke University Press, 2006), 171–87. Nancy S. Landale and R. S. Oropesa noted that Puerto Ricans on the island were more likely to conform to the categories of the Census than mainland Puerto Ricans did, who preferred the "Latino or Hispanic" identification over the racial categorical ones. See Landale and Oropesa, "White, Black, or Puerto Rican?"

48. See David R. Roediger, *The Wages of Whiteness: Race and the Making of the American Working Class* (New York: Verso, 1991); Joe Feagin, *White Racism* (New York: Routledge, 2001); and George Lipsitz, *The Possessive Investment in Whiteness: How White People Profit from Identity Politics* (Philadelphia: Temple University Press, 2006).

49. See Lawrence Bobo and Vincent L. Hutchings, "Perceptions of Racial Group

Competition: Extending Blumer's Theory of Group Position to a Multiracial Social Context," *American Sociological Review* 61 (1996): 951–72; Steven Tuch and Jack Martin, eds., *Racial Attitudes in the 1990s: Continuity and Change* (Westport, Conn.: Praeger, 1997), chapters 2, 3, 4; Eduardo Bonilla-Silva, *Racism without Racists: Color-blind Racism and the Persistence of Racial Inequality* (Lanham, Md.: Rowman & Littlefield, 2006); and John F. Dovidio and Samuel L. Gaertner, "Aversive Racism," *Advances in Experimental Social Psychology* 36 (2004): 1–52.

50. Interview, February 5, 2004.

51. Interview, October 31, 2003.

52. Jorge Duany, "Caribbean Migration to Puerto Rico: A Comparison of Cubans and Dominicans," *International Migration Review* 26, no. 1 (Spring 1992): 61.

53. Godreau, "Slippery Semantics."

54. Jorge Duany, "Blanquitos," *El Nuevo Día*, December 9, 2009.

55. Interview, February 5, 2004.

56. Ibid.

57. Interview, October 24, 2003.

58. Tumin and Feldman, *Social Class and Social Change.*

59. Zaire Dinzey-Flores, "The Mask of Racial Superstructures: The Spatial Layout of Race in Puerto Rico's Housing," presented at the Association for the Study of the Worldwide African Diaspora (ASWAD), Rio de Janeiro, Brazil, October 5–7, 2005.

60. That is because "blackness" and "brownness" carry the stigma of criminality and lawlessness. Public housing and the gates around them have become "race symbols" of "habitual social significations" (see Loury, *The Anatomy of Racial Inequality*).

61. Interview, October 28, 2003.

62. United States Department of Justice Civil Rights Division,*Investigation of the Puerto Rico Police Department*, September 5, 2011, http://www.justice.gov/crt/about/spl/pr.php (accessed October 20, 2011).

63. João Costa Vargas, "Hyperconsciousness of Race and Its Negation: The Dialectic of White Supremacy in Brazil," *Identities: Global Studies in Culture and Power* 11, no. 4 (2004): 443–70.

64. Dianne Harris, "Little White Houses: Critical Race Theory and the Interpretation of Ordinary Dwellings in the United States, 1945–60," Proceedings from the Warren Center for American Studies Conference on Reinterpreting the History of the Built Environment in North America, August 3, 2005, p. 2, http://warrencenter.fas.harvard.edu/builtenv/Paper%20PDFs/Harris.pdf (accessed October 20, 2011).

65. Louis Althusser, *Lenin and Philosophy and Other Essays*, trans. Ben Brewster (New York: New Left Books, 1971).

66. Stuart Hall, "Race, Articulation and Societies Structured in Dominance," in *Sociological Theories: Race and Colonialism* (Paris: UNESCO, 1980), 305–45, 334–36.

67. Barbara Fields, "Slavery, Race, and Ideology in the United States of America," *New Left Review* 181 (May/June 1990): 95–118, 112. Also see Peter Wade's discussion on ideology in *Race and Ethnicity in Latin America* (London: Pluto Press), 5–24.

68. See Stuart Hall, "Race, Articulation and Societies," 340; Wade, *Race and Ethnicity*; and Harris, "Little White Houses."

69. Michel de Certeau, Luce Giard, and Pierre Mayol, *The Practice of Everyday Life*, trans. Timothy J. Tomasik (Minneapolis: University of Minnesota Press, 1998), 46.

70. Gates, in private and public housing, are part of what Wayne Brekhus calls "one of the most important facets of social identity: how people incorporate spatial and temporal variables into their social constructed identity." See Brekhus, *Peacocks, Chameleons, Centaurs*, 5–6.

71. Interview, February 5, 2004.

72. Henri Lefebvre, *The Production of Space*, trans. Donald Nicholson-Smith (Malden, Mass.: Blackwell, 1991), 183.

Epilogue

1. Interview, October 31, 2003.

2. Liz Serrano and Lilliam Rivera, *Biblioteca y Archivo Histórico Municipal, Lugar de Actividades Escolares—Ponce—Puerto Rico,* http://archivosmunicipales.blogspot.com/2008/08/biblioteca-y-archivo-histrico-municipal.html (accessed August 6, 2008).

3. Michel Foucault, *Discipline and Punish: The Birth of the Prison* (New York: Vintage, 1995), 113.

4. See Mike Davis, *City of Quartz* (London: Verso, 1990) for a discussion about unwelcoming city design and about the design of anti-homeless architecture, including divided benches to prevent people from lying down on them.

5. In March 2005 Puerto Rico's Housing Authority announced an investment of $10 million to $14 million dollars to install security systems in public housing communities, which included the reactivation of the controlled access systems in those public housing sites where the system had collapsed as well as the installation of security cameras in ten public housing sites. Joanisabel González, "Millonario Plan de Seguridad," *El Nuevo Día* (February 1, 2005), http://www.adendi.com/archivo.asp?num=1697&year=2005&month=2&keyword=millonario%20plan%20de%20seguridad (accessed May 30, 2012).

6. See Robert E. Park, Ernest W. Burgess, R. D. McKenzie, and Louis Wirth, *The City* (Chicago: University of Chicago Press, 1925); Louis Wirth, "Urbanism as a Way of Life," *American Journal of Sociology* 44, no. 1 (1938): 1–24; and Jane Jacobs, *The Death and Life of Great American Cities* (New York: Vintage, 1961). Also Iris Marion Young, in *Justice and the Politics of Difference* (Princeton: Princeton University Press, 1990), writes: "City life instantiates social relations of difference without exclusion. Different groups dwell in the city alongside one another, of necessity interacting with each other" (227).

7. Lewis Mumford, *The City in History* (New York: Harcourt, 1961), 9–10.

8. Jon C. Teaford proposes that, after 1945, Americans entered a posturban era of metropolitan living, "which defied traditional notions of a city" (4). See Teaford, *The Metropolitan Revolution: The Rise of Post-Urban America* (New York: Columbia University Press, 2006).

9. David Sibley, *Geographies of Exclusion: Society and Difference in the West* (New York: Routledge, 1995).

10. Giorgio Agamben, *Homo Sacer: Sovereign Power and Bare Life,* trans. Daniel Heller-Roazen (Stanford, Calif.: Stanford University Press, 1998).

11. Young, in *Justice and the Politics of Difference,* 242, notes the idea of community and how it helps enforce exclusion. David Harvey, in turn, has noted the capitalist organization of the city and its inevitable enforcement of inequality.

12. The clearance of substandard housing, the building of housing complexes for the poor, the provision of temporary housing, suburbanization movements, mortgage loan policies that expand homeownership, new urbanist designs that push for mixed-income communities, urban revitalization, individual home-improvement investments, community development organizations, and housing choice selections all point to the social value that the house holds in twenty-first-century society.

13. Kenneth Clark found that in America ghettos are colonies of "invisible walls" (Kenneth Clark, *Dark Ghetto: Dilemmas of Social Power* [New York: Harper & Row, 1965], 11) while St. Clair Drake and Horace Roscoe Cayton described the processes that kept communities of African Americans segregated in Chicago's Black Belt as the "invisible barbed-wire fence of restrictive covenants (St. Clair Drake and Horace Roscoe Cayton, *Black Metropolis: A Study of Negro Life in a Northern City* [1945; Chicago: University of Chicago, 1993], 382). With the gates, these separations are made visible.

14. Gordon W. Allport, *The Nature of Prejudice* (New York: Perseus, 1954).

15. The effect of a neighborhood on poor residents' well-being is unclear. Specifically, evaluation of Section 8 and moving to opportunity voucher programs, Hope VI policies, as well as examinations of processes of gentrification, have yielded mixed results with respects to how poor and ex-public housing residents fair in scattered and mixed-income, or gentrifying, neighborhoods. See James E. Rosenbaum, "Changing the Geography of Opportunity by Expanding Residential Choice: Lessons from the Gautreaux Program," *Housing Policy Debate* 6, no. 1 (1995): 231–69; Ingrid Gould Ellen and Margery Austin Turner, "Does Neighborhood Matter? Assessing Recent Evidence," *Housing Policy Debate* 8, no. 4 (1997): 833–66; Jerry J. Salama, "The Redevelopment of Distressed Public Housing: Early Results from HOPE VI Projects in Atlanta, Chicago, and San Antonio," *Housing Policy Debate* 10, no. 1 (1999): 95–142; Lawrence F. Katz, Jeffrey R. Kling, and Jeffrey B. Liebman, "Moving to Opportunity in Boston: Early Results of a Randomized Mobility Experiment," *Quarterly Journal of Economics* 114, no. 2 (2001): 607–54; Larry Burton et al., *The HOPE VI Resident Tracking Study: A Snapshot of the Current Living Situation of Original Residents from Eight Sites* (U.S. Department of Housing and Urban Development Office of Public Housing Investments, November 1, 2002); G. Thomas Kingsley, Jennifer Johnson, and Kathryn L. S. Pettit, "Patterns of Section 8 Relocation in the Hope VI Program," *Journal of Urban Affairs* 25 (2003): 427–47; William G. Grigsby and Steven C. Bourassa, "Trying to Understand Low-income Housing Subsidies: Lessons from the United States," *Urban Studies* 40, nos. 5–6 (May 2003): 973–92; Susan Clampet-Lundquist, "HOPE VI Relocation: Moving to

New Neighborhoods and Building New Ties," *Housing Policy Debate* 15, no. 2 (2004): 415–47; Susan J. Popkin et al., "The HOPE VI Program: What About the Residents?" *Housing Policy Debate* 15, no. 2 (2004): 385–414; Rachel G Kleit, "HOPE VI New Communities: Neighborhood Relationships in Mixed-Income Housing," *Environment and Planning A* 37, no. 8 (2005): 1413–41; Rebecca C. Fauth, Tama Leventhal, and Jeanne Brooks-Gunn, "Seven Years Later: Effects of a Neighborhood Mobility Program on Poor Black and Latino Adults' Well-being," *Journal of Health and Social Behavior* 49, no. 2 (June 2008): 119–30; Loretta Lees, "Gentrification and Social Mixing: Towards an Inclusive Urban Renaissance?" *Urban Studies* 45, no. 12 (November 2008): 2449–70; Geoffrey DeVerteuil, "Evidence of Gentrification-Induced Displacement among Social Services in London and Los Angeles," *Urban Studies* 48 (June 2011): 1563–80; Frank Gaffikin and Mike Morrissey, "Community Cohesion and Social Inclusion: Unravelling a Complex Relationship," *Urban Studies* 48 (May 1, 2011): 1089–118; and Lynne C. Manzo, Rachel G. Kleit, and Dawn Couch, "Moving Three Times Is Like Having Your House on Fire Once: The Experience of Place and Impending Displacement among Public Housing Residents," *Urban Studies* 45 (2008): 1855–78.

16. *Cabrini Green: Mixing It Up,* in production, directed by Ronit Bezalel, screened at Society for American City and Regional Planning History, Thirteenth National Conference on Planning History (Oakland, Calif., October 15–18, 2009). See the preview at http://ronitfilms.com/films/mixingitup.html (accessed May 31, 2012).

17. Sharon Zukin, "Space and Symbols in an Age of Decline," in *The City Cultures Reader,* ed. Malcolm Miles, Tim Hall, and Iain Borden (New York: Routledge, 2000), 81.

18. David Harvey, *Justice, Nature and the Geography of Difference* (Cambridge: Blackwell, 1996).

19. John R. Logan and Harvey L. Molotch, *Urban Fortunes: The Political Economy of Place* (Berkeley: University of California Press, 1989).

20. See, for example, Richard Sennett's lecture, "The Architecture of Cooperation," Harvard Graduate School of Design, February 28, 2012, http://www.youtube.com/watch?v=tcXE4NEgLn8 (accessed May 30, 2012); and Claire Cooper Marcus and Carolyn Francis, eds., *People Places: Design Guidelines for Open Urban Space,* 2nd ed. (New York: John Wiley, 1998). Also see Andy Merrifield, *Dialectical Urbanism* (New York: Monthly Review Press, 2002), for ways in which a city can live up to its promise of inclusion.

21. Sepúlveda Rivera, "Viejos Cañaverales, Casa Nuevas: Muñoz versus el Síndrome Long," in *Luis Muñoz Marín, Perfiles de su Gobernación, 1948–1964,* ed. Fernando Picó (Río Piedras: Fundación Luis Muñoz Marín, 2003), 166–207, 200–207.

22. Robert D. Putnam, *Bowling Alone: The Collapse and Revival of American Community* (New York: Simon & Schuster, 2000).

Methodology

1. When I selected these sites for study, I was unaware of who managed the sites and whether or not they were managed by one company.

2. The fear was that I would be perceived as a law enforcement representative or somebody who was snooping around for suspicious reasons.

3. Although there may be more criteria involved in deciding whether someone was "safe" for me to talk to and to include in my research study, I understood the residents' insistence on safety as being a sincere concern that I not become a victim of crime. However, I do not doubt that interpersonal dynamics, such as concern for credibility, political affiliations and orientations, residential proximity, familial and friendship ties, the desire of portraying the community in a specific way, or other factors influenced whom they decided to refer to me.

4. See the flyer utilized for recruitment for Dr. Pila that is reprinted in Chapter 4.

5. It is impossible to calculate the average reported yearly income in Gándara because most families did not report their income in dollar amounts, instead choosing to identify the source of their income.

6. See Larry B. Mohr, *Impact Analysis for Program Evaluation*, 2nd ed. (Thousand Oaks, Calif.: Sage, 1995).

7. Norman K. Denzin, *The Research Act*, 2nd ed. (New York: McGraw-Hill, 1978).

8. Todd D. Jick, "Mixing Qualitative and Quantitative Methods: Triangulation in Action," *Administrative Science Quarterly* 24 (1979): 602–11, 603.

9. Ibid., 603.

10. Judith Freidenberg, *The Anthropology of Lower Income Urban Enclaves: The Case of East Harlem* (New York: New York Academy of Sciences, 1995), 133.

11. Eviatar Zerubavel, "Generally Speaking: The Logic and Mechanics of Social Pattern Analysis," *Sociological Forum* 22, no. 2 (2007): 131–45.

Index

Acknowledgments

Although readers will get to know only their made-up names, the people whose words are featured here are more real and complex than this book can ever relay. I am indebted to the residents of Residencial Dr. Manuel A. de la Pila, Residencial José N. Gándara, Urbanización Alhambra, and Urbanización Extensión Alhambra for sharing their stories, their experiences, and their communities with me. My gratitude also extends to the many people and entities in Puerto Rico, and in Ponce, who aided this research effort. Thanks to the Westbrook Management staff, Biblioteca de la Junta de Planificación Urbana, Oficina de Tierras y Planificación del Municipio de Ponce, HUD Puerto Rico, Administración de Vivienda Pública, Oficina de Estadísticas de la Policía de Puerto Rico, Departamento de Justicia de Puerto Rico, Archivo Municipio de Ponce, Fundación Luis Muñoz Marín, and staff at Ponce's Biblioteca Mariana Suarez de Longo. Special thanks to Emma Balbuena Linares, Fernando G. Defilló Kourie, Miguel Elías Díaz, Rafael Pagán Marrero, Treeny Rodríguez Flores, Awilda Vázquez, and Michael Siegel of Rutgers Cartography, for their generous contributions to this research effort. My thanks to Eric Schroeder Vivas, who designed the beautiful cover, which so adeptly captures the essence of the book.

I would like to recognize the generous funding support by a University of Michigan National Poverty Center Grant, the Department of Housing and Urban Development (HUD) Research Grant program, and a Ford Foundation Fellowship. The Mellon Foundation's Postdoctoral Fellowship in Race, Crime, and Justice, at the Vera Institute of Justice, allowed me valuable time and space for beginning to conceptualize this book. And my gratitude to the *Singapore Journal of Tropical Geography*, where an earlier version of Chapter 4 was published (33, no. 2 [July 2012]: 198–211).

My deepest gratitude to Peter Agree, of the University of Pennsylvania Press, for supporting this book from beginning to end. Thanks to him and Erica Ginsburg for their confident guidance through publication. The reviewers provided feedback that, in my view, made the book better. My thanks to them for offering their insights and expertise.

In Michigan, where this project first began to take form, I received great support and encouragement from Jossianna Arroyo, Mary Corcoran, Donald R. Deskins, Alford Young, Jr., Earl Lewis, Sylvia Pedraza, Jeff Morenoff, and David Thacher. In my four years living in Ann Arbor I enjoyed an intellectually rich and fun community. Tasleem Padamsee and Chavella Pittman have witnessed the daily production of my work and life for almost a decade. I am privileged to have their friendship and eternally thankful for their support. Thanks to the many friends who, beginning in Michigan, have allowed me to lean on them and share unforgettable experiences, especially Beverly Araujo, María Elena Gil, Danny Méndez, Beatriz Ramírez-Betances, Mérida Rúa, Edna Viruell-Fuentes, and Rochelle Woods. Colleagues at Rutgers have been an important source of encouragement, intellectual inspiration, and personal support. My sincere thanks to Ulla Berg, Ethel Brooks, Deborah Carr, Sandra Rocío Castro, Karen Cerulo, Phaedra Daipha, Judith Friedman, Judith Gerson, Daniel Goldstein, Paul Hirschfield, Lauren Krivo, Asela Laguna-Díaz, Niki Dickerson von Lockette, Aldo Lauria-Santiago, Catherine Lee, Kathy López, Ann Mische, Donna Murch, Julie Phillips, Joanna Regulska, Sarah Rosenfield, Patricia Roos, Zakia Salime, Kristen Springer, Silismar Suriel, and Eviatar Zerubavel. Thanks also to Alexis Merdjanoff and to Samantha Galarza, the best undergraduate student ever, for their assistance.

Understanding that I am a part of and not apart from the topic of this book took convincing. The late Paul Ederer, my high school English literature teacher, the late William Alonso and J. Lorand Matory at Harvard, began to cultivate my interest in research and underscored the importance of being me in my work, while working on things that "matter." I wish to honor their lasting influence on me. Although Jeannette Hopkins wasn't able to escort this work to its completion, she spiritedly challenged me to be myself in my scholarship. As she edited the first drafts of this manuscript, she gave me a lifetime of lessons. As I dream of our conversations while taking in the ocean breeze in Portsmouth, I feel fortunate to have had the opportunity to work with such an extraordinary editor. As my interactions with Jeannette underscored, a book demands a special kind of confidence. I am grateful to those who, with collegial support, intellectual insights, and gifts of friendship, helped nurture that confidence. My deepest appreciation and respect go to Ana Aparicio, Daisy Auger-Dominguez, Carolina Bank Muñoz, Antonino D'Ambrosio, Arlene Dávila, Junot Díaz, Jorge Duany, Juan Flores, Tyrone Forman, Isar

Godreau, Megan Golden, Christina Gómez, Carolina González, Alison Isenberg, Rivke Jaffe, Miriam Jiménez Román, Sara Johnson, Dominique Jones, Zainab Latif, Tracey Lazsloffy, Van Luu, Minkah Makalani, Keesha Middlemass, Khalil G. Muhammad, Jacqueline Olvera, Ginette Palés, Anita Price, Martiza Quiñones, Ana Yolanda Ramos-Zayas, Julissa Reynoso, Robyn Rodríguez, Helen Safa, Kelvin Santiago-Valles, Mika Sampson Robinson, Tanya Saunders, Alexandra Soriano-Taveras, Maribel Tineo, Arlene Torres, Lucia Trimbur, Fiona True, Fritz Umbach, and Carlos Vargas-Ramos. I continue to be inspired by all of you and thank you, also, for your friendship.

This book came to life in Bedford-Stuyvesant, Brooklyn, a place that I am proud to call home. Brooklyn has offered an ideal urban landing place from where to think about the ideas of urbanism and city life discussed here. In a true measure of urbanity, it has offered great writing spaces and plenty of opportunities to connect with others, strangers and familiars alike. But most of all it has given me a community. For their friendship and support of me and my young family, thanks to all the friends there who model urban community-making; there are too many to name them all but I want to mention Esther Bukai, my neighbors Mrs. Beulah Grant and Leroy Glemond Nurse, Denise Henry, José Magro and Thandi Baxter-Magro, Hope McGrath, Doreen Mensah-Hinds, and Sarah Zeller-Berkman. Miguelina Polanco, Patricia Vélez, Tía Miriam Veras, y Tía Teresa Llaca han hecho posible la maroma esta de ser una madre académica. Siempre estaré agradecida por su amor hacia mi y mis hijos. Thanks also to my dear cousin, Guillermo David, for his unending solidarity. A Mercedes Díaz, que cogió un viaje adelantado a otros mundos, y a Delia Paulino, gracias por su apoyo.

The architects of my life in Ponce, my parents Esperanza Aurora Flores Romero and Juan Vicente Dinzey Hazle, were the first to encourage me to do whatever I wanted to do. Against so many odds, some of which I detail in this book, they created a dream of a life. They have shown me what love, pride, energy, and perseverance can accomplish. Gracias, Papi y Mami, por todo lo que han sido y por todo lo que son. My siblings Yrthya and Juancho will know parts of this book better than anyone. I am so very fortunate and thankful to have your love and to have had you as comrades on the Ponce journey. Our love and unique kind of family lives on in our beautifully interconnected children: Ambar Cloé, Ciara Mía, Amara Lorien. They bring nothing but joy to my, Lelolai's, and Caribe's lives. My brother Johnny and his daughters Johnmarie and Johnlin are always on my mind and in my heart. Los amo, mi familia, mis caras lindas.

Three amazing, perfect beings share my Brooklyn nest: Edward Paulino, Lelolai Palmares Paulino-Dinzey, and Caribe Macandel Paulino-Dinzey. Thank you, Eddie, for being a partner, friend, and my most enthusiastic fan. You energize me to continue moving forward positively. My children, Lelolai Palmares and Caribe Macandel, changed my life. You both have taught me more in the last five years than I knew in the thirty years before I met you. I am awed by this most magnificent, most important, of adventures that we're taking together. I live to make you proud, and I seek to offer, to demonstrate a life that is dictated not by fear but by discovery, promise, joy, justice, and hope. "Yo respiro amor . . ." This, everything, is for you.